Music

Noise/ Music

A HISTORY

Paul Hegarty

B L O O M S B U R Y

NEW YORK • LONDON • NEW DELHI • SYDNEY

Bloomsbury Academic
An imprint of Bloomsbury Publishing Inc

1385 Broadway	50 Bedford Square
New York	London
NY 10018	WC1B 3DP
USA	UK

www.bloomsbury.com

Bloomsbury is a registered trade mark of Bloomsbury Publishing Plc

First published in 2007 by the Continuum International Publishing Group Inc
Reprinted by Bloomsbury Academic 2013

Library of Congress Cataloging-in-Publication Data
Hegarty, Paul, 1967—
Noise/music : a history / Paul Hegarty.
p. cm.
Includes bibliographical references (p.), discography (p.), and index.
ISBN-13: 978-0-8264-1726-8 (hardcover :alk. paper)
ISBN-10: 0-8264-1726-4 (hardcover :alk. paper)
ISBN-13: 978-0-8264-1727-5 (pbk. :alk. paper)
ISBN-10: 0-8264-1727-2 (pbk. :alk. paper) 1. Noise music—History and
criticism. I. Title.
ML3534.H43 2007
781.64—dc22
2007024836

ISBN: HB: 978-0-8264-1726-8
PB: 978-0-8264-1727-5

Printed and bound in the United States of America

Contents

Acknowledgements

Thanks to: Graham Allen, Ben Andrews, Jackie Clarke, Bernadette Cronin, Patrick Crowley, Toby Dawson, Mike Gane, Malcolm Garrard, Gary Genosko, Greg Hainge, Martin Halliwell, Colin Harrison, Phil Hawkins, Michael Hoar, Phil James, Arthur and Marilouise Kroker, Caitríona Leahy, Brian O'Shaughnessy, Keith Reader, Judith Still, Times, Alex Walsh, Matt Whitman, John Younge.

Special thanks for reading and comments: Graham Allen, Patrick Crowley, Greg Hainge, Colin Harrison.

Thanks to the Faculty of Arts, University College Cork, for the Arts Faculty Research award, 2005–06.

Thanks to all at Continuum, and to David Barker for his interest and patience.

In memoriam: John Peel, Tommy Vance, Koji Tano, Jean Baudrillard.

Preface

Noise/Music is about noise, about how noise relates to music, and the different ways we arrive at noise music, even if such a combination would seem contradictory, impossible, doomed to fail. It is a history of how, in the twentieth century, noise has become a resource, was incorporated into musicality and rejected musicality, while all the while occurring in the place of music. Although the book works through movements, approaches and practices historically, the question of whether we can legitimately do this is implicit throughout (and explicit in chapter 1). What exactly noise is, or what it should do, alters through history, and this means that any account of noise is a history of disruptions and disturbances. This means that the history of noise is like a history of the avant-garde—while we can identify what looks like a linear succession of avant-gardes, if we consider the idea of an avant-garde, or of noise, then we should recognize that at any one moment, however briefly, when something is avant-garde, it is specifically outside of linear progression, and is a question posed about progression. Noise itself constantly dissipates, as what is judged noise at one point is music or meaning at another. As well as this disruptive element, noise must also be thought of as constantly failing—failing to stay noise, as it becomes familiar, or acceptable practice. Furthermore, a history of noise has to recognize it can only work as a consciously retrospective attribution. In practice, this means that although the book follows noise in its relation to music in a forward direction, I argue that we have only begun to think about noise music recently, and we work backwards to find the notional forward movement from Russolo, Cage, Fluxus, and so on. I argue that noise music acquires a sense (whether wanted or not) in the wake of industrial music and Japanese noise music—i.e. from the late 1970s onwards.

Noise/Music is a theoretical whole, if not a unity: underlying the whole is the idea that noise is a negativity (it can never be positively, definitively and timelessly located), a resistance, but also defined by what society resists. It works as a deconstruction, so, in practice, this means that identifying the noise in a piece of music is only the initial step; the next is to see noise as the relation between that first, explicit noise and that which is not noise. This can be internal to the piece, or in how it relates to institutional practices, musical conventions, society as a whole, or to anything else that seems to be in play against the noise, but intimately connected to it and its definition at any one time. Individual chapters deal with different musical styles, presumptions, uses and locations of noise, so each of these produces different specific models, all of which presume the overall theorization. The chapters also accrete, so that by the time of chapter 9, on Japanese noise, all previous noise is there (to be worked back from). Chapter 1 is about the first moments noise is identified, used or appropriated and what it means to identify these moments as significant. It lays out the general issues about what noise is. The next chapter continues from here to address Cage, Fluxus and technological developments, arguing that new machinery is a subset of the technologies in and around noise, not just a cause. Chapter 3 looks at Adorno and the movement of jazz away from its own conventions. Chapter 4 combines electrification of the guitar and repetition to think about noise in rock of the late 1960s and early 1970s. Chapter 5 asks whether and how progressive rock can have anything to do with noise, and chapter 6 continues a question asked there, about whether we can really divide rock music into pre- and post-punk, and covers ineptitude from Dubuffet through to punk. Chapter 7 sees many earlier strategies of experimental music used in the first few years of industrial music, and chapter 8 assesses how noise and power cross into one another in industrial music and also in Public Enemy. Chapter 9 is a theorized overview and analysis of Japanese noise music, and chapter 10 continues this with a dedicated reading of Merzbow. Chapter 11 is on sound art, critically approaching the question of how it tries to be noise, or if it does. Chapter 12 looks at interventions on pre-existing materials, in the form of vinyl manipulation, sampling and glitch. Chapter 13 closes the book with a thought about the utopianism of promoting listening. Some chapters are theoretically more straightforward than others, according to the material dealt with, but all presume the ideas of chapter 1, and the general method mentioned above.

Noise/Music does not cover all the possibilities of noise in music. As it is first of all a theory, some artists simply ended up without a place, or sometimes what seems a more modest place than they might merit. I could cite arbitrariness of examples as a questioning of exemplarity, and this would not misrepresent how I approached the book, or the music dealt with. However, while some artists were left out consciously, others I am at a loss to explain. The book finished, I noticed there was little or no reference to Nurse With Wound, Current 93, Coil, The New Blockaders, The Haters, Maurizio Bianchi, My Bloody Valentine, Sonic Youth.[1] On reflection, the reason for this was that they did not fit into the schema of the chapters' thematic interests, and would be of interest when dealt with individually rather than as part of one of those themes. Beyond this, there is no reason there could not be more noise analysis of metal or techno, and a further thematic could be that of speed. In finally closing down the choices, I was also aware that comprehensiveness would be a problem—there is no reason noise cannot be found everywhere. For that reason, none of the chapters, even on Japanese noise, tries to list all the possible variants of the type of noise dealt with, even though the temptation might be to display the breadth of one's record collection. Lastly, the decision to include or exclude is not one of quality, and neither is the judgement of noise or noisiness. Even if noise is something like the avant-garde, it is not a synonym for experimental or avant-garde music.

NOTES

1. For a substantial account of the first three of these, see David Keenan, *England's Hidden Reverse: A Secret History of the Esoteric Underground* (London: SAF, 2003).

1
FIRST

> Existence and the world seem justified only as an aesthetic phenomenon. In this sense, it is precisely the tragic myth that has to convince us that even the ugly and disharmonic are part of an artistic game that the will in the eternal amplitude of its pleasure plays with itself. But this primordial phenomenon of Dionysian art is difficult to grasp, and there is only one direct way to make it intelligible and grasp it immediately: through the wonderful significance of *musical dissonance*.[1]

Noise is not an objective fact. It occurs in relation to perception—both direct (sensory) and according to presumptions made by an individual. These are going to vary according to historical, geographical and cultural location. Whether noise is happening or not will depend also on the source of what is being called noise—who the producer is, when and where, and how it impinges on the perceiver of noise. Noise is not the same as noises. Noises are sounds until further qualified (e.g. as unpleasant noises, loud noises, and so on), but noise is already that qualification; it is already a *judgement* that noise is occurring. Although noise can occur outside of cognition (i.e. without us understanding its purpose, form, source), a judgement is made in reaction to it. Noise then is something we are forced to react to, and this reaction, certainly for humans, is a judgement, even if only physical.

Noise is not only a judgement on noises, it is a negative reaction, and then, usually, a negative response to a sound or set of sounds. Biologists, sound ecologists and psychoacoustics would have us believe that noise is sound that damages us, and that a defensive reaction is simply natural, even if, at an individual level, it might be learned. This would imply that certain frequencies or volumes of noise are inherently noisy. Let's imagine that this is the case—we still need to think on how it works, and this will show that the idea of some things being noisy deconstructs itself. First, even in this model, noise needs a listener—probably some sort of animal or a non-organic machine with hearing capacities (both can be classified as 'hearing machines'), in the vicinity of the noise so that the soundwaves can be heard. The sound then has to be perceived as dangerous to the functioning of the hearing machine. Without these two moments, we might have a sound, but we do not have noise. I am sure that few would disagree with this interaction being necessary, but would then insist that certain frequencies or volumes are fundamentally and always damaging to particular organisms or machines; but the tolerance of individual hearing machines varies, however, and this is not just due to biological factors. Many organic hearing machines (and not just humans) will split the world into loud sounds that are fine and dangerous sounds that are noise, whose reception must be avoided, and this is as much to do with learned social behaviour as physical pain, or the threat of same. *Noise is cultural*, and different groups of hearing machines will process sounds differently. Primarily, here, I am interested in human hearing of noise, and human cultures display a variety we can understand more clearly than the range of sound ecologies for dolphins, whales, primates or birds. Whether a noise is *there* or not, it comes to be as sound, or as noise perhaps, only retrospectively. The Big Bang can be said to have occurred at a given moment, even if time did not exist until just after it, but it betrays itself retrospectively as humans (or others) come to understand it, and also because its evidence only comes to you over time, as the universe expands. And the Big Bang has a sound—it is the final static that can never quite be removed—so the universe itself (this universe anyway) can be imagined as noise, as residue, unexpected by-product, and the last sound will also be the first.

Humans can be physically affected by certain sounds or noises: very high frequencies or very loud sounds measured can damage hearing. Very low frequencies affect other areas of the body, and have commonly been used in torture—digestive systems can be disturbed, the functioning of the heart disrupted. Many types of sound can be mentally disturbing. To think of these effects is only to begin to see how noise works, and the element that links all noise, all judgements that noise is happening, is that noise is something that one is subject, submitted or subjected to. Further on in the book, we will see that subjection in the context of noise can be mobilized more positively, but for now, I want to argue that noise happens to 'me', is beyond my control, and somehow exceeds my level of comfort with the soundworld I or we inhabit. In some way, noise threatens me, is part of the other I define myself against. Noise is a phenomenology of noise, insofar as it exists in relation to individuals, who define themselves as being subject to noise (a community forms around the hearing of a house or car alarm).

Certain types of noise are to do with the sounds of 'other people', and these are the ones that are most complicit with power, and lead to noise control regulations. As a result, practices that are not in any way loud enough to constitute a physical threat or even irritation are thought of as noisy. Different subcultural or cultural traditions or practices that are thought of as other are noisier, hence perceptions of people speaking in 'foreign' languages being loud, or to take a peculiar case, the reaction of some pubs or cafés to groups of deaf people using sign language. This last example raises another key part of what noise is: although it can be loud, it is much more about what is deemed to disturb, and loudness is only part of that overall *sense* of noise. So, noise is an excess, is thought of as being too much, and for human hearing, this occurs almost entirely through cultural perceptions, and individual reactions within that framework. This is why Jean-Luc Nancy, for example, tries to build up an ethics based on listening, as listening suggests openness, receptiveness, and this leads to understanding. You don't need poststructuralism to tell you that, as we have come to believe that listening is almost enough to have a society or community that gels together and conquers its neuroses or issues, but what Nancy and other writers who will feature in this book identify is that hearing has been neglected within western philosophical reflection, and this neglect has reduced our appreciation for the difference between hearing and listening.

Generally speaking, hearing is thought of as less reflective, a physical process we can do nothing about (the tired truism of not being able to close our ears as we can our eyes adding to the impression that seeing has correctly been imagined as the dominant human sense). To hear is to be subject, though, and writers such as Jacques Derrida would argue that western philosophy ('metaphysics') is based on a presumption that I hear myself speaking, and that is how I know I am here. But, he claims, 'here' is always 'there', and there is never truly a moment where 'I' am simply present, all in one place, at the same time.[2] The common presumption today, whether coming from human resource management, counselling or politicians, is that listening is a good. But who listens? Too often it is supposed that there is a 'me' that is in a position to control 'my' listening. I want to claim, as Nancy has done, that listening is not under 'my' control. As Stanley Fish has it, you do not have culture, it has you, and any listening, including the belief that listening is good, ethically sound, productive, and so on, comes from within a culture. Or, as Arthur Kroker puts it, 'Hearing has always been alchemical, a violent zone where sound waves mutate into a sedimentary layer of cultural meanings, where historical referents secrete into contemporary states of subjectivity, and where there is no stability, only an aural logic of imminent reversibility' (*Spasm*, 52).[3] Noise, and the music that comes from an engagement with it, tests commonplace notions of hearing and listening, and tries to destabilize not just our expectations of content or artistic form, but how we relate to those, to the point where the most interesting point of encounter might be a loss of controlled listening, a failure of adequate hearing, even if this is only temporary.

Noise is negative: it is unwanted, other, not something ordered. It is negatively defined—i.e. by what it is not (not acceptable sound, not music, not valid, not a message or a meaning), but it is also a negativity. In other words, it does not exist independently, as it exists only in relation to what it is not. In turn, it helps structure and define its opposite (the world of meaning, law, regulation, goodness, beauty, and so on). Noise is something like a process, and whether it creates a result (positive in the form of avant-garde transformation, negative in the form of social restrictions) or remains process is one of the major issues in how music and noise relate.

Noise has a history. Noise occurs not in isolation, but in a differential relation to society, to sound, and to music. Against the backdrop of Enlightenment, and then Romantic, notions of music and its place, modernist thought about music tries to branch out, to address the world of sound and human interaction with and/or construction of that world. The first key moment occurs with Futurism. Filippo Tomaso Marinetti, the leader of the movement, had already introduced the notion of 'sound poetry', but it is Luigi Russolo's *The Art of Noises* that provides the theorisation of futurist ideas on sound. According to Russolo, 'ancient life was all silence. In the 19th century, with the invention of machines, Noise was born' (23).[4] Mel Gordon glosses this claim with the statement that 'the cacophony of sounds in the 19th century street, factory, shop and mine—seemingly random and meaningless—could not be easily isolated and identified' ('Songs from the Museum of the Future', 197).[5] So instead of silence being the premodern state, we have a soundworld based on recognition and incorporation. As John Cage 'discovered', there is no such thing as silence, even when all sound seems to be removed.

In fact, the next canonical moment in the thought of noise is silence, in the guise of Cage's piece *4' 33"*, inspired by a visit to an anechoic chamber. In this ostensibly soundless room, he still heard something. He was informed that what he was hearing was 'the nerve's [sic] operation, blood's circulation' (*Silence*, 13).[6] From this came the 'silent' piece, where the audience's attention is drawn to all the other sounds to be heard in a concert hall (many of which are from outside the room). The world, then, is revealed as infinitely musical: musicality is about our attentiveness to the sounds of the world. This returns us to a Platonic conception of the universe: the forms of all things are there—we just create versions of them. Douglas Kahn argues that this movement illustrates the central role of neo-Pythagorean conceptions of sound within modernism—i.e. the music of the spheres being out there, even if presently inaudible to humans. This notion is ambiguous as well as significant: 'the legacy of neo-Pythagoreanism within modernism, however, has been fairly peculiar, as it pertains to both notions of the breadth of *all sound* and the capability of a line to represent many attributes of the world, including a range of sounds' (Kahn, *Noise Water Meat*, 74).[7] In the case of music's relation to noise, Russolo and composers such as Erik Satie and Edgard Varèse sought to bring this broadened musicality of the world into music. The Futurists invented a range of machines that would make popping, hissing, crackling sounds—and these would be mobilized into compositions. As well as the presumption of finding sounds and music inherent to the universe, we also have the question of 'material': the world would be a source of music when harnessed in some way, a 'material for' in order to be material. Can music be immanent? Music cannot just be out there, as it implies human organization. But just because that has been the view does not mean it has to stay the case. It would seem that music has to at least pass through agency, if only historically, for there to be, as there is in certain forms of contemporary Japanese noise music, a sense of such an immanence.

While the non-immanence of music might seem to be given, how far can we say sound or noise is 'for itself', a something in the world? Even the place of sound has to be historicized, for while the world was not silent until the mid-nineteenth century, other than in its 'musical' aspects such as water running, or birdsong, nature was at least quiet, except at moments of danger. Urbanization is one factor in the coming of noise: first at the obvious level of there being more people, machines, vehicles, and so on. But with population comes a concentration of wealth, in the proto-capitalist sixteenth to eighteenth centuries. This, combined with a growing concentration of lower classes, brings the phenomenon of street music and performance. Early noise abatement legislation (i.e. from that period) targets street criers and street music. R. Murray Schafer writes that the perception, which heightens in the nineteenth century, is that 'the street had now become the home of non-music, where it mixed with other kinds of sound-swill and sewage' ('Music, Non-music and the Soundscape', 36).[8] Jacques Attali adds, in his book *Noise*, that this is the period where the threat of those without power was crystallizing in the spaces of the city, and their culture was increasingly deemed 'noisy'. So what we think of as perhaps inherent to an idea of noise, its unwantedness, comes initially, and over a long period of time, with an undesirability that goes beyond the auditive unpleasantness of certain sounds.

This situation is of course exacerbated in the nineteenth-century industrializing city—machines add a layer of volume and continuity to unwanted sound. With mechanization, the perception of noise widens and the sounds of industry are associated with the 'noisier' working class, and retain their status as unwanted because low, because not acceptably hierarchized into the forms of 'high' music or meaning.

For Schafer it is not just class and hierarchies that count—it is the division of space, and, importantly in the history of thinking about sound, the enclosure of space, that has a huge bearing on what is thought of as noisy. He argues that there is a transition to 'indoor living', especially where the upper classes are concerned, notably with the development of plate glass for windows in the late seventeenth century. At this point, 'high' music is private, taking place in people's houses. This is the basis for the modern concert hall, where people are to attend to the music generated from a given spot within that space, and nothing else. They are certainly not to be allowed to make noises themselves, except at conventionally agreed moments, e.g. to applaud at the end. But what's on the outside? Now more than ever, there is a sense of sounds not generated by someone or something else, outside, being intrusive, unwanted. Music heightens the separation of the world into desired, organized sounds, and unwanted noise. For Hegel, 'music acquires an especially architectonic character because, freed from expressing emotion, it constructs on its own account, with a wealth of invention, a musically regular building of sound' (*Aesthetics*, vol. II, 894).[9] What goes on at the speculative level has its corollary in the world of class, of private and public. Schafer writes that 'with indoor living, two things developed antonymously: the high art of music and noise pollution—for noises were the sounds that were kept outside' ('Music, Non-music and the Soundscape', 35). The status of western art music depends on this excluded other, and even doubles this exclusion when it attempts to represent nature or specific sounds within it.

Noise and music were not always so separate. According to Attali, after Nietzsche, music was not autonomous, even in the west, until the early modern period. Even in Greek society, music and sound were part of a whole, part of a general sacrificial economy: although the sacrifice brought the threat of the divine, it was part of the process of the sacred, without which there is no sacred (at least in the terms laid out by Georges Bataille).[10] For Attali, the development of music, and even that it develops (over history, over time), is part of a continual creation of an outside, where noise is disorder:

> Primordially the production of music has as its function the creation, legitimation and maintenance of order. Its primary function is not to be sought in aesthetics, which is a modern invention, but in the effectiveness of its participation in social regulation. Music—pleasure in the spectacle of murder, organiser of the simulacrum masked beneath festival and transgression—creates order. (*Noise*, 30)[11]

When music is central to ritual, to sanctioned transgression, it is effectively not music: it is the noise that will gradually, progressively be excised in the same way that, for Bataille, we move cemeteries and abattoirs to the outskirts of towns. But that which music excludes can come back: Antonin Artaud uses the plague as a metaphor for theatre, for how a sacrificial, mobile, unwanted form of theatre would operate.[12] According to Attali, noise is returning, in the form of the omnipresence of purposeful muzak and advertising: this is the price for excluding certain practices as noise.

Within aesthetics, the tradition has it that the beautiful is so, in different ways, because of its link/reference/belonging to nature. For Kant, music can be pure or 'free beauty' (*Critique of Judgement*, 76–7),[13] but nature will always offer a better version. Music always runs the risk of being as if it were natural, either through imitation, which is cheating (169),[14] of being 'only an agreeable noise' (173), or too intrusive. On religious singing, Kant has the following to say: 'those who have recommended that the singing of hymns be included at family prayer have failed to consider that by such a *noisy* (and precisely because of this usually pharisaical) worship they impose great hardship on the public' (200n) [Kant's emphasis]. This neatly brings together the dual problematic of a society reducing the sacred in its ritual and possibly threatening forms, and the unwantedness of noise. Excessive celebration is out because it offends 'the public', the protestant, privatizing, proto-secular public. While nature is, for Kant, good to society's bad, or to its bad lowering of nature, perhaps we should ask where exactly the boundary of nature and culture is. Nowadays we might talk of a sound environment or even a sound ecology, but even when Kant writes what he is in favour of, in terms of sound or music, it is the natural music of birdsong, for example (80), because it is not being aesthetically directed. Maybe we should see the loud singing by someone else as an internalized nature–culture divide. Even if this new 'nature' is largely deemed offensive, it is closer *for the listener* to nature.

This brings us back to the twentieth century: for Russolo, the industrial world was humanity's environment—as we would always be interacting with our surroundings, we should regard those as our environment, and treat any sounds emanating from it in the same way. Attali, too, insists that 'life is full of noise and [. . .] death alone is silent: work noise, noise of man, noise of beast' (*Noise*, 3), and as for Cage, he writes that 'wherever we are, what we hear is mostly noise' (*Silence*, 3).[15]

When we combine Enlightenment views of nature versus culture and twentieth century thought on noise, we encounter something we're very familiar with by now: the notion that nature is a product of culture: the product that acquires a real status, often higher than culture, setting up a process of mutual legitimation, as now nature justifies cultural practices. Noise threatens this divide, as Theodor Adorno illustrates, unwittingly, in *Aesthetic Theory*. Here he complains about aeroplane noise ruining walks in the forest (311): but what is being ruined is precisely that acculturated form of nature that forgets, endlessly, its acculturatedness. While ostensibly it is a human noise that disrupts the tranquillity of the forest, what is actually being disturbed is the walk, a cultural phenomenon, with its human demand for calmness, with its foreknowledge of just how much nature you're going to get.[16]

Certain sounds within nature are deemed musical. For Rousseau, even early human communication falls into this category, but 'natural musical sounds' are separated off from meaningful communication just as surely as any other noise by virtue of not being humanly structured.[17] The music of Aube (Akifumi Nakajima) represents one way around this set of problems, in that it poses the question of what might count as music, in terms of naturalness, faithfulness to nature and human intervention. Most of his albums consist exclusively of one sound source (the sounds of nerves in the brain, water, the pages of the bible being torn, metal— are a few of the many sources), which is then heavily processed and turned into sound 'pieces'. The sounds have something musical about them (sometimes rhythm, sometimes a form of tonal progression), but tend not to settle into that, and in any case, do not consist of the narrow range of tones western music identifies as notes.

It is a common argument that noises can be soothing, due to our experience in the womb, and also our early pre-linguistic time of life. The experience of sound immerses us in our environment (it is often claimed). John Shepherd writes that 'while a sound may have a discrete material source [. . .] it is experienced as a phenomenon that encompasses and touches the listener in a cocoon-like fashion' ('Music as Cultural Text', 147); for Richard Leppert, 'sound, by its enveloping character, brings us closer to everything alive' ('Desire, Power and the Sonoric Landscape', 305).[18] Aube's sounds often recall this immersive, soothing quality, but ironically distort the source so that it is not as nature would have it. Often his processing of non-natural sounds might lead to something that sounds 'more natural'. In *Quadrotation* we see four different sources set up against one another. They are: steel, blood, fluorescent and glow-lamp, water. This suggestion of a new 'four elements' that would cross many traditional categories offers a way of approaching the divides outlined above.

Does Aube bring noise into music, make noise music, or noise? This question applies across the spectrum of 'noise music'. In other words, the question is, how do music and noise relate? The answer will vary of course, but there might be some general theoretical assumptions to be made, and these too might vary, according to when and where we think noise is. If noise is fundamental within nature, then maybe the invention of music (or language in general), as the human organization of sounds, is the way awareness or perception of noise spreads. If noise is fundamental to culture (including listeners within cultures), then it arises in contrast to other sounds we do not categorize as noise; these can be noises which we no longer hear, or the exact opposite, sounds organized into meaningful structures. The only difference between noise as natural and noise as cultural is temporal. Both are about the 'discovery' of noise, even if recognized as something of a reconstruction, a retrospective awareness that noise 'has always been there'. For humans, noise is nothing without having meaning, or law, or structure, or music as its other.

According to Attali, the relation is even more specific, as 'music is a channelization of noise' (*Noise*, 26). His vision is a quasi-Hegelian one, where noise is endlessly brought into culture and meaning, essentially through music, which acts as a key tool of power throughout western history. Music transforms amorphousness and something like natural freedom (i.e. that present in a 'state of nature') into society. As western history rolls on, a series of avant-garde musics and associated behaviours (nomadism, for example, subcultural behaviours, or lifestyles in general) accretes into a core of a developing society that combines progress with oppression:

> With noise is born disorder and its opposite: the world. With music is born power and its opposite: subversion. In noise can be read the codes of life, the relations among men [. . .], when it becomes sound, noise is the source of purpose and power, of the dream—Music. It is at the heart of the progressive rationalization of aesthetics, and it is a refuge for residual irrationality. (*Noise*, 6)

While parts of Attali's theory match the complexity of Hegel's vision of the dialectical development of Spirit, his view is more of a transformation of existing matter, from natural to cultural to political. Noise is originally threatening, a threat that is mobilized by humans, which gradually makes it lose its noisiness, or at least means it can only ever be noise temporarily. He writes that 'noise is a weapon and music, primordially, is the formation, domestication, and ritualization of that weapon as a simulacrum of ritual murder' (24).[19] So when noise is first part of the human world, it remains threatening, part of sacrifice. Nowhere is this more literally in evidence than in the 'brazen bull' of Phalaris, ruler of Acragas, in Sicily, in the sixth century BCE. Phalaris had Perilaus construct a bull in bronze, within which a human could be placed. A fire would be lit under the bull, and the heat would roast the victim. All the while, reeds placed in the nostrils of the bull would convert the screams into sounds like the bellowing of a bull. It seems that Perilaus was 'allowed' by Phalaris to test it himself.

Attali follows the Nietzsche of *The Birth of Tragedy* in privileging the Dionysian element of ancient Greek culture, where noise exhibits something of the threatening sacred world.[20] This gradually gets formalized into musical gestures, and in so doing illustrates, or, more accurately, provides the model for centralized control of death in the shape of ritual sacrifice. Attali is not clear whether sacrifice precedes mobilization of noise, but we can imagine earlier sacrifice not imagining representation in the noises it made, but conceiving of its noises as directly powerful, divine etc., and later, this becoming ritualized (in the thin sense of the word) in the shape of music. Music then replaces the sacrifice, suggesting it instead of making it happen or accompanying it (hence the 'residualness' of irrationality in music).

From that point on, in Attali's story, music operates at the spatial and temporal edges of what goes on to become western society, and mostly it comes to work as a prophetic indication of further social change. It 'is a herald, for change is inscribed in noise faster than it transforms society' (*Noise*, 5) and 'the noises of a society are in advance of its images and material conflicts' (11). I am not interested in the accuracy of these statements as such, and therefore the looseness of the term 'noise' can be ignored. What is of interest is the continual process opened up by this perspective, where music becomes an avant-garde, and in so doing is always, initially, at least, identified as noise. Only later does the old noise come to be seen as legitimate music. The moment of recuperation, though, signals the loss of something for musics that have willingly taken on their categorization as noise, and I think this is most telling for experimental and/or radical music in the latter part of the twentieth century (although dada and its 'museification' experienced the strange moment of failing while being too successful). Ultimately, for Attali, we will resist these recuperations, and he offers a naive vision of how new technology will make us all musicians, music producers, and so on, and that this will have positive implications for democracy (this is where the 2001 edition of his book is most self-congratulatory, and at its weakest).

Music is there to save us from the chaos it unwittingly reveals as its other and as its sources (i.e. if music is organized sound, then sound must need arranging), and while Kant gets very confused about music in his *Critique of Judgement*, Hegel offers pure certainty, while still showing that music's order can only function by rejecting noise, and in so doing, noise as something we are aware of as threat, comes to be, at least as potential:

On the one hand, we demand an expression of th[e] regularity [of the beat] as such so that this action can come to the individual's apprehension in a way itself subjective, and on the other hand we desire an interest less empty than this uniformity. Both are afforded by a musical accompaniment. It is thus that music accompanies the march of troops; this attunes the mind to the regularity of the step, immerses the individual in the business of marching, and concentrates his mind on what he has to do. For the same sort of reason, the disorderly restlessness of a lot of people in a restaurant and the unsatisfying excitement it causes is burdensome; this walking to and fro, this clattering and chattering should be regulated, and since in the intervals of eating and drinking we have to do with empty time, this emptiness should be filled. This is an occasion, like so many others, when music comes to the rescue and in addition wards off other thoughts, distractions, and ideas. (Hegel, *Aesthetics*, vol. II, 907)

Music can organize our bodies and keep our minds in order—long before Foucault supplies the critique of disciplined societies, philosophers and 'classical' music are harnessing notions of beauty as order. Long before 'background' music, Hegel is aware of the thin line between order and disorder, and this latter appears even in something like emptiness. Why? Because the empty is formless, a threatening emptiness that is not as simple as a lack. At the same time, the formless makes us think too much, and think 'badly' (i.e. thoughts that need to be warded off, if they cannot be corralled into a system).

It is unfortunate, but unavoidable, that a structuring of the history of noise has not only been Hegelian, tautological, and based on the notion of noise music driving musical progress. So we have a canon of the greats, the precursors, the moments that count. We cannot avoid this, but we can be aware of the paradox of relating a continuous history of what is by definition discontinuous, what is about disruption and disturbance. Noise is like the avant-garde—always what seeks to be ahead, even if assimilable to a history of those that were ahead (so contemporary art books that are surveys of art history praise progress and innovation as a result of modernist avant-garde values of progress and innovation, and then work back to reinterpret earlier art in this context—but this canon-formation is based on mutability, a mutability that got hidden, then lost, then denied). The canon is not to be ignored, but it can be messed about, broken down. One of the ways we can do this is to continually remind ourselves that a precursor (for example, Varèse) only becomes a precursor later on: comes to *always have been a precursor*.[21]

Michael Nyman makes an important move in this direction, when he identifies a categorical difference between avant-garde and experimental music. The former is produced by composers (Boulez, Stockhausen, and so on) and 'is conceived and executed along the well-trodden but sanctified path of the post-Renaissance tradition' (*Experimental Music*, 1).[22] In other words, the score, the orchestra, the composer, the persistence of western tonal schemes (however dissonant) are avant-garde, but only in a limited way. The true avant-garde is engaged in practices which undermine and dispute western art music as a whole, and is therefore to be seen as experimental. Notions of finished pieces, competence of performers, composition, means of production (of sounds, of pieces) are all to be questioned.

For Nyman, as for many, the pivotal figure is John Cage, and in particular, his piece 4' 33". This is now widely accepted, but Nyman wrote this in the early 1970s, very much as an active participant in 'the future of music', so his intervention is also one of the moments Cage is moved to the centre, to the pivotal position, so more than a simple observation of fact. Of course, there are earlier moments we can point to, and Nyman's distinction can work just as clearly when we look at the more experimental composers of the earlier part of the twentieth century.

There is then, a key difference between the use of dissonance or unfamiliar elements (such as quotation of folk songs in Stravinsky or Bartók) in orchestral or chamber music in or around tonality, and the experiments Satie, Russolo, Kurt Schwitters, or (at a push) Varèse, were engaged in. The distinction is not a pure one, and if you were to insist too strongly on it, it could be easily deconstructed. We need to acknowledge that this difference occurs *after*, or as a result of Nyman's distinction, and applies retrospectively, in light of the proliferation of noise musics. For me, we can talk about dissonance in Beethoven, Berlioz, Wagner, Richard Strauss or Arnold Schoenberg, but it can only be thought of as noise in newness (essentially as seen by Attali), while Futurists such as Russolo signal a world where the arrangement of musical notes is secondary.

Noise cannot be imagined as a synonym for dissonance, even if the judgement of noise by the then-surprised publics is imposed on modernist dissonance. Dissonance works through its rethinking of consonance, and composers using it tended to think of their work as reinvigorating the western tradition of music. Schoenberg's twelve-tone system was often imagined to be 'atonal', and it does diminish one hierarchy (of dominant tones), but this dissonance was not there to wreck or disturb music: 'dissonances need not be a spicy addition to dull sounds. They are natural and logical outgrowths of an organism' (Schoenberg, 'My Evolution', 91). He rejected the idea that he was doing anything other than continuing the project of 'classical' music, with a 'more inclusive sound-material', so that '*nothing essential changes in all this!*' ('The New Music', 137).[23] Despite my claim for a fundamental difference between those who sought to renew music and those who were against the existing institution of music, all imagined, at some level, that they were contributing to advancing music. Russolo himself notes that 'noise instruments expand the chromatic-diatonic system without destroying it' (*The Art of Noises*, 80). Russolo, Satie, Varèse and Charles Ives all wrote scores to be performed, but the essential difference is that they wished to incorporate non- or extra-musical sounds. Audiences, though, heard non-musical sounds in Debussy, Stravinsky or Schoenberg, and in terms of initial reception, all have moments where performances are disrupted by the unwanted noise of audience protest (such as the riot at a performance of Stravinsky's *Rite of Spring*, in Paris, on 29 May 1913, or the uproar at the first public performance of noise music (as Russolo puts it) in Milan, 21 April 1914).[24] To the first distinction of wishing to use sounds previously thought of not as bad music, but as non-music, we can add a second that is the wish to provoke, to expand the field of the rethinking of art into a rejection of how it had thus far been done. This precisely matches (but without mapping directly on to) the shift in visual art from Impressionism and Cubism to Futurism and dada. It is not that the practitioners necessarily saw themselves as competitors, but how they associated with the art institutions (including the public) differed. Futurism, through Russolo in particular, is the key to this shift.

Russolo himself took his inspiration for his 'art of noises' from Marinetti's poetry, which he describes as the first poetry capable of living in the new age of technology, cities and mass warfare. This latter, in particular, called for 'the noise instrumentation of Futurist *free words*' (*The Art of Noises*, 49). Marinetti's poems used onomatopoeia to bring noise into language, usually the noise of bombs, bullets, and so on. What is also important is that this poetry be read, and the noisiness would inflect even the more straightforwardly written parts. Similarly, also in the 1910s and early 1920s, dada would bring this element into their performances, further disrupting the 'reading' by pitting it against other simultaneous performances of music, plays or more shouting/poetry. In a way, this type of poetry, tied in with performance, would continue without great changes, throughout Fluxus's time and on into the 1960s, and beyond, in the shape of 'sound poetry'.

Futurism also announced a technological aesthetic. Rather than just representing or illustrating the relatively newly industrialized, militarized and technologized urban environment, this world would be brought directly into art. It would be recognized as being of aesthetic value in itself, and also mobilized into artworks to raise awareness of the beauty of machinery, warfare and industry. An endless stream of manifestos hammers the point home. Marinetti's 'The Founding and Manifesto of Futurism' (1909) proclaims the glory of war, the beauty of industry, and above all, the 'beauty of speed' (*Futurist Manifestos*, 21).[25] Futurism saw technology and mechanical aggression as the death knell for polite art and society. Balilla Pratella attacked the conservatism of music, particularly in Italy, and although he praises composers such as Debussy and Richard Strauss, he is already trying to look beyond symphonic renovation ('Manifesto of Futurist Musicians' [1910], 32).[26] But it is Luigi Russolo who synthesizes these ideas in his *Art of Noises*, which first appeared in 1913.

Like many of the Futurists, Russolo's ideas were way ahead of the actual art he produced: after several rousing chapters on our new ways of seeing and hearing, and the shiny but harsh world of modern noise, he still returns to the question of finding the right pitches for noises, and carefully shaping and moulding the new noise instruments he had devised (*The Art of Noises*, 86–7). His ideas about what noise is and how it can constitute art and even be aesthetically pleasing in the most simple sense are what make this book important. Having stated that noise was 'born' in the nineteenth century, he adds that 'today, noise is triumphant and reigns sovereign over the sensibility of men. Through many centuries life unfolded silently, or at least quietly' (23). Russolo seems to be offering a very clear 'when' for the advent of noise, but life itself is noisy: 'every manifestation of life is accompanied by noise' (27), and noises in nature should actually be interesting to us in their own right (see 41–3). So there had always been noise, or at least noises, but this seems to have been heightened in the expanding urban environment of the west (arguably this applies elsewhere too, but the conclusions drawn about noise by Russolo [or Satie or Cage etc.] refer back to the western art music tradition, and produce an aesthetic of progress, in the shape of avant-gardes, to combat it, so for now, the new noisy environment is largely in the west). Noise music would try to capture the inherent richness of noise (39) and its newly acquired intensity in cities. But Russolo is not simply adhering to the Pythagorean idea of capturing sounds from the infinite musicality of the universe. For Russolo, modern society has added to and developed the already noisy universe, and drawn our attention through its sonic intensity to that very noisiness. Instead of one continuum of noise that humans feature in, noise is supplemented by urban industrial soundworlds, and from that point on, we recognize the noisiness of nature. His conclusion is that modern listeners now exist who are ready for noise music (24, 85), and that in harnessing this, 'our multiplied sensibility, having been conquered by Futurist eyes, will finally have Futurist ears' (29).

Russolo designed and built his noise machines, his *intonarumori*, in order to replace the old orchestra. Among the many types (which would later be combined in 'noise harmoniums' of various sizes) were hummers, bursters, rubbers, cracklers. Instead of musical tones, sounds would be created, often inspired by machinery, which although pitched, would work between and link different pitches, using microtones and overtones—so the instruments would remain noisy. Although the machines would not represent the sound of hammers or sirens, they could certainly imitate already existing sounds; appropriately, Russolo is the complete antithesis of Kant, in that the former praises imitation (*The Art of Noises*, 44). In harnessing noise, the realm of music would be made infinite, and 'for him who *understands* it, noise represents instead an inexhaustible source of sensations' (41). Two things stand out in this statement: first, the emphasis, as witnessed elsewhere in *The Art of Noises*, on the listener. This shows a recognition that noise music will be something different from music, in that the musical piece is not a finished product under the control of a composer. On the other hand, the statement also shows that while you might not have to be classically trained to like the new music, there are still better and worse listeners.

Many of Russolo's contemporaries might not have been seen by him as listening well enough, for the predominant reaction among even experimental composers was of being interested but unwilling to accept the ultimate usefulness of music created only from noises, and would, at best only incorporate 'non-musical' elements. Debussy is fairly typical in identifying Futurist music as limited in comparison to more overtly musical forms: '[Futurist music] claims to reassemble all the noises of a modern capital city and bring them together in a symphony [. . .]. It's a very practical way of recruiting an orchestra, but can it ever really compete with that wonderful sound of a steel mill in full swing?' (*Debussy on Music*, 288). In other words, yes it is a beautiful sound, but stick to the real thing. Varèse also had doubts, and Fernand Ouellette glosses his view like this: the Futurists 'never succeeded in progressing any further than mere noise. They produced no work of art. There was no attempt to go beyond the simple imitation or unmodified utilization of familiar noises—such as the klaxon—on stage' (*Edgard Varèse*, 38).[27] Ironically, Russolo and others who used his *intonarumori* were closer to Varèse than either side would have liked, as they ended up mostly combining the noise instruments with more traditional ones, and Varèse incorporated sounds such as sirens into his music.[28] Schoenberg, meanwhile, while revolutionizing the concept of tonality (i.e. it was always to be re-established anew) and accepting that art could stray far from beauty (see his 'Eartraining through Composing', 380, on this last point) was uninterested in the use of noises. We must 'force nature', he writes, 'otherwise we can either not grasp it, or else, if one lets the sounds run as they please, it remains a children's game, like electrical experiments with elderberries or tobogganing or the like' ('Theory of Form', 253).[29] Unwittingly, Schoenberg shows how far he is from the more radical experimental art of Futurism, dada, or even Surrealism, which would be more than happy to be associated with such fripperies, even if his thoughts correctly highlight the utopianism in imagining you can bring nature into art without in some way processing it.

So far, it might seem as if 'real' noise music is very literal, very directly using noise (e.g. Russolo), but from Wagner to Schoenberg, and later on in Boulez and Stockhausen, there is noise, of a very clear form, as signalled by Attali: that of temporarily being misheard, the noise of a dissonance that is later accepted. Schoenberg represents the highly didactic strain of composing: 'what I am doing is perfectly musical, and one day you will all catch up and understand me'. He is far from wrong, but this is a search for acceptance, for the acknowledgement of the renewal of a moribund art, while all around other art movements are doing something else, something more noisy (even if those noises too, whatever the intention of its producers, become intelligible over time).

In stark opposition to Schoenberg's self-importance and validation of art music are Ives and Satie, both of whom introduce a different form of noise to concert music—in the shape of popular music, referring to it, but also writing it. Ives combined extensive use of dissonance with the writing of songs that have gradually come to be seen as essential to the identity of twentieth-century America. He was not trying to disturb audiences as such: the composer Henry Cowell (with Sidney Cowell) notes that 'at a time when consecutive extreme dissonances were unknown, Ives used them constantly whenever, in his judgement, they constituted the most powerful harmonic force for his purpose. He had no sense of their being ugly, or undesirable, or in any way unpleasant' (*Charles Ives and His Music*, 155).[30] But I think the Cowells' judgement is of its time. Composers and musicians would bolster each other through claims of musicality rather than noisiness, or disruption. However radical the composer, most were dismayed at the violent reactions against their music and the almost total commercial failure of their work.

As well as the dissonant elements in the music, Ives disturbs the genres of music, something essential in all 'noise music', where expectations are supposed, however temporarily, to be upset. While not crucial to the noisiness or otherwise of Ives, it is important to note his relation to the music publishing industry. Although he was a successful businessman, his ideas were definitely left-wing, and he refused to have copyright on his work, to the puzzlement and annoyance of publishers who would assign him it, and then be argued against until it was removed. So what? Attali identifies the invention of copyright as a key control over music production, bringing it into the capitalist realm of regulation and profit (*Noise*, 51–5). The question of ownership of music is significant for noise as economic disruption, notably via sampling (see chapter 12), but contrast Ives' position with that of Schoenberg, who complains that intellectual property seems to be the only type to be allowed to be taken away ('Human Rights', 509).[31] Schoenberg's position is still against the functioning of the existing institutions, and in line with the vast majority of musicians, but Ives stands here as precursor to values of musicians from later decades of the twentieth century.

Satie is well known for his tranquil piano music, but even that can be seen as rebellion against the growing complexity of 'classical' music of the late nineteenth and early twentieth century (as with minimalism in the 1960s and 1970s). But he also created stranger works, incorporating non-musical sounds, notably in *Parade*, for Cocteau's ballet. Here there are sirens, a gun, a typewriter, a spinning lottery wheel, a *bouteillophone* (made of bottles), and extensive percussion. These short bursts of 'non-musical' sound are integrated into what is still a recognisable piece of music, if quite a repetitive piece. Satie imagined many different futures for music: 'the mysterious frontiers which separate the realm of noise from that of music are tending increasingly to disappear [tendent de plus en plus à s'effacer]' (Satie, *Écrits*, 140).[32] There should also be a 'musique d'ameublement'—furniture music. Normally, he argues, music has nothing to do, so why not have music for specific purposes, or actions. This would largely be in the background, literally ambient, but just like lighting, there would be different musics for different settings.[33] He imagines an advertisement: 'Don't go to sleep without listening to a track of "musique d'ameublement" or you'll sleep badly' (*Écrits*, 190). This new type of music steps outside all of the existing genres of the time (even if the boundaries between music and other activities would have been much more fluid prior to the eighteenth century), and rethinks incidental music as something positive. In terms of noise, it could even be seen as a counter to it, controlling your own surrounding soundworld, but it is just as much a mobilization of noise as a way of preventing or combating it, and above all, the relation between music and noise is rethought. Lastly, his piece *Vexations* stands as an essential moment in the reconceptualizing of what music is and how it works. This reasonably short piece is to be played 840 times, which would take over a day to perform. The player is at least as tested as any audience. Noise is built into this piece as it directly poses the question of musical competence and consistency. Prefiguring Fluxus and the performance art of the 1960s and 1970s, this is an endurance test, without, for example, the narrative 'reward' of Wagner's 'Ring' cycle. Content becomes irrelevant, expression hard to control, as fatigue and trance set in. This most fixed of pieces becomes aleatory, fluid. Also, maybe it was never meant to be played, and its concept is far more important than any realization it might have.

Satie was a major inspiration for John Cage (as acknowledged in the latter's *Cheap Imitation*), who takes all those experimental and/or noisy elements of Satie and expands on them. The growth of noise is just that, and exponential in the case of Cage. From experiments with turntables and radios, to percussive music, to chance generation of work, through the incorporation of any and all sound to the recentring of music as simply 'organized sound' for and only existing through the listener, Cage is a central figure in any thought about noise, and his *4' 33"* the moment we can pick to illustrate this (as Nyman argues, *Experimental Music*, 2, and the first two chapters expand on this). *4' 33"* is a piece lasting 4 minutes and 33 seconds. The first time it was played, in 1952, David Tudor 'played' it on a piano. The instructions are that there be three movements, indicated by the performer, and these movements are to be silent. The piece can vary, and be 'played' on any instrument. But Tudor or anyone else is only the framing device: like Piero Manzoni's *Socle du monde* (where an upside down plinth is placed on the earth, making the world the art object), everything else becomes the material. The listeners will not hear everything else, though, if they are today's humans, but will instead have a specific sound environment for the duration of the piece. What was noise (including sounds made by the audience) becomes the piece. In Cage's thoughts, as Kahn clearly shows, this meant accessing some form of the 'music of the spheres', the inherent musicality of the universe, even if also raising the question of whether this would be the case without listeners.[34] Noise is not abolished when 'all sound' is let in—unpredictability means a more subtle (less literal) form of noise and the interplay of noise and music persist alike. *4' 33"* and Cage's other silent pieces have become an ironic moment in the history of audience reaction to experimental music, as instead of jeering or complaining, the later audiences sit attentively, waiting for 'music' to come to them. Of course, if they make lots of noise, then they might be diminishing the strength of the piece (through controlling it, perhaps as a defence mechanism), but the piece *cannot fail*, and ultimately, failure is something that is increasingly important in the linking of noise and music. *4' 33"* is still didactic; it still tries to teach us about music we have missed up until now, caught as we were in tonality, or our own mundane sound production.

Kahn goes further, arguing that Cage needs to silence in order to 'let silence be'. The silence of the performer of *4' 33"* can be understood as an extension of the traditional silencing of the audience to better appreciate the music being performed (*Noise Water Meat*, 166). Music itself is silenced, sacrificed to the musicality of the world: '[Cage] not only filled music up; he left no sonorous (or potentially sonorous) place outside music and left no more means to materially regenerate music. He opened music up into an emancipatory endgame' (164). In so doing, Cage also closed off the unwantedness of sounds, or certain sounds. All sound was good, so how could there be noise—and for noise here, read also diversity, social and aural dissonance (162). Kahn's point is well made: within music and sound art, Cage is unquestioningly accepted as a major authority, and this needs balancing, but Kahn's impatience with the worship of Cage's genius means that he spends a lot of time on subtly undermining Cage, and ends up reinforcing the centrality of his influence. But once this job is done, I think we can reassess Cage in terms of individual pieces or strategies, and these will show an avant-gardism in spite of Cage's limits or obsession with 'letting noises be', to the point where they cannot be noise. Although many of these works precede *4' 33"*, that work is still within the Futurist lineage, and works such as the *Imaginary Landscapes* belong in the next phase, in terms of noise: where electricity expands audition.

NOTES

1. Nietzsche, *The Birth of Tragedy and The Case of Wagner* (New York: Vintage, 1967). Emphasis is Nietzsche's.
2. We should not imagine that Derrida's reprivileging of writing (écriture) and challenges to the authenticity of speech means he is inattentive to the problem of listening (see 'Tympan', in *Margins of Philosophy* [Chicago: Chicago University Press, 1984], *Ulysses Gramophone: Hear Say Yes in Joyce* [London: Routledge, 1992], among many) and to the human voice as different to speech (see his *Artaud le Moma* [Paris: Galilée, 2002], for example).
3. Kroker, *Spasm: Virtual Reality, Android Music, Electric Flesh* (New York: St Martin's Press, 1993).
4. Russolo, *The Art of Noises* (New York: Pendragon, 1986).
5. Gordon, 'Songs from the Museum of the Future: Russian Sound Creation (1910–1930)', in Douglas Kahn and Gregory Whitehead (eds), *Wireless Imagination: Sound, Radio and the Avant-Garde* (Cambridge, MA: MIT Press, 1994), 197–243.
6. Cage, *Silence: Lectures and Writings* (London: Marion Boyars, 1968).
7. Kahn, *Noise Water Meat: A History of Sound in the Arts* (Cambridge, MA: MIT Press, 1999).
8. Schafer, 'Music, Non-music and the Soundscape', in John Paynter et al. (eds), *The Companion to Contemporary Musical Thought*, vol. I (London: Routledge, 1992), 34–45.

9. Hegel, *Aesthetics*, vol. II (Oxford: Clarendon, 1975).

10. On this, see in particular Georges *Bataille, Visions of Excess, Selected Writings, 1927–1939* (ed. Allan Stoekl) (Minneapolis: University of Minnesota Press, 1985), and Bataille, *The Accursed Share* (New York: Zone, 1991).

11. Attali, *Noise: The Political Economy of Music* (Minneapolis: University of Minnesota Press, 1985). This book, first published in 1977, has itself become part of the 'when' of noise, part of the history of thinking about noise. Unfortunately, Attali has substantially rewritten his book (*Bruits: essai sur l'économie politique de la musique* [Paris: PUF/Fayard, 2001], and effectively diminished the Nietzschean thinking in order to compound some of the problems of the first edition. He overstates his prescience of 1977, and shows an embarrassingly feeble grasp of the music he is using to 'update' his book. I will largely be referring to the first version of this text.

12. Artaud*, The Theatre and Its Double* (London: John Calder, 1970), 7–22.

13. Kant, *Critique of Judgement* (Indianapolis: Hackett, 1987): 'Many birds (the parrot, the humming-bird, the bird of paradise) and a lot of crustaceans in the sea are free beauties themselves and belong to no object determined by concepts as to its purpose, but we like them freely and on their own account. [. . .] What we call fantasias in music (namely music without a topic [Thema], indeed all music not set to words) may also be included in the same class' (76–7).

14. The nightingale's song is among the most beautiful sounds, writes Kant, so in the absence of one, a 'jovial innkeeper' would 'hid[e] in the bush some roguish youngster who (with a reed or a rush in his mouth) knew how to copy that song in a way very similar to nature's. But as soon as one realises that it was all deception, no one will long endure listening to this song that before he considered so charming'.

15. This sentence is much more curious than I imagine Cage intended it to be: are we always a we, 'wherever we are'? If what we hear is noise, how do we understand where we are, or that we exists as an entity? Is noise just there, and we stumble across it, or is our hearing effectively the producer of noise as the thing 'we' hear? Is it noise before we hear it? Or if we don't? Or if we are not 'we'? Noise is a constant, it would appear, and there is a large amount of it, but the 'mostly' is still letting us hear more than it says: is all that we hear 'mostly noise'? Or is it that most of the sounds we hear are noise (while some are not)? Is our hearing mostly occupied with noise? Could we not also say that what we mostly do not hear is noise? (i.e. that there is always noise occurring, but actually 'we', 'wherever "we" are' are mostly not hearing that noise even as 'what we hear is mostly noise'). The noise that comes to 'our' ear is made background, if it is 'mostly noise', so our hearing both makes and unmakes noise. None of this even touches the question of whether we listen or can choose to listen, wherever we are, to noise. Or whether it would still be 'mostly noise'.

16. Adorno, *Aesthetic Theory* (Minneapolis: University of Minnesota Press, 1997).

17. See Rousseau, *Discourse on the Origin of Languages* (Oxford: Oxford University Press, 1999).

18. Shepherd, 'Music as Cultural Text', in Paynter et al. (eds), *The Companion to Contemporary Musical Thought*, vol. I, 128–55; Leppert, 'Desire, Power and the Sonoric Landscape', in Andrew Leyshon, David Matless, George Revil (eds), *The Place of Music* (New York and London: Guilford Press, 1998), 291–321.

19. Here Attali directly 'echoes' Nietzsche, who writes that 'optimistic dialectic drives music out of tragedy with the scourges of its syllogisms; that is, it destroys the essence of tragedy, which can be interpreted only as a manifestation and projection into images of Dionysian states, as the visible symbolizing of music, as the dream-world of a Dionysian intoxication' (*The Birth of Tragedy*, 92). Nietzsche, in turn, is much more Hegelian than he might wish, in bringing the Apollonian and Dionysian together (see 128–33 and passim).

20. Adorno also ties Hegel and the Dionysian, when writing that 'the "Spirit" in Beethoven, the Hegelian element, the totality, is nothing other than nature becoming aware of itself, the chthonic element' (*Beethoven: The Philosophy of Music* [Cambridge: Polity, 1998], 166). Furthermore, this is both 'demonic' and 'ideal' (rather than just being a resolution of the difference between them) (167).

21. Debussy offers another take on this idea: 'the more music was written, the more precursors there were. If certain periods were lacking precursors, the following period would

simply have to invent some' (*Debussy, Writings on Music* [London: Secker & Warburg, 1977]).

22. Nyman, *Experimental Music: Cage and Beyond*, second edition (Cambridge: Cambridge University Press, 1999).

23. Schoenberg, 'My Evolution', 'The New Music', in *Style and Idea: Selected Writings* (London: Faber & Faber, 1975), 79–92, 137–9 respectively. Emphasis in the original.

24. The Futurists quelled this particular 'uproar' by launching themselves into the crowd, beating up the dissenters (*The Art of Noises*, 33).

25. Marinetti, 'The Founding and Manifesto of Futurism', in Umbro Apollonio (ed), *Futurist Manifestos* (London: Thames & Hudson, 1973), 19–24.

26. Pratella, 'Manifesto of Futurist Musicians', in *Futurist Manifestos*, 31–8.

27. Ouellette, *Edgard Varèse* (London: Calder and Boyars, 1973). Ouellette is referring to Varèse's own manifesto that appeared in *391*, no. 5.

28. Varèse certainly also saw himself renewing, even as he innovated within, the world of orchestral music. His work was largely percussion based, and the ensembles unusual as a result. He, like Satie before him, would incorporate sirens, and other non-musical sources of sound (mostly percussive). His aggressive, relatively simple works stand in stark contrast to most other musical avant-gardism of the mid-twentieth century, and hence it is only with the growth of *musique concrète* and electronic music that he came to be regarded as significant.

29. Schoenberg, 'Eartraining through Composing', and 'Theory of Form', in *Style and Idea*, 377–82, 253–5 respectively.

30. Henry and Sidney Cowell, *Charles Ives and His Music* (New York: Oxford University Press, 1955).

31. Schoenberg, 'Human Rights', in *Style and Idea*, 506–12.

32. Satie, *Écrits* (Paris: Éditions Champ Libre, 1977). Translations my own.

33. For the connection between Satie's 'furniture music' and John Cage's use of silence, see Kahn, *Noise Water Meat*, 179–81. Kahn also notes the initial involvement of Darius Milhaud (179).

34. Kahn also argues the move to 'silence' is one 'from noise to panaurality' (*Noise Water Meat*, 159), where listening makes musical, and noise disappears, even as it ostensibly occurs.

2
TECHNOLOGIES

So far, I have focused on the conceptual change that led to the incorporation of what had been perceived as noises into music, and also how some tried to resist this incorporation, even as they drew noises to the attention of culture. In the case of sound and noise, the role of technology, through electricity and electronics in particular, is directly vital to all developments in the history of noise and noise music. Technology has both offered a spur and a means for expanding, exploring or exploding the world of cultured sound. In this chapter, I want to propose a way of linking technology to conceptual technologies or strategies which help us to clarify new noises in art and music leading up to 1960. To begin with, we should note that technology has to be seen in the widest sense, before assessing the impact of specific instances. Martin Heidegger argues that technology is relational, a mode that defines how humans interact with the world, and, above all, that it is 'a way of revealing', or a 'realm of revealing, i.e. of truth' ('The Question Concerning Technology', 318).[1]

This means it is part of our being, being as part of, or as counterpart to, the world. The modern world has literalized this, and limited it to tools we use for work in the world. As a result, we imagine that beings, tools and the world all occupy distinct places (or are discrete categories) and we lose contact with a more authentic way of being. As technology in the usual, limited sense is so central to noise (as it is to music), this insight about technology can at least provide us with a way of refusing obsessions with machine technology in its own right. For the moment, though, the significance of Heidegger's idea is that there can be no separation of technology from other human activities.

This was also clear to writers such as Paul Valéry and Walter Benjamin, who both posited a modern society where technological inventions would come to alter our ways of living and being. Their visions, similarly to the later Marshall McLuhan, tend to emphasize the force material technology has on creativity and culture, altering how art is produced, and then what kind of art. Benjamin argues, for example, that photography not only influenced the Impressionists, but also that it freed painters in general from traditional (or at least standardized), representational concerns. They would now be free to experiment, as the camera could document. Even if we accept this argument (as many do), we could add that in reality, Daguerre's patenting of 1839 did not signal anything like what we would recognize as photographic documentation of the instant. This would only really arrive in the late nineteenth century, after the strangely monumental records made of the American civil war and the Franco-Prussian war and Paris Commune of 1870–1.

Joel Chadabe, in his book *Electric Sound*, offers a similar genealogy for the development of experimental electronic music.[2] He writes of a series of 'milestones', where the first is the Telharmonium, an instrument created by Thaddeus Cahill in 1906; the second is the 'opening up of music to all sounds' (ix), which he identifies as starting in the 1930s, and then running concurrently with the development of that first machinic milestone (which ends up in the synthesizers of the 1950s). The third and fourth are purely machine developments, and the fifth is, unironically, a synthesis, where 'the fifth milestone will mark the resolution of still-unresolved design issues and the crystallization of still-forming concepts into the many potential forms of the electronic musical instrument' (xi)—perhaps forming some new sort of cyborg, a Kraftwerk dream.

This sort of determinism is rejected by Kahn. Writing on the specific example of *musique concrète*'s use or otherwise of tape, he says:

> Obviously, with the precedence of phonograph lathes and optical sound film in the 1920s, the inheritance from the German military of the magnetic audio-tape recorder by post-World War II composers and artists did not have the technologically determinist effect upon artistic practice so often attributed to it; that is, its mere availability did not engender an art appropriate to it. ('Introduction: Histories of Sound Once Removed', 12)[3]

Neither I, nor, I imagine, Kahn, would argue that Benjamin or even McLuhan are determinist, but it can already be too much to emphasize the way machines have influence, making it seem as if the process goes in only one direction. For example, we could argue that the way Impressionists painted drove the search for machinery that could truly capture an instant, or, better still, that photography and Impressionism were part of a larger discourse about both capture and experimentation. This is the best way to approach how technology and new ideas about sound interacted in the early twentieth century. Kahn goes some of the way towards this in proposing a model of three 'figures': vibration, inscription and transmission ('Introduction', 14–22). The first of these is the notion, remaining from classical Greek culture, that all is in vibration, and that musicians and music instruments capture fragments of the celestial music. This thinking is doubled in the machinery used to produce music up until the late nineteenth century. At that point, the inscription of actual sounds completes a process started in the shape of the musical score, and the phonograph inspires a new way of imagining sound as something that is present when brought out, and becomes more human as a result. Last, transmission alters the spatial element, so that sound can be separated from its object. So sound is revealed as not being autonomous in any way at all: what we have are different ways of thinking sound (and music), and these different ways of thinking are paralleled by specific material technologies, so that there is no fundamental primacy of either machine or idea/discourse.

This model can be developed further: we might imagine that the relative importance of technological and conceptual elements (in music or sound production) might vary, and we could also imagine that Kahn's three types could all be present but in different degrees—particularly in terms of noise as something sought rather than rejected. In addition, although it is technically right, historically, to order those three moments that way, the gap between them is not so clear—transmission is intimately linked almost from the beginning with inscription. This is primarily through amplification, as Kahn notes elsewhere (*Noise Water Meat*, 194, 202). Amplification increases the range of the audible, both in terms of breadth (variety of sounds to be heard) and depth (distance of audibility).

Phonograph and gramophone technology is entirely bound up with amplification (whether through horns, circuits or chips), and amplification is not just behind transmission; it *is* transmission. Kahn's notion of transmission is one where the location of the first sound is literally unconnected to the second (where it is heard), through wireless technology ('Introduction', 22). It would seem perfectly possible to argue, however, that in the wider sense, we are already talking about transmission when we think of cables linking phones or a Telharmonium to restaurants on Broadway (see Chadabe, *Electric Sound*, 5). This transmission can be extended to the phonograph, where there is already a gap between the first sound ('recorded') by the needle and the second sound emerging from the loudspeaker. The inscription of the record in the first place is also a form of transmission, albeit a fully material one, where solids are the means of transmission. Benjamin argues that mechanical reproduction alters the status of the original artwork, and it does this through *dissemination*.[4]

Technological dissemination of sound (and 'sound objects' such as cylinders or records) can be set in opposition to sound as acoustic vibration. A sound heard by humans will be some sort of acoustic vibration of the air, but the production of that vibration has to be rethought once amplification, radio, the phonograph, and new instruments such as the ethereal theremin come into play. Electricity catalyzes the new sounds of the late nineteenth and early twentieth century, and the notion of a direct relation between movement (of a musician's fingers, for example) creating a movement (of e.g. strings) leading to another movement (air) and another (of the ear) is broken up. Electricity is the noise of acoustics and of psychological space (just as phenomenology of the early twentieth century resituates the subject in continual relation to object). This space is opened up on the inside of buildings, and across and between buildings, while the industrialized cities expand and periodically war as transmission (through bombs) intervenes.[5]

Radio expands the soundworld literally, but also often as a side-effect of its main purpose (of broadcasting information, music, drama, and so on). Between the signals lurks endless variation of static, different 'colours' of noise—some of which is the background radiation of the universe (just as it is discovered to be such, radio technology seeks to eliminate it through digitalization and compression). The signal itself can come and go, and weather conditions will alter which signals can be picked up—'interference' is a key part of the spectrum of what humans hear as sound via radios. Artists such as Kurt Weill and Berthold Brecht were keen to use the radio for formal dramatic experimentation, while John Cage would imagine a different usage—or misuse, in his *Imaginary Landscapes*, where radios would be the instruments. Rather than a passive conductor of artworks as 'radio', the plurality of radio across multiple radios would free even very straightforward broadcasts from their limited aims. Orson Welles would disturb the American public with his adaptation of *The War of the Worlds* (in 1938), and Antonin Artaud would disturb the French radio station that commissioned his *Pour en finir avec le jugement de Dieu* ('To be done with the Judgement of God') to the point where they refused to broadcast it.[6]

Artaud's piece is a great example of how literal noise becomes a more interesting threat. *Pour en finir* is a sequence of pieces that combine shots, screaming, approximate drumming and rants about God, America, shit, aliens, and so on. The content and form work together, as a genuine Sadean philosophy unravels to the point where it cannot be heard as philosophy. At the same time, the work cannot be heard as aimless noise, as it continually insists on its content. The suspicion that it is all an elaborate joke—not instead of being serious, but as well as—never leaves either. In his *Theatre and Its Double*, Artaud had thought of theatre as plague, and good theatre must work by contagion—so what better than to use the French state's broadcast company to infiltrate into peoples' homes—he was, after all, a known writer, and it would take some time for the outraged to switch off. *Pour en finir* is a prime example of Attali's notion of noise—where something is deemed to be noise as it offends, and this judgement occurs via officialdom. It is also transgressive in more than its scatological content. It crosses genres, does not tie together neatly, except parodically, through the repeated outbursts of squealing and percussion. Unfortunately, the release of Artaud's 'broadcast' (which was heard on radio only many years after it was scheduled) on CD comes complete with a CD of remixes which restrain whatever residual oddness it may have had, replacing it with already dated sampling and dancification strategies (i.e. putting beats to samples from the broadcast, and, 'crazily' [sic], messing up the samples through editing). The final product makes the initial work seem as nostalgic as the new accompanying use of it.

At more or less the same time, though, the French state was sanctioning the creation of studios and studio work by Pierre Schaeffer, who coined the term *musique concrète* to describe collages or mixes of found sounds. Such patronage of music 'research', with its futuristic and futurological rhetoric of scientific exploration of sound and listening, would continue in France, through the Maison de la Radio of Radio France, and be paralleled in Germany, up to and beyond the work at Darmstadt. There is a sense, in radio, editing/collage work and the invention of new instruments and sounds, that experimental music really was some sort of laboratory, although Cage saw the 'experiment' element differently: instead of attempting to achieve a particular outcome, one should 'set about discovering means to let sounds be themselves rather than vehicles for man-made theories or expressions of human sentiments' ('Experimental Music', 10). While experimenters around him were attempting to attain particular outcomes, Cage wanted both more and less: more than something musical or technical, and less because less specific. What we will have, he writes, is 'new music, new listening' (*ibid.*): no hierarchy, no cause and effect, instead a sort of unpredictable and ever-changing harmony.

Cage also used turntables/gramophones and radios in his *Imaginary Landscapes*. The combination of sounds produced from multiple recordings simultaneously would form part of the material, but so too would the workings of the machinery, through the changing of speeds, the inclusion of other incidental noises from the needle, or from the records. In his *Cartridge Music*, he went further, using the record players themselves as instruments (as turntablists would today, notably, for us, Otomo Yoshihide, DJ/Rupture, Christian Marclay [in a more sound art format], Martin Tétreault). The noises that come from playing records have become a commonplace ambience since sampling took off—signalling nostalgia, authenticity, warmth—or, less often, attempting to disturb the smoothness of digitality, but even early recording operated in the realm of noise. Edison sought to capture the voices of the dead on wax cylinders (and this carried on with Konstantin Raudive's tape recording, where it is precisely the unexpected sounds, difficult to understand, that are scanned, slowed down, reversed, and so on, to get to the spirit voices). The excess of what we now refer to as analogue recording suggested an extension of the soundworld in all directions, including time, and despite Cage and others taking this to be a sound utopia unfolding, it was in the reduction through force or perversion of function that noise could interfere.

Radio, recording and new instruments (eventually leading to the synthesizer, if we want to impose a spurious idea of evolution) all challenge the borders of the soundworld and of music. They all also recall something that had somehow been lost: instruments are machines. They can be conceived of as being vehicular machines for human ideas or feelings, but also as physical machines for displacing air (eventually), via a huge variety of material forms. Only when 'synthetic' instruments come along (like the *intonarumori* of Russolo) can we go back, via the criticism of or resistance to, new music and instruments, to de-idealize machines like the violin or piano. Awareness of technology as relational helps to see that no particular music or sound machine can claim superiority. Noise, and use of it, helps reduce the belief that machines are mere means to higher musical or conceptual goals. This is because it highlights material production of sound, and this is further signalled through technical limitations, incidental unwanted noises, resistance to avant-garde soundworks. As noise-oriented technologies persist, there is a gradual move away from ideas of musical competence being only about capacity to play instruments. On this last point, it is not that, say, a theremin is inherently simpler to play than a violin, even if it looks like waving your hands around wires must be easier than picking out notes, as to play standard tones on either involves a reasonable amount of skill. The important thing is that the mystique of the musical instrument is reduced (this process continues at accelerated pace through the mass production of home keyboards, and the spread of software for playing, producing or mixing music and sounds) at the same time as the effective possibilities for sound and listening are almost infinitely expanded.

Fluxus

Fluxus is not a reaction to technology, even if it could be construed as resistance to capitalism and the commodification of art. It certainly isn't an embrace of technology either. I would make the case that Fluxus, particularly in terms of what it does with music and conceptions of what counts as music (and/or performance), emerges with the growth of technology (in music). Tape recording, gramophones, modernist notions of noise all feature in Fluxus. The conceptualism that ties it together (however messily) is also a technology. Fluxus was an art movement that, in the early 1960s, brought together artists who were working outside of the dominant avant-garde strategies such as abstract expressionism (or painting itself), or the increasingly complex forms of 'classical' music that came about after Schoenberg (serialism, stochasticism). High culture was going too high, and had lost the crucial spark that made it indigestible to the culture industry, many thought. Fluxus followed on from dada, and aimed to shock, confuse and be messy. Like *arte povera*, it would stray far from the accepted 'proper' artistic materials and conventions. High and low art would both be used and taken apart.

Like dada, Fluxus mostly worked through events where several artworks would be presented, performed, made, destroyed or consumed. They also made many multiples, which have since become collectible, but at the time represented a Duchampian critique of art as saleable culture (the many copies threatening the idea of an individual artwork, the materials [could be anything] undermining the idea of the artist as a genius creator, and the accessibility not only made ownership of art more democratic, it actually constituted a questioning of artwork as saleable object). Fluxus would cross artistic disciplines and dispense with notions of artistic skill. It was messy, with gallery events comprising works in many media or genres, including music or early versions of sound art. Meanwhile other events took place at a purely notional level (i.e. as concepts) or outside of conventional art spaces. This was a bringing of noise as practice through noise as form and content. Sound, particularly if not overly polite, disrupts contemplation, directly and also philosophically, in that the 'highest' of the senses—vision—cannot operate unimpeded for understanding/feeling/sublimity, and so on. Fluxus music was also noisy in its refusal to operate by any accepted codes of music-making, but as it occurred in place of, or the place of, music, it would act noisily on our sense of music and its boundaries.

Dick Higgins theorized this as 'intermedia'. He referred to the music of John Cage and Philip Corner as 'the intermedia between music and philosophy' (*Horizons*, 23).[7] The term is redolent of intertextuality, particularly the version which would imagine an easily definable 'intertext', but Higgins' term is much more interesting, and heads to the dissemination model of intertextuality. For Higgins, arts were only separated from each other in the Renaissance, and whether that was valid or not, it no longer is (*Horizons*, 19). Intermedia is not just a mingling of media, not just something that is of 'mixed media' either (24). An intermedia is between two media, suspending the discrete media it sits amongst. Intermedia in general is the space that these works create, or re-open. It would be working with both music and philosophy (as in Higgins' example) in a way that it was not bound by them, nor would it resolve them into a new unity.[8] He is scathing about Wagner's attempts to bring all art together in the *Gesamtkunstwerk*, writing, with 'slight' exaggeration, that 'the catharsis of Wagner's *Götterdämmerung* leads inexorably to Buchenwald' (*Horizons*, 63).

The idea or practice of intermedia is not restricted to any one time, and perhaps is like Attali's definition of noise, or the markers of something like Foucault's epistemic shifts, in that what is 'intermedial' today can constitute a new body/institution/form another day. The implication would be that nothing is either inherently or permanently intermedia. In a salutary warning to those who work across media, or who believe in the promise of Nicolas Bourriaud's 'relational aesthetics', Higgins states that 'no work was ever good because it was intermedial' (26). To imagine that what you do is inherently interesting or avant-garde is to misplace the sense of form, and replace it with an empty signifier of form ('this is what happens' rather than it happening, and being subject to judgement). No sound, noise, process, practice is inherently good or avant-garde.

In practice, Fluxus offers a range of approaches to music and soundmaking, although 'approaches' suggests a coherent and purposeful methodology in itself, which was not really the Fluxus way. It represents an intrusion into the art world, and a mutation of the purposiveness and/or expressivity of music. The score is transformed into a conceptual strategy rather than a simple set of instructions, attaining this through a simplification or minimalizaton of what a score demands. The score becomes a recommendation, a way of encouraging chance sounds or actions. Retaining the instructions prevents chance or aleatoriness from turning into personal interpretation of 'mood' or 'moment'.

George Brecht offers numerous examples of how this works, and produced works (many of which are the instructions rather than the realizations). Perhaps the most renowned, or at least emblematic, is *Drip Music (Drip Event)*:

Drip Music (Drip Event)
For single or multiple performance.
A source of dripping water and an empty vessel are arranged so that the water falls into the vessel.
Second version: Dripping.
G. Brecht
(1959–62)[9]

As with the performances of Cage, or the art of Yves Klein and Manzoni, questions would be asked as to whether this was art, whether this was music? In art terms, it ties in with conceptual art, and was performed in art contexts; in music terms, sound is produced by a performer, and forms of both variation and repetition feature. So what is missing? Artistic or musical skill. Canonical tones of western music. Expression. Controlling intention manipulating outcomes. Not all music has the latter, not least in the wake of Cage and Fluxus, so we should add that *Drip Music* removes personal intervention for altering outcomes. The intervention happens at the beginning only, perhaps in a reference to pure creation releasing some sort of ideal object. Listening to this, or to Lamonte Young's *Composition 1960 #2*, where a fire is lit and left to burn, we are drawn away from music consisting of human-derived tones (however dissonant these can be). As with Cage's silent pieces, the musicality of the universe is revealed. This idealism is tempered only by ridiculousness, or at least its potential, even in the most po-faced performance. The seriousness of Charlotte Moorman's realizations of Nam June Paik's cello-based works gives them an absurdity both meaningful and pleasingly silly. Moorman has crawled over a beach with the cello strapped to her, played TV screens, played cello nude (*Opera sextronique,* 1967), played Paik (Cage, *26'1.1499 for a String Player,* 1965). These culminate in Paik's *TV Cello* (2000), where an approximation of a cello is formed by TV screens, showing Moorman's performances, general Fluxus stuff and news events. Paik, though, is perhaps nearest to noise when not addressing music directly. His TV installations intercut images and sound, and often feature detuned screens, sometimes in installations where the TVs compete with each other. Here, noise environments are set up where several media are made to function noisily, despite themselves. In terms of the idea of 'intermedia', one of Paik's multiple TV installations attains the goal of intermedia not through the installation but when the perceiver experiences the pieces and the media being exceeded.

Many Fluxus pieces involved the destruction or abuse of musical instruments, in an ultimate literalization of an attack on musical norms and forms.[10] Brecht, of course, engaged in this, as did Paik (*Integral Piano* [1958–63]—a piano covered and filled with household items and waste, toys, machines, being one of many times pianos suffered for his art) and Joseph Beuys.[11]

Musique brut

Further from the art world is the possibility of a raw music outside of all conventions and probably unaware of its avant-garde likenesses. From the 1940s on, the

French artist Jean Dubuffet championed the cause of 'art brut' (now generally referred to as 'outsider art')—produced by children, the insane, the untutored—as this would be closer to pure creativity. It is not so much lack of awareness of art conventions that drives art brut, but a disregard for those conventions. Dubuffet himself attempted to produce childlike works, or works made from 'unartistic' materials such as dirt (this around 1950), but he was well aware of the contradiction (or possible bad faith) in an artist making stuff as if he or she were mad (as Surrealism did on many occasions), and would refer to those formally (e.g. through simulating the use of unartistic materials, or in the presentation of his works) and in his writings. Dubuffet made albums using instruments he did not know how to play, by himself and with the Cobra artist Asger Jorn.

There is a whole continuum and possibly even canon of 'musique brut', ranging from Adolf Wölffli's almost infinite scores which seem to generate an entire world and worldview, to singer-songwriters such as Jandek, and the motivations of the musicians are highly varied, but the audience for 'outsider music' has expectations, the key to which is the authenticity of the performance or recording. This is where the rawness comes in, offering an excess of honesty because not interested in it, and also because the musical capacity is limited. So we are brought to a very basic music, one that can work as a comment on the aspirations of what seems to be more purposive. Musique brut is not outside music, but something that operates at its edges, raising the question of music, of what it is or should be. For this reason, someone who is not totally without awareness of what they are doing can still produce work of this kind (just as in performance art).[12]

For audience and performer, the voice is an essential part of music at its rawest (arguably as it has the capacity not only to denote rawness, but also to connote it), and Artaud's *Pour en finir* is a striking example of this. Artaud is in a privileged position with regard to 'outsider art', having experienced a host of psychological and mental disorders, and with long experience of incarceration. At the same time, he was also a highly respected and prolific writer, and played these different parts of himself against each other, perturbing audience's expectations. His radio work *Pour en finir* shows us an early version of what 'industrial culture' would see as bodily performance, bodily technology. This is in combination with the theoretical machine of the 'body with organs' with which he more or less ends *Pour en finir* (61). This idea, later extensively developed by Deleuze and Guattari, entails moving beyond the body as a collection of useful machines, and toward the creation of a machinic body that is porous to the world. Artaud's radio play takes the voice away from discourse or expression of subjectivity, and in combining it with gleefully thumped percussion, offers a way in which the voice becomes part of musique brut—a raw material that is neither actually genuinely raw nor material, in the sense of providing a means to an (other) end.

Voice has a claim to transcendence that has not gone away since Kant and Rousseau. It represents the supposed interior life or existence of the speaker, and therefore has a link to the ideal, to contemplation, rationality, self-reflection *and* acknowledgement of the other. A voice that eluded these, while suggesting them, might offer the other to the Ideal Voice, as long as the bodily processes took over from ways of thinking 'the body' as idealized location of identity (as insisted on by a lot of 'performance', performance theory etc., even though these proffer an older, less interesting position than even so-called 'mind–body dualism').

One such voice is that which courses through Artaud, unwitting discoverer of his own 'body without organs'. His is the body without self, and also a body dismantling itself. One way Artaud is able to observe this process is through the mutation of voice: 'neither my cry nor my fever are mine' (*Collected Works*, vol. I, 80), and this in the context of his perilous embodiment: 'with each of my tongue's vibrations I retrace all the paths of my thought through my flesh' (165).[13] This flesh is not a new body, a surrogate self, but living as 'apprehension', an apprehension caught in the circuit of breath and exhaled sound. In the course of learning to work this strange situation, he stresses the expelling of breath, where he would be 'expelling not air but the very capacity to make sound' (vol. II, 113).

In so doing, he builds a subjectivity that always comes apart, that fails, that *is* only as expelled. The most obvious way this occurs is in glossolalia, vocal sound seemingly without form, without conscious control (although there is a para-linguistic structure to the seemingly random sections of *Pour en finir*), and in screaming—most importantly in taking your voice outside of its 'natural' pitch (to question whether a natural pitch exists for me, or in reception of me, or in me as reception of me, and so on). It is not, then, just the loss of words and meaning that counts, but the alteration that creates noise, creates a way of being other than rational, controlled, anchored in 'me'. There is something very hackneyed in thinking screaming is more authentic than speaking or singing, or alternatively that it is good for avoiding claims of authenticity, so with Artaud what gets his screaming out of that bind is that it occurs in contrast to and in the context of discursive speech. This speech is itself broken by its rhythm, which undermines the claims of the content (such as the Americans, who are taking over the world, being resisted through microbes of God). Screaming and percussion offer interludes in *Pour en finir*, parodying a play, or musical narrative. Within the scripted elements, the attention of Artaud and his collaborators continually drifts to the form of their vocal performance, which exceeds both content and form of the discourse, while emphasizing its effect. There is, in other words, a use-value in screaming and shouting as if possessed if the script talks of shit and God, God and shit, shit as God, we are all shit; but instead of seeing a tidy relation between form and content—expressive form—we should take the vocalizing in the context of Artaud's belief in exhalation, voice, breath as *weakening* the power of the self and the self's utterance, and take it as a bad use-value, unproductive.

What Artaud expels is a voice which is different to the voice of reason and subjectivity, as even Derrida acknowledges: 'breath [le souffle] is not the same thing as the voice, not the voice of language, discourse, the verb and the word, in any case' ('Forcener le subjectile', 85).[14] This is a material voice that realizes a low immateriality (like Bataille's low materialism) as opposed to the highness of the cultured speaking or singing voice. Artaud realizes Lucretius' idea of the voice as material: 'when atoms of voice in greater numbers than usual have begun to squeeze out through the narrow outlet, the doorway of the overcrowded mouth gets scraped. Undoubtedly, if voices and words have this power of causing pain, they must consist of corporeal particles' (*On the Nature of the Universe*, 146).[15] And while we're with the low, the same process could be heard, felt, seen, in reverse, in the dematerialization of Artaud's shit, Artaud's insides.

Barthes might offer us a more literal perspective: for him the voice is something added to breath, there is a 'grain' which is the product of internal percussions

and channellings, of the physical form of the person emitting the sounds ('L'Écoute', 226).[16] This voice has nothing to do with talent, training or even correct phy-
sique, but with the lowness of voice, as ultimately uncontrollable. This perspective
takes away the possibility of expression being controlled by the subject/individual
and democratizes the listening judgement to be made. In addition, this grain creates the individuality of the voice in its own right. There is a simple way that this
applies to a singer you might like, but, more interesting is his assertion that this
individualization further minimizes the singer/speaker's role in producing 'their'
voice, because he claims this 'individuality' is not a *personal* one, it is not someone's property ('The Grain of the Voice', 182).[17] Artaud is of course ahead of
Barthes here, and aware that 'grain' is not another term for 'timbre'. Intonation is
part of it, but only as a means of attacking intonation (as carrier of significance, of
emotion, expression in general).[18] The voice(s) of *Pour en finir* lose their individualized grain, as the 'grain' takes over, and crosses from one participant to the next,
regardless of gender.

The concept of grain might seem to encourage a consideration of sexual difference, or presumptions about it, but when the voice is becoming noise, it is also
losing gender, for example in the loss of unified pitch, or 'natural' pitch. *Pour en
finir* becomes a realization of Artaud as not Artaud, as not God, as not shit, only to
become all those things again, only ever failing to fully become. This noise can
only occur by making the noise cross from one level to another, from content to
form and vice-versa, from shit to God, from Artaud to Blin to Grain in Artaud is an
undoing, a bringing to be as expulsion rather than an expulsion realizing voice.

13,000,000 pure notes: *Musique concrète*

In 1948, Pierre Schaeffer came up with the term *musique concrète*, noting it in his
diary of 15 May. The 'concrete' would oppose what he thought of as the abstraction
of music made for musical instruments. The real world, the 'sonic givens', would
form the basis of a new musical material. *Musique concrète* would be made up of
'sonorous fragments that have a real existence [existant concrètement], and that
are thought of as being clearly defined and complete sonic objects' (Schaeffer, *À
la recherche d'une musique concrète*, 22).[19] Many avant-garde musicians in the
post-war period were disappointed that standard music seemed to have reached
some sort of limit with serialism, but did not want to ditch musicality altogether.
Alongside experiments happening more or less outside of music, a new type of
composition was emerging, which worked with new recording technologies as an
integral part of its construction. For Schaeffer and Pierre Henry, found sounds
were transcribed directly into records. In the early 1950s, recording tape simplified
the process. In parallel to these recording media, electronic music was developing,
building up tones from oscillators (Schaeffer found this very limiting, and is mildly
critical of Karlheinz Stockhausen).[20] These types of music seem to owe as much
to a scientific approach as they do to aesthetics. The studio, often state-funded,
particularly in France, was the laboratory, sounds the object of the experiment.
Without this institutional support, the practical and financial difficulties would have
prevented such awkwardly created works being produced.

Schaeffer imagined a new form of music where research and art would combine, with the quasi-scientific research leading to an artistic outcome (*À la recher-*

che, 137, 140–1). At a very literal level, composers and musicians were also inventors, and this would remain the case well into the 1960s. The arrival of synthesizers and, ultimately, computer-based music, has taken this necessity away. The thought technologies have not altered that dramatically; sampling, montage, the use of the studio (even if this could be a laptop) all come out of *musique concrète*'s experimentation. In the early twenty-first century it is not too unusual to encounter albums made entirely of processed sounds made musical, often concentrating on a particular set of sounds, such as Matthew Herbert's *Plat du Jour* (food), or Matmos' *A Chance to Cut Is a Chance to Cure*, where the sounds are from plastic surgery operations. However, in the late 1940s and early 1950s, it was acceptable neither to mainstream listeners nor to the existing avant-gardes.

Schaeffer wanted to expand the realm of music, and bring in sounds that were musical, even if not matching expectations of being specific notes. Non-musical sounds would be richer, fuller, and the amount of combinations available almost infinite (André Moles, in a burst of literal-mindedness, claimed there were 13,000,000 pure tones [cited by Schaeffer, *À la recherche*, 119]). Western music, whether tonal or 'atonal', was severely and inherently limited. To experiment, we would have to listen, and listen outside music, in order to hear what music was currently withholding (*À la recherche*, 180). Music had become obsessed with form, Schaeffer argues, whereas real interest could only come from material [matière] (21). Paying attention to the stuff of music—sounds as themselves— would reconcile material and form, not, as Adorno saw in Beethoven, in terms of a dialectical coming together, but as a new immanent body. Form and material would no longer be distinguishable, at least in traditional terms. Schaeffer is quick to point out that this does not mean you can string any old sounds together; this new music would still need organization (76).

In practice, any old sounds *would* get recorded, but the bulk of the work happens after that. Schaeffer and Henry would alter the speed of their recordings, recombine sounds and so on, and eventually a piece would exist. The world was now a source of endless sounds (23), and this endlessness filters down into every sound, which is now a carrier of multiple possibilities. Each sound, in manipulation, remains open, potential.[21] Schaeffer's first completed piece (*Étude aux chemins de fer*) is built from the sounds of trains. Whether using a single sound source (which would be layered, altered, distorted, cut-up) or multiple sources, the key principle in *musique concrète* was montage. If the first part of the process is listening, then the last is recombination. In between these, we have the crucial notion, for Schaeffer, that sounds must be removed from their 'dramatic context' (32, 46). This is important when dealing with 'sounds as they are', because we could be misled that 'what a sound is' means recognizing its provenance. We can only get to the sound itself once we have defamiliarized the listener as to the source of the sound. This does not preclude some recognition, but the sounds must then be manipulated or restaged such that their origin loses its significance. So we might hear a piece that uses plastic bags as its material. We can recognize it as such, but the piece should get us to move on from there, and to not ascribe the meaning of the music to its origin, so we get beyond 'ah, music from plastic bags' to the sounds that *incidentally* get produced via the bags. Music itself was far from excluded from *musique concrète*, and while Schaeffer decided music and the rest of the soundworld did not really go well together in a concert setting, Henry would combine live, performed music and other sounds in many later pieces (such as *Messe pour le temps présent*). Primarily, though, music was just one source of sound among all the rest, and it too had to lose its 'dramatic context'—i.e. its self-sufficiency as an autonomous piece of music. Prerecorded music would be brought in as part of the collage of sounds making up a piece, on the basis that music was out there in the world, only now it would be taken and reprocessed as resource. Sampling, mixing, looping, citation all sprang from these European musicians and Cage's 'mix' pieces (*Fontana Mix*, *Williams Mix*).

Working with this 'concrete' sound does not entail passivity, or idealization of the material (although this could happen, of course). Even field recordings require selection, editing, production. Beyond selection is the alteration of the sound, and the montage. With every stage, the sound is becoming more 'musical', more ordered, and Schaeffer is clear: 'I love order' [je suis [. . .] fanatique de l'ordre] (*À la recherche*, 99). Ordering is the human intervention that creates music (this would apply even to attributing purposiveness to natural sounds, I would argue). Schaeffer, though, perhaps to justify his new approach to musical sound, really does stress this, and I think that is what is behind his strange valorization of eye over ear:

> The experiment in concrete music uncovers, inside the ear, and this almost unconnected to the musical ear, a sonorous eye, sensitive to the form and colour of sounds, and, because there are two ears as there are two eyes, also to the contours of sounds.

> [*L'expérience concrète découvre à l'intérieur de l'oreille, et presque sans rapport avec l'oreille musicale, un œil sonore, sensible aux formes et aux couleurs des sons, et aussi, puisqu'il y a deux oreilles comme des yeux, au relief de ces sons*]. (194)[22]

Why have an eye at all? Would it be worth investigating the 'world of all sounds' when the outcome is to refuse the ears? The implication seems to be that an eye is more knowledgeable, more discerning. This can only be because of the apparent close connection between vision and rationality; the eye can order its world in ways the ear cannot (even if the eye itself does only a small part of that). The ear, on the other hand, is imagined as being subject to the world, so as the entire world comes into audition, the only thing to do is move to vision's organizing skills. This passage gives us a strong clue as to the place of noise here: in bringing noise into music, it becomes musical, therefore losing noisiness. *Musique concrète* goes beyond composers like Satie and Varèse in making the entirety of a piece from found sounds, but actually goes further, in so doing, in countering noisiness. In a way, it is the most structured of music that understands noise as other, while Schaeffer is making the world musical, performing a noise reduction. Fellow concrete composer François Bayle writes that '*musique concrète* wasn't at all a music of noises, not at all a music of provocation. It was the contrary'.[23] Noise here crosses into music—the music, or at least the strategy of it, retains a capacity for noise—jumps, cuts, gaps, alterations all allow this, hence the continued vibrancy of those strategies in electronica.

For Adorno, there is nothing at stake in sampled, collaged sounds, and he probably speaks for many in arguing that it is a form of tinkering, a sort of alienated hobby.[24] While he spends more time criticizing the 'new music' of serialism as a form of misguided application of science ('The Aging of the New Music', 193),[25] *musique concrète* is the logical endpoint of the problem as Adorno hears it: 'in music, however, that is all construction; nothing at all is composed anymore. Music regresses to the pre-musical, the pre-artistic tone. Many of its adepts logically pursue *musique concrète* or the electronic production of tones' (194). The utopian views of those composers, musicians or engineers is dismissed as a primitivist fallacy, a backwards move. Here, and throughout his œuvre, Adorno is caught in a regressive (or recursive) avant-gardism of his own. He continually complains that music is not advancing, but in order to do so, has to insist on the continued primacy of modernist orchestral music. There are those who imagine that mainstream pop music is too mainstream because they know nothing outside of it and are unaware of their self-imposed limited listening. Adorno, who would have made exactly that argument against pop music and its listeners, has closed himself in in the same way. From the perspective of noise, though, these limits are precisely what makes Adorno interesting because all the advocates of something like noise music tend (in the 1950s certainly) to want to harmonize sound, music and noise into a greater music. Adorno criticizes the imagined authenticity of sounds that get us out of the apparent limits of western compositional practices, criticizing the 'trust that the discovery of intentionless layers, like new snow still unmarked by the imprint of the subject and the objectivation of the subject's traces in the form of conventionalizations of expression, would make pure immediacy possible' ('The Aging of the New Music', 190). Although he is not directly addressing *musique concrète* in that sentence, the notion applies clearly to it, particularly in the light of what he has to say about 'material', which goes directly counter to Schaeffer's notion of the worth of 'pre-existing sounds':

> The work of art without content, the epitome of a mere sensuous presence, would be nothing more than a slice of empirical reality, the opposite of which would be a work of art consisting of mere rationality devoid of all enchantment. The unmediated identity of content and appearance would annul the idea of art. (*Sound Figures*, 197)[26]

The musical artwork must work dialectically, and let technique and content continually work each other. What must not happen is something that cannot be structured linearly, or at least that does not construct itself as a function of its wholeness and conclusion. In order to do that, the music must stay within its boundaries, even if ideally it is pressing against them, because we cannot get outside of musical tradition. First, because we cannot look for non-musical material (argues Adorno); secondly, because we cannot ignore the languages of music that have accreted and will present themselves to any listener; thirdly, and most importantly, because this tradition has set itself up as a dialectic with a historical mission, and this has to be played out in the artwork for it to be relevant. Contemporary writers thinking about noise divide into those who dismiss Adorno (due, in particular, to his rickety readings of jazz) and those who back Adorno up, at least to the extent of criticizing a reification of extreme music as something fully beyond music, structures, predigested and culture industry-led reception and so on. Adorno might well be right in his framing of his criticisms of everything after Schoenberg and Webern, but the various noisy 'formless' musics that would argue against him operate despite this correctness, and are defined against as well as through those theoretical limits. In other words, experimental music working with noise is mostly well aware of the limits on it to escape any and all meaning, control, reification, and so on.

Adorno is not always predictable, either, complaining more about Stockhausen than Schaeffer (see *Sound Figures*, 212, as well as 'The Aging of the New Music', 194). This is generally on technological grounds: firstly, there is, in electronic music, an overinsistence on an unreflective (i.e. merely functional) technology; second, this technology is rubbish, producing very limited sounds for a lot of work ('as though Webern were being played on a Wurlitzer organ' ['The Aging of the New Music', 195]).[27] Schaeffer fully agrees (*À la recherche*, 15), but Adorno will go much further and refuse the potential of non-instruments, arguing that 'there has never been any gramophone-specific music' ('The Form of the Phonograph Record', 277).[28] He was writing that in 1934, but did not seem to change his mind subsequently, on either the record player or the radio. Records were to become key source material, via manipulation, and Stockhausen would make the microphone a productive as well as reproductive technology (*Stockhausen on Music*, 80). Adorno, then, seems caught in an incapacity to see new technologies, whether machinic, conceptual or performative, as ever being able to supersede the musical technology laid out in the form of orchestral music.

NOTES

1. Heidegger, 'The Question Concerning Technology', in *Basic Writings* (London: Routledge, 1993), 311–41.

2. Chadabe, *Electric Sound: The Past and Promise of Electronic Music* (Upper Saddle River, NJ: Prentice Hall, 1997).

3. Kahn, 'Introduction: Histories of Sound Once Removed', in Douglas Kahn and Gregory Whitehead (eds), *Wireless Imagination: Sound, Radio and the Avant-garde* (Cambridge, MA: MIT Press, 1994), 1–29.

4. Benjamin, 'The Work of Art in the Era of Mechanical Reproduction', in *Illuminations* (London: Fontana, 1992), 211–44.

5. Benjamin argues that the 'aura' of the original is lost in an era of perfect reproduction—so a film, for example, has no original; it is only copies, and any original painting begins to lose its aura as perfect photographic reproductions more or less take its place. Whether that is the case as much as he imagines, it is worth noting that mass warfare, conducted at a distance, has the same effect on the individual: 'instead of draining rivers, society directs a human stream into a bed of trenches; instead of dropping seeds from airplanes, it drops incendiary bombs over cities; and through gas warfare the aura is abolished in a new way' ('The Work of Art', 235).

6. Artaud, *Pour en finir avec le jugement de Dieu* (Paris: Gallimard, 2003).

7. Higgins, *Horizons: The Poetics and Theory of the Intermedia* (Carbondale and Edwardsville: Southern Illinois University Press, 1984). The essay 'Intermedia' (18–28) was originally published in 1966.

8. In 'Music without Catharsis' (Horizons, 53–63), Higgins builds on this idea in terms of musical resolution. He argued that Fluxus was non-cathartic. In that case, it was because there was nearly always a score, so it could not fall into the illusion of self-expression (58–9). Even music like that of Stockhausen was cathartic, where, surprisingly perhaps, Steve Reich was not. His argument is that in 'modular music' (56) (or 'minimalism), we get climaxes without catharsis (56–7). A similar case can be made for much of post-1975 'noise music', of

post-progressive music such as that of Guapo, whose riffs mount endlessly over whole albums, or Om's *Variations on a Theme* (2005), where there is no macro-evolution at all, despite the continual promise (through the repeated riff and periodically climactic percussion moments).

9. Cited in Nyman, *Experimental Music*, 77.

10. Nam June Paik, like Brecht, moved from music to performance, never completing the move—so music in their hands was something capable of being endlessly wrecked, and not quite destroyed. Paik also made Cagean processes into something more dynamic and aggressive (including going over to Cage, cutting his tie off and covering Cage and John Tudor in shampoo as part of his *Étude for Piano* [1959]). Also of interest in this context is performance artist Kazuo Shiraga.

11. The piano, as symbol of the harmonious western musical system developed in early modern times, came to suffer extensively at the hands of Fluxus. Philip Corner's *Piano Activities* involved many aggressive physical actions on the machine, and the assistance of many Fluxists: Emmett Williams, Wolf Vostell, Nam June Paik, Dick Higgins, Ben Patterson, George Maciunas, in Wiesbaden, Germany (1962).

12. There is a fairly cynical industry around 'outsiders'—witness the recent breakthrough of Daniel Johnston.

13. Artaud, *Collected Works, vols I–IV* (London: Calder, 1974–99).

14. 'Cette hiérarchie entre l'audible et le visible [in Van Gogh's painting] semble reconstituer des schémas bien classiques; mais elle ne rapporte pas l'une à l'autre la parole ou la langue d'une part, "l'image sur papier" d'autre part. Le souffle ne se confond pas avec la voix, en tout cas pas avec la voix de la langue ou du discours, celle du verbe ou du mot.' Derrida, 'Forcener le subjectile' in Paule Thévenin and Jacques Derrida, *Antonin Artaud: dessins et portraits* (Paris: Gallimard, 1986).

15. Lucretius, *On the Nature of the Universe* (London: Penguin, 1951).

16. Barthes, 'Écoute', in *L'Obvie et l'obtus* (Paris: Le Seuil, 1982), 217–30.

17. Barthes, 'The Grain of the Voice', in *Image Music Text* (London: Fontana, 1977), 179–89.

18. Again, Derrida is happy for this to be the case in Artaud, although, significantly it is in the context of painting and Artaud's comments on painting ('Forcener le subjectile', 62).

19. Schaeffer, *À la recherche d'une musique concrète* (Paris: Le Seuil, 1952).

20. *À la recherche*, 15. For a summary of the various groups working in studios with tape, electronics, vinyl, processing techniques, see Chadabe, *Electric Sound*, 26–53.

21. Pierre Boulez imagines his own works in this way, as he continually revisits and reworks them. He did a couple of early pieces (*Études* I and II) with Schaeffer, but then returned to more accepted instrumentation.

22. 'Sonore' here has a double meaning: firstly it implies resonance—a place sound can occur, and secondly, it is to do with capacity to 'hear'. For another misplaced eye, see Georges Bataille, *The Story of the Eye* (London: Penguin, 1979), 66.

23. Cited by Chadabe, *Electric Sound*, 35.

24. See, for example, Adorno, 'On the Fetish-Character in Music', in *Essays on Music* (Berkeley and Los Angeles: University of California Press, 2002), 288–317.

25. Adorno, 'The Aging of the New Music', in *Essays on Music*, 181–202.

26. Adorno, *Sound Figures* (Stanford, CA: Stanford University Press, 1999). Schaeffer writes that '[the sound object] forces us to listen to it, not as an index [référence], but as it is, in all of its actual substance' (*À la recherche*, 177).

27. The term 'electronic music' meant something much more specific in the 1950s and 1960s. For Stockhausen and followers in Germany, at any rate, it was about much more than the use of electronically generated sounds, or an argument about their musicality. It was also about the possibility of building up sounds, or, alternatively, breaking them down into constituent parts (Stockhausen, *Stockhausen on Music: Lectures and Interviews*, ed. Robin Maconie [London: Marion Boyars, 1991], 97).

28. Adorno, 'The Form of the Phonograph Record', in *Essays on Music*, 277–82.

3
FREE

Outside of the confines of the avant-garde, another cultural revolution was taking place. Between the steady rise of jazz, the dramatic arrival of rock 'n' roll and rapid developments in recording and reproduction technology, the face of music was changing. The late 1940s and 1950s saw popular culture and music undergo a paradigm shift that had been signalled since the 1920s. Adorno was one who spotted this trend early, and despised it, rejecting jazz and other popular music as false expressions of the dominant ideology of capitalism, i.e. commodity fetishism, via a consumerism that imagined mass acceptance of that culture as individualistic. Critics have often vehemently taken sides on his attitude, especially with regard to jazz, but gradually a middle path emerged, where Adorno's general view of 'the culture industry' is accepted, but his harsher pronouncements are recognized as exaggeration.[1] It has often astonished people that the modernist Adorno is so scathing about jazz, which has such strong claims to be a key part of the modernist experience in America at least. Robert Witkin argues that Adorno feels obliged to take on jazz because unlike other forms of the culture industry (like Hollywood films), there are many who defend jazz as a legitimate type of avant-gardism (*Adorno on Music*, 173). So we have to see Adorno's position against jazz as a reflection of his critique of the consumerist commodity that is the culture industry. According to Leppert, what Adorno listened to, in 1930s Germany, was 'hardly what today would characteristically be incorporated under the label' ('Commentary', 349). So, in both cases, the writers claim that it is ignorance of the wider context that would lead to a simple dismissal of Adorno.

But here is the problem: Adorno went out of his way to criticize the single most advanced music of the time other than orchestral music, as he does with *musique concrète* in later years. It is worth taking a balanced view of Adorno's take on popular culture because so much of what he complained about had barely begun, and his views, if applied carefully, are even more valid as time goes on. However, there is much to suggest that, for Adorno, any avant-gardism outside of the historical march of 'classical' music would not be allowed as a progressive or authentically subversive development. There are hints of this view in Witkin. He offers this very succinct summary of Adorno's complaint that jazz is not what it seems or claims to be: 'Adorno uses this opposition between superficial irregularity and underlying conformity [i.e. of the beat] to establish the groundwork of a musicological critique of jazz' (*Adorno on Music*, 163). The contrast betrays the falsity of jazz—'its apparently liberatory gestures—those improvisatory movements which account for its success—express only the attempt to break out of the fetishized commodity world without ever changing it' (165). The practice of jazz is inherently false, offering a pretence of freedom, but this goes deeper than the improvisation or expressivity being a con. Jazz does not fit into the dialectic of western history, in the way that classical music does. Classical music offers a whole that builds coherently, and therefore reflects the process of living in society. Music from Beethoven on must also offer dissonance in order not to spuriously represent a harmonious worldview ('here and now music is able to do nothing but portray within its own structure the social antinomies which are also responsible for its own isolation' [Adorno, 'On the

Social Situation of Music', 393]).[2] Even worse, though, would be to have mock dissonance:

> to be sure, dissonances occur in jazz practice, and even techniques of intentional 'misplaying' [*Falchspielens*] have developed. But an appearance of harmlessness accompanies all these customs; every extravagant sonority must be so produced that the listener can recognize it as a substitute for a 'normal' one. (Adorno, 'On the Fetish-Character in Music', 306)[3]

The atonality of Schoenberg, like the writing of Beckett after the Second World War, is the authentic alienated expression of an alienated world. In music terms, only music that builds on the tradition of bourgeois music can address the historical accretions of that society. You cannot step outside, in Adorno's view:

> The terror which Schoenberg and Webern spread today as in the past, comes not from their incomprehensibility but from the fact they are all too correctly understood. Their music gives form to that anxiety, that terror, that catastrophic situation which others merely evade by regressing. They are called individualists, and yet their work is nothing but a dialogue with the powers that destroy individuality. ('On the Fetish-Character in Music', 315)

Accepting Adorno's wider theory about cultural production will disqualify all such production from being a genuine avant-garde that offers a new comment on social processes and the position of art. Accepting that Adorno had only limited access to jazz (limited historically and geographically) is to neglect his attempt to theoretically destroy any rivals to the music that clearly comes from the classical tradition. If we are to think of jazz in terms of noise, then for Adorno, it is not a genuinely dissonant disruption, but a distraction from culturally creative noise. It is only noise in the sense of its unavoidability, its promotion as part of the culture industry.

Adorno is scathing about the claims of jazz in his article 'On Jazz'.[4] As Witkin points out in his partial defence of Adorno, the claims of jazz are that it has reclaimed a primitive form of expression, that it is in tune with modern visual art, that it expresses the state of humans in the modern city, and that the role of performance and improvisation bring a greater access to subjectivity for both listener and performer (*Adorno on Music*, 161–2). As noted above, Adorno does not believe that the form of jazz expresses anything authentically (therefore that should suffice, for him, one might imagine). He criticizes the assertion of 'the primitive' in jazz at several levels: most notably for those reading today perhaps, he offers a proto-postcolonialist critique, arguing that this primitivism, like that in the visual arts of the early part of the twentieth century, is a white, western construct:

> The extent to which jazz has anything at all to do with genuine black music is highly questionable; the fact that it is frequently performed by blacks and that the public clamors for 'black jazz' as a sort of brand name doesn't say much more about it, even if folkloric research should confirm the African origin of many of its practices [. . .] the manufacture [*Herstellung*] of jazz is also an urban phenomenon, and the skin of the black man functions as much as a coloristic effect as does the silver of the saxophone. In no way does a trium-

phant vitality make its entrance in these bright musical commodities. ('On Jazz', 477)

Much European jazz and a certain amount of jazz encountered by whites in America in the 1920s and 1930s would suggest this 'blackness' to be a front, a cynical co-option by white bands. But once performed by blacks it could be seen as a bit strong to suggest they are being inauthentically black. If nothing else, it is simple assertion. On the other hand, Adorno is addressing audience expectations which have been created by the culture industry, and the expression of 'black soul' a white audience goes to see and hear (although he would probably have included black audiences here too) is false, even if something more substantial is also going on. It is peculiar, given Adorno's stridency, that he hedges his claim about the 'supposed' African origins of jazz. This mirrors his doubt about that authenticity, but it could also be seen as a rejection of the possibility of jazz as authentic black expression (by this I do not mean soulfulness etc. but valid, meaningful cultural expression that connects, reflects and possibly alters the movement of culture). Adorno can be defended if we are selective about what statements we pick. He suggests that jazz has been appropriated and packaged by the culture industry, as he does in 1933, writing that 'jazz no more has anything to do with authentic Negro music, which has long since been falsified and industrially smoothed out here' ('Farewell to Jazz', 496).[5] This can be taken as a critique of the culture industry and not of jazz as such, but for Adorno, actually this has occurred because jazz is inherently terrible: 'rather, what hollowed jazz out is its own stupidity' (497).

Jazz, then, is complicit in its own co-option; what little merit it had it has lost for itself. For Adorno, this is because its very origins are a corruption of what was already not very advanced culture. Adorno contradicts himself when looking at early jazz, because he departs from the claims that primitivism is a culture industry construct to a more 'profound' claim that the primitive can be of no interest (it is Adorno, not me, making these claims one way or another):

> To the extent that we can speak of black elements in the beginnings of jazz, in ragtime perhaps, it is still less archaic-primitive self-expression than the music of slaves; even in the indigenous music of the African interior, syncopation within the example of a maintained measured time seems only to belong to the lower (social) level. Psychologically, the primal structure of jazz [Ur-jazz] may closely suggest the spontaneous singing of servant girls. Society has drawn its vital music—provided that it has not been made to order from the very beginning—not from the wild, but from the domesticated body in bondage. The sado-masochistic elements in jazz could be clearly connected to this. The archaic stance of jazz is as modern as the 'primitives' who fabricate it. ('On Jazz', 478)

As with his earlier points, as a critique of the attribution of primitiveness, this is pretty much unquestionable, but Adorno wants to strip all African-American and African music of musical or social interest because American blacks were enslaved and because African music-makers were not drawn from the elite (according to him) . . . Firstly, it is hard to see this as anything other than racist, and secondly, it directly contradicts Adorno's own take on music, which is that it must emerge dialectically from its social and musical tradition. He goes on to hint that this is where 'vital' music comes from, but it seems there is no place for this 'vitality' to go (see also 471) and that it must stay caught up in a neurotic immanence rather than a productive, progressive dialectic. Adorno is right to question the exoticist praise of people deemed primitive that was rife not only among jazz fans, but also among writers in general, notably within Bataille's *Documents* group,[6] but there is no place for the music after the criticism, it seems.

Adorno criticizes the practice of jazz as performance. It would aspire to bringing performer and material closer together, and therefore to create a novel and powerful reaction among listeners, including performers, whose improvisations will be driven further, higher and so on. Jazz is no freer than any other form, and is worse because it offers itself as illusion of freedom. Improvisation is limited to standard moves and is only allowed to move so far away from original, relatively simple outlines and contours (this all applies much more to pre-war jazz than to what comes later). This gives the vision of breaking out, but one which more effectively reins in protest ('On Jazz', 480), just like any culture industry appeal to individualism through commodities. Once more, Adorno stretches further to challenge the idea that group composition occurs, claiming that 'the division of labor in jazz merely outlines the parody of a future collective process of composition' (482), the classic Marxist refusal to see the possibility of anarchistic community. Expressivity in jazz is neurotic, pathological, connected to a failure to complete the Freudian journey to selfhood that Adorno subscribes to almost parodically, here at least. He claims that the vibrating of notes and the ways in which jazz singing seeks expression of the singer's being are to do with weakness (488–91). This is immensely more interesting an idea than Adorno imagines; for him it is a straightforward dismissal, and I will return to it in the next section of this chapter, connecting it to the possibility that Adorno's writing does leave a place for free jazz.

Free jazz

Jazz has had, in all its phases, elements of Attali's notion of noisiness. It has been seen as being beyond social norms and rules, that which threatened order. In extreme cases, such as Nazi Germany, jazz was banned (except for jazz that could be used for marching) and was defined as 'decadent music' in the exhibition *Entartete Musik* of 1938, the publicity for which featured a caricature of a black saxophone player, complete with star of David on his lapel. Even within jazz, each new innovation or style would provoke claim and counterclaim about what was really jazz (this even more so after the war, and reaching its height with the advent of free jazz in the late 1950s). But formally, jazz was far from dissonance and atonality, it was more as a practice that it stood apart from western norms (the combination of improvisation and written/composed elements, the alteration of notes). It was incredibly successful as a whole, and this is one reason Adorno is quick to complain about it, but distribution, getting concerts, getting paid for them and so on was far from straightforward, and the genre itself could not at any stage be legitimately described in terms of the homogenous caricature he proposes.

Far from Adorno's attention, jazz moved on, through the explorations of bebop (Charlie Parker at the forefront) and early 'free-ish' jazz like that of pianist Lennie Tristano (this in the late 1940s), and gradually lost many of the constraints Adorno was at least partially correct in criticizing. He had complained that jazz flirted with 'new music's [i.e. orchestral, chamber] realm of dissonance' ('Farewell to Jazz', 497), and then went on to allow some space for a more authentic jazz to appear:

> His ['the virtuoso saxophonist or clarinetist, or even percussionist'] realm was considered to be the realm of freedom; here the solid wall between production and reproduction was evidently demolished, the longed-for immediacy restored, the alienation of man and music mastered out of vital force. It was not, and the fact it was not constituted the betrayal and downfall of jazz. (497–8).

Presumably, then, if a music emerged which did this, jazz would no longer be betrayed but restored. This would be a highly deconstructive restoration, because it would be of an origin that had not, up until now, been there. It would also be one that Adorno does not really imagine to be possible. Nonetheless, negatively or dialectically, he consciously offers jazz as potential for the realization of itself, possibly, and then, retrospectively making a historical dialectic. From forgetting Hegel, in talking of slave music, to jazz *as* Hegel.[7]

Neither did free jazz emerge from out of nowhere: bebop had driven not only avant-garde jazz, but the *idea* of a jazz avant-garde, of jazz as avant-garde. Central to this was the notion of virtuosity. Bebop exponents explicitly aimed to break down the possible division between technique and expressivity, so technical skill became a way of asserting 'jazzness' just as much as rhythmical strategies or flattened chords, and so on. Jazz players would have to prove themselves as players, and as players with skill, and this is one of the key factors in resistance to Ornette Coleman, whose 1960 album *Free Jazz* accidentally provided the term for the new genre. Coleman's playing did not seem to match the expectations of more experienced jazz musicians and critics, it didn't seem to be following the rules, and, at a pragmatic level, not all the musicians he worked with had 'paid their dues' to merit taking valuable slots playing in major clubs. The first group to be threatened by free jazz was not Adorno-driven conservatives, but jazz musicians.[8] Although Coleman had started to leave rules/generic expectations behind in his numerous 1958–9 recordings, it was *Free Jazz* that changed the concept of how jazz could function. It supplies a method to improvised music across an increasing range of genres (for convenience sometimes later labelled 'Improv'). Instead of a soloist working out variations and tangents from themes, the aim was to have a group improvisation.[9] Almost fifty years on, the record does not live up to its promise, but still sounds odd, almost because, rather than in spite of, the difficulties and resistances of some of the contributors. There is still a clear sense of soloists taking a turn, but they are impeded and encouraged by group interventions. The piece was highly unusual in its length—37 minutes—and the sleeve notes emphasize that what you hear is exactly how the piece was recorded (even if vinyl's time limits meant it had to be cut in two).[10] Coltrane had already been producing extended solos in concert, but *Free Jazz* loses the line between composed and improvised elements.[11] It is not completely free at all: while it fights against identifiable rhythms and fixed keys, it has a 'tonal centre'; connections can be followed through 'motivic chain-associations' (Ekkehard Jost, *Free Jazz*, 59).[12] In other words, although there are no set rules, there has to be referencing, the construction of sequences, and the possibility of reintroducing the basic written material. Jost also notes that *Free Jazz* does not really go anywhere, and picks this out, admittedly as a disappointed aside, as something essential to its strangeness, and success as a piece:

> Despite an abundance of motivic interaction, the overall character of *Free Jazz* must be called static rather than dynamic. Only rarely do emotional climaxes occur, and there is hardly any differentiation of expression. [. . .] perhaps Coleman and his musicians were too occupied in articulating a newly acquired vocabulary and conquering a musical *terra incognita* [. . .] It may also be that Coleman set out to create a static, homogeneous whole, his main point being the integration of individual ideas to form an interlocking collective. (*Free Jazz*, 60).

The idea of collective improvisation is muddied by the doubling of the groups, one in each channel of the recording. This must essentially have been about recording clarity, but the double structure is maintained by Coleman in various of his bands, notably Prime Time. It makes *Free Jazz* into a questioning of binarism. Instead of a Derridean interplay of supposed opposites, which then colour each other, I think we should take *Free Jazz* as more of a rotating binary, where the two are never synchronized or separate. The interplay between soloist and group (which never fully goes away, except fleetingly) means that instead of a high-handed dismissal of the distinction, the piece works to comment on how the two work together.

The freeness is where the noise in the 'new thing' jazz lies, precisely because it is not fully free. The interaction of generic instrumentation (although in a peculiar combination in *Free Jazz*), semi-standardized improvisational practices and rhythms on the one hand with the failing of these on the other, is how noise occurs here, as opposed to being in the messiness itself, or the abandon. Noise is not a freedom, and vice-versa, but the free is a raising of noise and its relation to music (as enactment of rules, standards, specified full or half tones).[13] Even Adorno would concede that 'immediacy', as he terms it, is not impossible in music, and although he is thinking about the prospects of 'informal' music as something beyond (but not completely) serial composition, he allows for improvisation (*Quasi una fantasia*, 295–6) and could just as well be talking of the free jazz he does not know about when writing the following (in 1961):

> Whatever manifests itself as immediate, ultimate, as the fundamental given, will turn out, according to the insights of dialectical logic, to be already mediated or postulated. This holds good for the individual note. No doubt, a certain immediacy is undeniable in such elements, as is the fact of a spontaneous, specifically musical experience. Of undoubted significance for music theory is Hegel's insight that *although all immediacy is mediated and dependent on its opposite, the concept of an unmediated thing—that is, of something which has become or has been set free—is not wholly engulfed by mediation.* (*Quasi una fantasia*, 299, emphasis added)

Generally, Adorno insists on the first idea, that mediation will always catch you, and that the avant-garde must demonstrate its being beholden to the dialectics of mediation. Here, though, there is a recognition that one term cannot simply subsume and engulf the other. The implication for any sort of 'informal' music is that it can offer something of the freedom it proposes. Free jazz acts *as if* it had escaped, and in so doing recalls Bataille's departure from Hegel, in claiming that there could be a dialectic without conclusion, without realization or *Aufhebung*. The musicians involved in free jazz know they cannot be outside form or the making of form. The emphasis on performance (and lack of editing in recording) tries to get at music as not just creation, but also dissipation of form. The attack on tonality and the introduction of non-musical noises into play makes the form of a piece oscillate between form and formlessness—which Bataille identified as 'formless'.[14]

Free jazz is part of modernism's drive to abstraction, but it is not a formalism, or cannot be read as that alone. The idea of 'the free' implies a jettisoning of content, even of purpose, as the emerging form is the only outcome (there can be no means and ends at the level of form). Just like abstract expressionism, though, this is only barely the case. The content is displaced: expression, ever purer as it becomes expression of expression, is the new 'content', with subjectivity being created as interaction and performance, through the combination (or interference) of technique and expressiveness/emotionality. Writing of 'fire music', that is, free jazz from the mid to late 1960s, David Keenan says:

> Fire music was an attempt to break on through to a primal and sensually liberating state, to create a total music unmediated by the mind. [. . .] They believed they were furthering black music by opening up the range of 'legitimate' sounds and techniques it could draw on, in an effort to communicate beyond words (or notes) the contents of their soul. ('The Primer: Fire Music', 42)[15]

The attack on musical convention is literalized in performance, non-music coming from 'improper' playing of saxophone or piano in particular. The literalization adds to the expressive potential, which becomes part of what is conveyed, prowess undoing itself to the gain of subjectivity.

Beyond this, free jazz occurs in a particular historical context, that of the demand for civil rights for blacks, and then Black Power and associated movements. But before getting to that, there is also the question of a more purposive content or *idea* within free jazz. If it is about individual and collective expression (so the content is the form), it is also about what could be beyond that. John Coltrane, Albert Ayler, Pharoah Sanders, Alice Coltrane, among others, saw free jazz as getting beyond normal human experience, into a type of ecstatic spirituality. Sun Ra proposed a whole space mythology and tried to actualize this in his music.[16] This ecstatic experience is the 'freeing up' that comes out fleetingly in the experience of 'freeing up' music. It can never attain full immediacy or communion with the universe, and so on, but it can signal the limits of the mundane world in trying to leave that world behind. Its failure is a sovereign one, a worthwhile one that remains impossible to quantify or value.

Coltrane's *Ascension* (1965) is one of a series of albums where he tries to get music outside, beyond and above itself. Unlike Bataille, *Ascension* aspires to transcendence, some sort of realization once beyond the rules of structured music, but formally it is not heading towards attainment (unlike Pharoah Sanders' 'The Creator Has a Masterplan' for example, with its sets of resolutions [beginning with an extended resolution with the entire band forming a solid chord-like moment]).[17]

The soloists are more Icarian than Apollonian, always brought back into the embodiment that is the band's continual, collective creation and destruction of community. Berendt and Huesmann sum up the conflict between spiritual transcendence and lower, less obviously spiritual directions in *Ascension*, writing that 'it is hymnlike, ecstatic music of the intensity of a forty-minute orgasm' (*The Jazz Book*, 117).[18] Just as Coltrane never set out to be Bataillean, this statement aims at an alternative, sexual sacred which simply supplants earlier forms, and it is not aiming at a Bataillean sacred where high and low merge, and where horror and death are central to the eroticism of the sacred experience than of the sacred conceived by Bataille. Nonetheless his general economy of expenditure, where loss replaces gain, where meaning and the law are threatened, but still menace and inform the attempts to escape them, is at work in free jazz.

Free jazz is sovereign in Bataille's sense. For Bataille, sovereignty is 'life beyond utility' (*The Accursed Share*, vol. III, 198) and also the 'miraculous realm of unknowing' (444n). It is connected to impossibility, because he or she who would be sovereign strives to get out of the restricted world, and success in this project is impossible. However, the sense of this impossibility, this living-on through failure, is exactly the only sovereignty (briefly) attainable. Unwittingly, Adorno follows a similar path when writing about jazz and weakness. The 'jazz subject' improvises to elude authority ('On Jazz', 488), but will fail (really fail, not fail in a 'good way') as it will not leave this impossible struggle behind, and seeks to wallow in this failing:

> the decisive intervention of jazz lies in the fact that the subject of weakness takes pleasure precisely in its own weakness, almost as if it should be rewarded for this, for adapting itself into the collective that made it so weak, whose standard its weakness can satisfy. ('On Jazz', 490)

Jazz, then, is a neurotic reaction to oppression (491), and its validation by audiences a reinforcement of that problem. Astonishingly, Adorno seems to think jazz is actually weak, musically (jazz thinks 'its seeming ineptitude is really a virtuosity of adaptation; that its "not-being-able-to" [and this is clearly tied in with the sexual meaning here] indicates an "ability-to"' [489]). Nonetheless, Adorno identifies a vital part of jazz in thinking about the performance of weakness alternating with potency, in spite of his opinions as to what that means for or in jazz. Weakness, in the form of the refusal of dogmatic supremacy or assertion of rules, will remain a central part of noise, and like much that constitutes noise, it arrives through negativity, here from a criticism of a new type of music.

The community constructed through collective improvisation is a violent, if not actually hostile one. Exclusions abound as colliding forces play off one another, and this both in and outside of the performing group. By the time of the advent of free jazz, the band and audience relation had been altered, notably by Charlie Parker, such that listeners would no longer be pandered to, expectations necessarily met.[19] This aloofness, or coolness, became a stylistic convention in its own right, but the relation between free jazz group and audience remains one where harmony is precluded. The society evolving through a piece will be one where conflicts are not resolved but put into play; only the agreement to have them put in play is decided consensually.

So in *Ascension*, there is a sequence of soloists, but this is a distraction, even if Sanders in particular forces out some great noises. The solos are overwhelmed by the group passages, which take up at least as much time as the short solos; the shortness of the solos also contributing to the group ethic. The large band sets off explosive blasts from which soloists emerge either fighting or almost struggling (as with the trumpets), and are subsumed in group bursts (sometimes launching themselves into these). The overall piece disrupts cognitive listening, and its duration is itself a force.

The drive to individual and collective freedom and realization has been seen as a key part of the struggle for black civil rights, equality and identity (by LeRoi Jones, for example), and abstractly, that would seem to be the case. Some musicians, like Archie Shepp, were more overtly militant, and directly referred to outside events in their music (for example 'Malcolm, Malcolm, Semper Malcolm' on *Fire Music*). Coltrane, among others, was, without being as overt, 'creating a climate of Afrocentrism' (Shipton, *A New History of* Jazz, 814), and this identity was being forged through a curious combination of avant-gardism and primitivism, this time different from that of the Surrealists and other European art movements, because a self-assertion of some sort of primal identity, in the wake of black consciousness writers of the 1950s like Aimé Césaire, James Baldwin and Frantz Fanon. *Ascension* itself can be thought of as 'as advanced as the most advanced contemporary jazz' (A. B. Spellman, 'Liner Notes' to *Ascension*) and at the same time be 'bringing jazz back to its natural state—totally improvised playing' (Bill Cole, *John Coltrane*, 167).[20] Free jazz is ultimately primordial, it is the original music and the original jazz (as jazz already draws, supposedly, on primal rhythms and musics). It does this as return—becoming the retrospective origin and the boundary between music and non-music. As it looks forward, it also 'anticipates' Afrofuturism of the late 1960s and 1970s, and so situates avant-gardism as a possibly fragmentary, community-based possibility, rather than there always being one specific avant-garde practice, outlook or artist.

It would be going too far to say that the violence in the music actually directly expresses black anger and rebellion of the 1960s—because it *is* itself rebellion, not a representation or account of some other rebellion.[21] Music and politics did combine in the shape of the AACM (Association for the Advancement of Creative Musicians) in Chicago and similar organizations in other US cities. These sought to build communities through artistic creativity, ensuring performances and recordings could happen (in the context of considerable functional racism, i.e. in how cities were divided up, as well as specific racial tensions), and keep up what today would be termed a 'dialogue' between community and art community. Jazz would take the ideas of identity and protest and radicalize them formally, even if not necessarily consciously, and also threatened the working of the culture industry, with small specialist labels (even if these are corralled by bigger ones), increasing avant-gardism and an anti-commercialism which goes beyond simple use of new formats, such as the 33 rpm LP (which both *Free Jazz* and *Ascension* effectively ignore, even though they were produced as recordings rather than recorded concerts). At the same time, the more acceptable face of rebellion—rock 'n' roll—itself a swiftly packaged and promoted commercialisation of black American blues and rhythm 'n' blues, was buying into the commodity form in the shape of the 7-inch, 45 rpm single. Whereas the old 78s were constricted by their short duration, the short time possible on a single was seen as positive, and songs constructed for, instead of despite, the format. In the 'culture industry', avant-garde jazz's refusal to adhere to such ideas separates it from the largely formulaic pop of the 1950s and early 1960s.[22]

Avant/improv

Free jazz would eventually have to forsake jazz conventions in pursuit of 'freeness' (for those of an avant-garde persuasion), and the Art Ensemble of Chicago and Anthony Braxton emerged from the AACM looking in just such directions.[23] Sun Ra was also heading off (bringing in both electronic music and rock aesthetics into his visionary attempt to formally bring the music of the universe to be, in improvised, or largely improvised music), and the mid 1960s saw musical categories or styles being disrupted and quickly reforming into new ones. In the realm of more 'programme'-based music, writers like Cornelius Cardew were moving away from orchestral conventions, students of Stockhausen were heading away from the limits of his electroacoustic strategies. The idea of improvisation would arguably dominate late 1960s music that saw itself as 'cutting edge'. The guitarist Derek Bailey and the improvising group AMM form one side of this, using the freeness specific to free jazz, to move away from jazz, while psychedelic music emerges differently, and will be discussed in the next chapter. The new improvisation of the late 1960s would move Cagean and *musique concrète* thinking into other genres where music was already occurring. So the idea of accessing the world of all sound, of all noises, is less important here, and the mobilization of whatever is there as performative strategy occupies a central position. For the guitarist Derek Bailey, the musical universe is not one containing the essence or idea of music, where this needs to be brought out. The improviser shapes material, brings it into the location of the performance through work, through an Aristotelian, dialectical relation to the world. The music occupies the time and space of its production, and only that. Like free jazz, 'free improvisation' claims to be at once the most primordial and the most developed music will ever be (although Bailey asserts it is not avant-gardist). He writes that 'historically, it pre-dates any other music—mankind's first musical performance couldn't have been anything other than a free improvisation' (*Improvisation*, 83).[24]

'Free improvisation', though, never quite leaves jazz behind, in reception terms at least. This has in fact become a self-fulfilling situation, where those who describe themselves as being part of 'Improv' are often closer to the jazz avant-garde than those who conceive of themselves as being part of 'noise music' or some other grouping. Those who imagine they are outside of all categorization are being idealistic. Bailey sees it quite clearly when stating that 'for me, the connection between this kind of playing and jazz is umbilical: the real possibilities start once you cut the cord' (cited in Ben Watson, *Derek Bailey and the Story of Free Improvisation*, 117).[25] The umbilical cord is thought of as a connecting metaphor, showing the interrelatedness and indebtedness of one object to another. Bailey might be suggesting that we move beyond this, cut ourselves free of this relation, but I think he is offering a more subtle and biologically consistent model: that the umbilical relation is essentially about cutting, about separation through a connection that has to be surpassed for there to be two things to relate to one another.

Bailey's practice is a realization of that cutting. Cynical about jazz, even the freest kind (see Bailey, *Improvisation*, 56–7), between the mid-1960s and his death in 2005, he collaborated with musicians from every conceivable style, and with every possible level of skill. He himself can be thought of as an anti-virtuosic virtuoso, his skill put to work as a destruction of standard beliefs about displaying instrumental genius through mastery of earlier modes of playing and the playing of canonically difficult works—just as much a convention in 1960s experimental jazz as in the programme music from classical music to Boulez.[26] Bailey sought to get outside of all conventions of playing, while simultaneously responding, musically rather than randomly, to his collaborators. While I do not think genre, style, category can be suspended except very fleetingly, the attempt is still worthwhile, and if the attempt is all we can have, then the attempt is the highest form of freedom to be aspired to, and must be maintained as an aim. Bailey fought guitar-playing convention at a material level. He was an early and regular user of feedback as an essential component of his music, with it becoming material in its own right, but also working as an arbitrariness that could never fully be harnessed. He would use extreme volume, but not dwell in it, and alternate between unamplified playings and scratchings and the power of the amplifier. Frequently, the note as played is left unheard, except peripherally, until amplified through volume pedal (many 'notes' are left unamplified)—a perfect working out of what Ben Watson describes as Bailey's 'aesthetically correct denial of guitar power' (*Derek Bailey*, 339). Bailey often plays these notes fiercely, and the audience can hear what we are not generally supposed to: the physical production of the sounds, as opposed to the idealized 'pure' musical tone instruments are supposed to be vectors for.

This material working through is part of what Watson thinks of as the 'militantly dialectical' approach of Bailey and free improvisation in general (9). Improvisation beyond categories ('non-idiomatic') is a late modernist 'return' to a primordial (if retrospective) musical moment, played over and over. The relations needed for music to occur are made present to the musicians and audience alike. Watson follows an avowedly Adornoian path, where all music of value exposes something about the economic and cultural systems that produced it and all other musics. He argues that free improvisation's dialectical approach is witnessed in its insistence on the concrete: the playing is not hidden away, not worked over and over in industrial production as recordings are (however aesthetically interesting many of these might be). The players are the producers, and the 'nowness' of the music offers an authentic social moment away from the capitalistically structured social world. Improvisation is socialist and collective, as long as the musicians are both listening and not resorting to preprepared sequences of chords (145).

This sense of a music that is Marxist in its practice and effect, even if not (often) in its avowed ideology, pervades the book, but Watson is also aware of the problem of valorizing collectivity and the 'nowness' of the music produced. The explicit need for live, active collaboration in improvisation means the notion of community is never far away, and as Watson rightly notes, this is a very cosy, liberal type of idea (254–5). In practice, he writes, the collective inspiration of free improvisation is essentially antagonistic (another key part of the dialectical process) (266), and the easy statement of 'community' represents an ideological distortion of the economically stratified world of capitalism.[27] The idea of a music that 'can only exist now' is a different one, but the problem, for Watson, is still to do with emphasizing the procedures of Marxist analysis:

> The very evanescence of Free Improvisation also represents a challenge to rational analysis. Absolute insistence on the specificity of a musical event abolishes the historical imagination and sociological perspective necessary for materialist-aesthetic comprehension and judgement. [. . .] Marxist musical analysis, which depends on a historical understanding of artistic form, is made impossible by such Zen insistence on the anthropological *hic et nunc*. (136)

Free music, like so much music since the advent of recording, insists (in opposition to the supposed distancing of recording), on the moment of musical creation, a moment of bringing to presence (through abstraction of music) of the group of people who are there, as a group. Philosophically, this implies something transcendent occurs, and that those present are taken outside of time, outside of socially constructed time and space, and can therefore seem or be presented as self-contained and immune from analysis, assessment or critique. It just is. A Marxist or 'Adornoist' position has to be wary of such claims of a community outside of all other contexts, but what Watson says applies to any attempt to stand back from the music. Ironically, free music needs to not be immanent, as 'only analysis and comprehension prevents a disappointed auditor from abandoning the entire racket' (304).

The Marxist, though, finds another layer to this problem, which is that to reject historical time and grounding is to deny that we inhabit a space–time built through surplus value extracted by capitalism, with a superstructure (or similar) which exists to mask this. I am sure this is right, but as with much of Marxism, if applied fully, most experimental art would be dismissed with the same argument, which, if nothing else, could not account for formal differences. If free music is dialectical, it can also work as something not just critical of the capitalist mode of production, but can fall outside it. As (the later) Adorno recognized, to *attempt* to get outside of that system is not false consciousness or denial, but all we can do. What is also curious is that free music seems to create a problem for Marxism, even as it offers its own parallel critique of the culture industry. Watson's 'Adornoist' argument relies on continually ignoring (while citing) Bailey's ideas about the absence of ideology in free music, and imagining an Adorno that was actually willing to extend the spirit of what he was saying to new forms of music. This is not to say that Watson is wrong, or that those intentions have to be obeyed, but it is to say that in order to make his Marxist case, he has to use a deconstructive method. This sits strangely with the determinism elsewhere in his argument—i.e. that free music must be Marxist because it operates semi-autonomously, economically speaking, in a way that challenges 'common sense' understandings about the inevitability of the market and the profit motive. Arguably any financially unsuccessful music does this to a large extent. Watson sees this in combination with the musical practice itself, but that too is a presumption. He specifically refuses to think of Bailey et al. as artisans (155), but it is unclear why one could not do this, except, I presume, that artisans, while potentially occupying a critical space, cannot offer the Marxist vanguard hope. In fact, maybe the free musicians are entrepreneurs, simply ahead of their business time? Even if we accept the necessity of grounding (which I do), why ground economically—as capitalism so desires?

Watson and Bailey share a suspicion about listening to recordings of improvised music. In most cases, the existence of a recording entails the logic of the music industry, although since the advent even of portable tape recorders, this is not a terminal problem for *all* recording. The point is that recording misses the truth of the particular spontaneity of the improvised concert, which includes the audience (see Bailey, *Improvisation*, 103). Bailey grudgingly goes along with existence of recordings, but, remembering that improvised music must be fleeting—and in this, it is *the* most pure of musics (142)—he writes that 'for many of the people involved in it, one of the enduring attractions of improvisation is its momentary existence: the absence of a residual document' (35). Watson's identification of the problem of the 'nowness' of free music does not even go halfway to the reification of the 'moment' in such ideas. How different is it to any 'you had to be there' statements about concerts? A music industry (including the artists) keen to salvage its profits has taken up this idea with a vengeance in the first few years of this century. It also ignores the possibility of passing on some awareness, however 'residual', to those who could not get to the 'precious now'. The 'residual document' highlights the fact that, contrary to Walter Benjamin's idea of reproduction diminishing the 'aura' of art, it actually heightens the value of the original, as that which is not only copy.

In the end, Watson's grapple with Bailey is itself messy, noisy, continually coming back to resistances and contradictions. The contradictions in his reading are not interesting, but the impedances are, because they precisely mirror the strange position that free music held compared with even experimental jazz of the time. From the 1980s onwards, not least due to Bailey's interventions, setting up events as well as in playing terms, this would alter. But as Watson rightly notes, free music thrives on opposition, on not being accepted, and even on disagreements between musicians.

For that reason, Watson is not keen on Bailey's peers AMM, arguing that they end up with too holistic a music (268). Their freedom, he thinks, is too disciplined, and its reticence incapable of the freedom attained by Bailey's harsher playing. It is fair to say that their concerts strongly cohere as they develop, but can still produce shocks, violent dissonances and so on. AMM stand between jazz and rock improvisation, with Keith Rowe (guitar) and Eddie Prévost (percussion) both 'preparing' their instruments as Cage 'prepared' pianos (with intrusive objects, machines, amplification, 'wrong' playing) at the centre (John Tilbury the other player for the bulk of their history). There are times when they approach a too-easy ambience, but these sections are always in anticipation of disruption. At the end of the 1960s, AMM, the messier Musica Elettronica Viva and Peter Brötzmann signal the removal of jazz from free music. This was an inevitable moment in the 'freeing up' of jazz, and while free music often features those who work within a jazz idiom or context, the 'freeness' itself extends far into other approaches. Its implied criticism of skill also plays out across more 'non-musical' groups like Smegma or the Nihilist Spasm Band (see chapter 6 of this volume). Once the jazz part has gone from free jazz, the free part has to go too. Once the vista opens up of playing any notes, incorporating any sound, taking any musical approach, then this infinite expanse itself becomes a limit, a pre-prepared instruction to 'explore' this musical universe, that can lead to the ossification of this exploration as simple style. Without resorting to the 'eclectic' (an updating of the idea of 'fusion'), freeness is to be sought within other methods, as in Ground Zero's combination of unpredictable elements, freer moments and compositions, or as a decision made for or in certain performances (Zorn's *Cobra* project) rather than an ideology or lifestyle. Freeness does not work without rules to play against. What if, in a further paradox, freeness had infiltrated simple, or even badly played, but structured music, such as in punk? The freedom of free jazz does not go away, but dissolves into other areas (including itself as genre); the freeness is caught within sets of paradoxes that not only do not prevent its existence, but are the reasons for it. The freeing up of playing, like the freeing up of 'all sound', filters into many musics, spreading noise even as they lose their initial moment as noise in their own right.

NOTES

1. See for example Robert W. Witkin, *Adorno on Music* (London and New York: Routledge, 1998) (160–80, on jazz), and also Richard Leppert's extensive commentaries in *Adorno, Essays on Music*. For an overview of the commentary on Adorno on jazz, see Leppert, 'Commentary' in *Adorno, Essays on Music*, 327–72 (343–60), and 346n, 351n for detailed references. I actually find these 'middle-path' writers to err in Adorno's favour, as will be seen below, in the case of Leppert.

2. Adorno, 'On the Social Situation of Music', in *Essays on Music*, 391–436. See the same essay for Adorno's view on how the 'qualified' bourgeois listener can maintain the sense of the goodness of his or her society through sanitized classical music, shorn of historical and potentially radical character (416–17, 422).

3. Adorno, 'On the Fetish-Character in Music and the Regression of Listening', in *Essays on Music*, 288–317. Adorno does not talk only of the regression of those (performers and audiences) duped by the culture industry, but also of their 'retardation'—he calls their interest in primitivism 'that of the forcibly retarded' (303).

4. Adorno, 'On Jazz', in *Essays on Music*, 470–95.

5. Adorno, 'Farewell to Jazz', in *Essays on Music*, 496–99.

6. 'We are rotting away with neurasthenia under our roofs, a cemetery and common grave of so much pathetic rubbish; while the blacks who (in America or elsewhere) are civilized along with us, and who, today, dance and cry out, are marshy emanations of the decomposition who are set aflame above this immense cemetery' (Bataille, 'Black Birds', in Bataille et al., *Encyclopaedia Acephalica* [London: Atlas, 1995]).

7. Adorno also looks forward to a music that looks forward internally as well as externally—such that its outcomes are not predetermined: 'in future, experimental music should not just confine itself to refusing to deal in the current coin; it should also be music whose end cannot be foreseen in the course of production' (*Quasi una fantasia*, 303).

8. See Shipton, *A New History of Jazz* (London and New York: Continuum, 2002), 777.

9. The full title of the album is *Free Jazz: A Collective Improvisation* by the Ornette Coleman Double Quartet (Atlantic, 1961, recorded December 1960).

10. Jazz recordings insist on this to the point of parody, particularly when technological concerns infiltrate the musical process so obviously as here—where the piece had to be split into two parts to fit the format of the 33 rpm LP. The idealism of the 'capture' of a performance is given away in the phrase 'heard here exactly as performed in the studio, without splicing or editing' (Free Jazz sleeve notes, Atlantic CD)—this is not the same as 'this is what was played in the studio'. It is further troubled by the addition of 'First Take'—an alternative version of the piece.

11. Coltrane had also been expanding the jazz sound 'vocabulary' to include squawks, howls and so on (Shipton, *A New History of Jazz*, 740). These noises therefore had very little time in which they were heard as noise (among avant-garde jazz musicians).

12. Jost, *Free Jazz* (New York: Da Capo Press, 1994 [originally 1974]).

13. Historically, its moment of noise has gone—at least to audiences familiar with experimental music—but as always, we should be aware of the elitism that insists everyone agrees that a certain type or piece of music is now fully normalized. Anachronistic noise can lurk like landmines or pockets of compressed methane.

14. Derek Bailey also highlights the idea that 'free improvisation' approximates formlessness, without simply being it: '[for those concerned with composed music] it seems that any overall pattern must be imposed to save music from its endemic formlessness [. . .] But generally speaking, improvisers don't avail themselves of the many "frameworks" on offer. They seem to prefer formlessness. More accurately, they prefer the music to dictate its own form' (Bailey, *Improvisation: Its Nature and Practice in Music* [New York: Da Capo, 1993], 111). Bailey mobilizes the idea of formlessness as critique, transforms it into a statement about all musicality, revalorizes it as genuine musical expression, and then to add that all this formlessness is not really without form. It is about a coming to form. On Bataille's idea of the 'formless' and how it differs from formlessness, see Patrick Crowley and Paul Hegarty (eds), *Formless; Ways In and Out of Form* (Oxford and Bern: Peter Lang, 2005).

15. Keenan, 'The Primer: Fire Music', *The Wire* 208 (June 2001), 42–9. This article is a very useful survey of free jazz, including later practitioners. Adorno would imagine his arguments about the rhetoric in and around jazz would be just as valid for free jazz as for other types, and that there was some simplistic primitivism going on in statements such as that of Keenan, but this would be undermined in that Keenan is writing about 'fire music' as precisely a modernist, avant-garde approach, whatever else it summons up.

16. Jost analyses how he does this in the two *Heliocentric Worlds* albums (*Free Jazz*, 188–9).

17. On Sanders, *Karma* (1969).

18. Berendt, *The Jazz Book: From Ragtime to Fusion and Beyond* (revised by Günther Huesmann, sixth edition) (New York: Lawrence Hill, 1992).

19. According to Shipton, the history of jazz before Parker had been one tied into other forms of black entertainment, conforming to more or less racist stereotypes not only of behaviour, but that blacks could be integrated as long as they followed set paths of behaviour. Parker made the music the only performance, which was highly unusual in the late 1940s (Shipton, *A New History of Jazz*, 505–6).

20. Bill Cole, *John Coltrane* (New York: Da Capo, 1993).

21. This ties in with Shepp's reading of 1960s free jazz: 'naturally, the music reflects that whole period . . . that whole time definitely influenced the way we played. I think that's where that really free form came into it' (Shepp, cited in Shipton, *A New History of Jazz*, 798). Shepp is not saying that the music illustrates that time, but that the events of the time have affected the approach to music. In other words, the racial violence, fight for rights, anti-war movements etc. do not become expressed content, but cross into form(less).

22. We all have some Adorno in us, and Leppert insists that even those who challenge him are very choosy in who they promote as good pop or rock (Adorno, *Essays on Music*, 345). I just think that rock 'n' roll, as the form that drove 'youth culture', clearly derived from other less mass-palatable musics, and promoted over messier white music like skiffle, is almost uniquely placed as a popular culture movement in matching Adorno's critiques.

23. Braxton pursuing a more modernist, quasi-scientific approach at times, the Art Ensemble of Chicago a much messier, and so noisier affair. As well as bringing in toy instruments, non-musical sources and non-jazz approaches, they would disrupt potentially weighty improvisations with incongruous folk or children's musics. While such disruption would ultimately become an even more annoying staple of 'serious' music of all categories, in the late 1960s, it contained a freshness and unexpectedness (and is one link between 'high' improvised music and the music of Frank Zappa, for example).

24. This begs the question of whether those first musicians saw or heard it that way, as Bailey's claim implies a secular, intentional subject, excluding the possibility of sacred intervention of an almost infinite variety, or even a simple wish to copy natural sounds—in which latter case, all music would be quotation.

25. Watson, *Derek Bailey and the Story of Free Improvisation* (London: Verso, 2004).

26. Bailey is not 'against' skill, nor does he simply claim that to improvise needs to come from a base of skill, but he rejects the ideas that formally trained instrumentalists will be the

best, and they may not even be capable of improvisation—in which case, they would not be making music.

27. There is a widely held belief in improvised music that it is a highly communal activity. John Zorn offers a slightly more anarchist version of a society working as a collective moderation of conflicts: 'I basically create a small society and everybody finds their own position in that society. It really becomes like a psychodrama. People are given power and it's very interesting to see which people like to run away from it, who are very docile and just do what they're told, others try very hard to get more control and more power. So it's very much like the political arena in a certain kind of sense' (cited in Bailey, *Improvisation*, 78). We might not agree or like the sound of all Zorn says, but it shows key elements of how improvisation is not anarchic, but anarchistic, in that de facto power exists—it is open to all, and is transitional (if the society is working). Like Foucault, Zorn does not pretend power can be dissipated, but recognizes that it is a creative force.

4

ELECTRIC

Electrification brings the guitar centre stage, changing group dynamics. Amplification of guitars was initially a defensive act, as guitar players tried to be heard in big band settings (in the late 1930s and 1940s), but in the 1950s, the new slimmed down electric guitar that is still the basic form of the instrument was in action. Blues and rock 'n' roll bands took the guitar away from being a backing instrument into not only a lead, but also a catalyst for heavier riff-based songs. Rock 'n' roll is the first musical form that consistently works with loudness: this was music to be played loud, as an assertion of youth identity. Meanwhile, in the songs, repetition, both musical and lyrical, would force home whatever 'message' a song had (often a self-referential one). This is really the extent of rock 'n' roll noisiness, until rock comes around in the mid 1960s, but that does not mean it was not taken as antisocial noise. As well as the moral panic around youth culture and loud music, there was resistance to the style of music itself, as it seemed to go against traditional skills: the singing was weird, involving shouting, or odd mannerisms; the lyrics were vacuous and simple, the music limited.[1] If there is noise in rock 'n' roll, it is here, in the refusal to value music according to what were thought to be timeless musical criteria. Meanwhile, a lot of rock 'n' roll was much closer to the style of the crooners, and did not trouble anyone. Ultimately, all styles of rock 'n' roll would create huge profits for the culture industry, which actually fully becomes itself thanks to rock 'n' roll, and the realization that rebellion is marketable as well as containable.

While rock 'n' roll in the 1950s had little awareness of what was going in *musique concrète*, or of John Cage, or Fluxus, nonetheless, the claim could be made that it is part of a simplification of music, a clearing-away that is just as productive, in the long run, of experimentation and noise as the tape-splicing labs around Europe and America. Institutionally sponsored experimentation can subsist within the confines of the lab, the relevant musical community, while rock occupies other locations, opens acoustic spaces that odder musics can move into. So rock is not just a clearing-away, but also a clearing.

Electricity threatened music as purity of human expression, and also of innate 'talent', as it first distanced the musician from the sound, and second, masked inadequacies of technique. This is not just the literal-mindedness of critics, but a crucial moment in the Bataillean dialectic (i.e. of oppositions and developments through negativity—via the other—but without resolution) of noise. Amplification takes over from the human voice, or music as expression of human feeling, emotion or subjectivity (often through approximation of voice). What you hear is revealed as electrically driven movements of air; sound is materialized, and becomes other to the expressing body. Music is now evidently a prosthetic, mediated through machinery, and this shakes the belief in the centeredness, intention and authenticity of musical creation. Even musics that were progressive in terms of form, content and politics—jazz and folk—held to the sense that true meaning would emerge the less mediated it was.[2] Jazz steered clear of electrics (Sun Ra being an instructive exception), but as rock quickly develops into a diversity of styles, jazz-fusion joins not only rock and jazz, but acoustic and electric. Similarly folk rock shrugs off folkist purity, in the slipstream of Bob Dylan's crossover.

Electricity, primarily through amplification, signifies. It is not just loudness, but the connotation of loudness, of aggression (particularly in the form of the electric guitar). It also allows a development of musical meaning, as notes are bent, stretched, made to vibrate (as in jazz since bebop). The insights of the lab-based experimenters are also played out on the fretboard of B. B. King. The electric guitar is not just connected with sex because it is 'wielded' as phallic object, or held suggestively; it connects into a more ecstatic eroticism through connection.[3] As the amplified guitar separates off (but not fully) from the guitarist, it approaches the crowd through loudness and also a continuous signal; even between tracks, the amps are live and setting up a bath of noise. This transfers into the music in the shape of solos, but also as extended notes: from B. B. King to Jimi Hendrix, the stretching of electric guitar sound is the nucleus of an erotic connectivity. Ultimately, this requires the death of the guitar. When Hendrix burns his guitar at Monterey Pop (1967), it is as the *consuming* element of sacrificial erotics. When Pete Townshend destroys his guitars, it initially comes from loss of control and the physical rendering of rage unleashed through aggressive performance, but in terms of sound, it is the loss of subjective control as feedback takes over—neither the band nor crowd can master this sound.[4]

Surplus sound is a key characteristic of electrified music, and as the 1960s go on, distortion and feedback, pushing the machinery beyond limits, offers another layer of noise that is both literal and noise in the sense of being unwanted, excess, waste. These noises are quickly used, and become techniques, but along the way, they operate as a way of maintaining a community. Paul Gilroy, citing Hendrix, refers to an 'electric church'. This would be 'a collective social body of musical celebrants that gathered periodically to engage the amplified modernist offshoots of the Mississippi delta and harness them in the causes of human creativity and liberation' ('Soundscapes of the Black Atlantic', 383).[5] We can take 'church' as meant in the most general sense, as a way of capturing an elective community that somehow bonds together, in this case through excessive performance. Gilroy goes on to say that Hendrix insisted on the necessity of loudness to convey the possibility of revolutionary change through both shock and the use of 'the correct frequency' (*ibid.*), the latter allowing a more direct connection, facilitated by the noisiness.[6]

Unfortunately, one of the central narratives of rock is the drive to virtuosity, and the strangeness of some of Hendrix's music gets subsumed under recognition of his 'talent'. Journalists and listeners colluded with musicians in heightening the 'greatness' of its central performers. What kind of validation is rock looking for in staging a discussion about who the best guitarist is (the possibility of there being one more important than the identity of the specific victor)? Rock was taking itself seriously, following the same path as jazz had taken, and justifying itself through continual assertion (in music and in discourse) as being valid and genuine art. This is one of the central narratives of rock, and is used as a weapon against rock, as the 1970s progress, and the point of interest becomes 'authenticity'.[7] In addition to the praising of skill, the performance of skill and the increasing wished-for or implied skill in being a rock listener, what begins to accrete is a story of rock, a story that many imagine was broken by punk, but in fact the rethinking of music history around punk is not the only narrative.

Organic

There are two major narratives of rock: the first is the steady development of a medium, and canon of great works. The other imagines itself differently, drawing up a history based on rebellion and moments when music and the commodification of music were disrupted. The first could be seen as premodernist, the second as modernist, but some would characterize the first as modernist, the second as post-modernist. [8] This latter definition would be based on the period in question, but would ignore the modernist thinking which insists on avant-garde production, and which arrived late in music, if we discount the 'avant-garde' of serialism. Beyond this slightly reductive presumption of two metanarratives of rock, which I am making in the interest of how noise works in and across rock, are a host of different contents for the thinking of the history of rock, and many different approaches to rock. Genealogies can be constructed with almost limitless variety, as can the meta-histories of how people have thought rock (see Simon Frith, Roy Shuker, Keith Negus, as examples of thinking how the history of rock has been written). In the case of 'noise' or of thematic and/or formal connections within rock and connecting rock to other genres, the temptation is to look for influence, explicit or otherwise, or at least confluence of approach (e.g. the use of electronics in the 1960s). So we might find *musique concrète* 'influencing' rock in the Beatles ('# 9 Dream'), Frank Zappa, Can, and so on. We could also take the influence of jazz, and see the experimentation with form crossing into rock, and probably ignore the music that usually goes under the rubric 'jazz rock' in favour of jazz-prog like the Soft Machine. The influence of jazz would not just be from improvisation, but also in the ecstatic overcoming of form, in favour of an apparently more direct, unmediated connection. Such connections work if we are putting together a 'high' or even pre-modernist type history where avant-gardists can be easily lined up in a sequential row, but as I am interested in noise as a mediation, this chapter needs therefore to find other ways of relating rock to its experimental fellow travellers in other genres. This would be the pursuit, by other means, of suggestions offered by Bailey and Zorn as to the value of improvisation. This will still entail consideration of central moments and figures in 1960s rock—Cream, Hendrix, the Grateful Dead, Zappa— but hopefully, in situating this music in the context of electricity, and the differences between the approaches of those artists, the creation of a canon can be avoided. [9]

Cream tend to fall outside the scope of studies of experimental music, as their approach is clearly delimited by blues conventions, and arguably the worst aspect of 1960s/1970s rock, virtuosity for its own sake. 'For its own sake' or 'emptiness' are continual reference points for writers thinking that the musical world changed with the advent of punk and real expression returned, but in Cream's case, it seems no one disputes this. Sheila Whiteley, in what is a positive take on Cream's influence, notes that 'it is generally established that along with Cream, Jimi Hendrix can be credited with establishing virtuosity as a major parameter in blues-based rock music' (*The Space Between the Notes*, 15). [10] Oddly, this is meant as a commendation, but Eric Clapton was even aware of the problem Cream had made for themselves: 'Everyone got into too much of a heavy ego-trip. Virtuosos and all that kind of rubbish' (cited in *The Space Between the Notes*, 10). Despite all this, for Whiteley, Cream are a central part of genuinely progressive rock.

There are two, linked elements in what constitutes progressive rock (at least of the 1960s). First, 'commentaries on "progressive rock" are generally framed in terms of *becoming*' (6). Whiteley is referring to rock becoming progressive, but is also including the idea that it must itself be about development, musical advances. Second, even if only abstractly, progressive rock aims to change society, or suggest alternatives. In the case of Cream, there is little on show of the latter, but some of the first. Cream's music represents a progression from and of the blues (7), and does this through literally extending the form, in concert at least. Their songs as they appear in recorded form are not especially long, but still broke away from the restrictions of the demand of the singles market, where songs had to be around three minutes or less in length.[11] Like Whiteley, John S. Cotner takes the idea of progression formally, but could go further. He writes that 'generally, the descriptor *progressive* is based on the root concept *progress*, which as David Brackett, Bill Martin and others explain, refers to *development* and *growth* by accumulation' ('Pink Floyd's 'Careful with That Axe, Eugene', 85). He is referring to the too-easy continuity between western art music and progressive rock, and seeks to get us out of easy categorizations, but the idea works at two levels. First, the high modernist notion of improvement and upwards development through experimentation more than matches 1960s ways of musical thinking. Second, improvisation, particularly when more straightforward than the 1960s jazz or free improvisation, enacts this development in the music.

Psychedelic music, acid-rock, blues rock, jazz-rock, space rock: all would take the song as pretext for extended improvisation, although 'jamming' might be the more relevant term. 'Spoonful', on the second, live, part of Cream's *Wheels of Fire*, is a good illustration of this. The more dissonant part of 'Spoonful' is actually the song, with the instrumental part building through straightforward explorations of keys and rhythm established early on, within the 'song' part. The performance closes with a reprise of/return to the song (after 13.30), with the audience applauding at that point. What that signals is not clear. Although the lengthy soloing by Clapton, and the band's performance strategy in general, recalls jazz structuring of tracks and concerts, and solos are rewarded by applause in that context, there is also recognition that the song has become of minor relevance; it is the instrumental working-out that counts. While debates on exactly when improvisation came into jazz (many arguing for it being there at its inception), pop and rock 'n' roll existed to do something else—pop with the song reduced to pretext was a new departure.

Wheels of Fire also raises the question of 'live recordings'. While fans, musicians and critics of all genres of music insist on the specificity of 'being there', live albums are widely listened to. Live albums represent a great commercial bonus (even more so since DVD), and are cheaper to make in the first place, particularly when dealing with 'virtuoso' rock bands. I would resist the over-purist idea that concerts cannot be captured, primarily because they are always being captured at some sort of remove, or with the possibility of distance. Where or when is the authentic experience? There would seem to be a clear answer to that, but is an audience member there as much as a performer? The question can also be asked the other way. How *much* are you there? Are you experiencing it fully? Correctly? Well? Badly? In other words, we imagine a self-conscious presence (even while commonly claiming that a great concert would entail 'losing yourself'). The live album is not just a bad copy, but constitutes the question 'what is it to be *there*'?

Album two of *Wheels of Fire* offers a very direct answer to this question: put the drums in both channels, Clapton's guitar in the right, Jack Bruce's bass in the left. This spatialization is presumably meant to make us feel like that we are on stage with the band, or, bizarrely, that they are playing acoustically, so where they are positioned matters. Instead of the electrically charged power trio, we get two groups with one and a half instruments in each, in an unhappy recreation of *Free Jazz*'s double quartet. On 'Spoonful', Clapton's solo meanders melodically, but not too far from a line, while Bruce alternates between riffs and runs and what on record sounds like a total lack of interest (8.45–9.30). 'Spoonful' is a display of jazz convention being transferred into rock as process of validation. It does not go beyond jazz, but seems to fall beneath it, not because of its lack of complexity or innovation, but because it aims for something else. This piece is not about resolution. Although I noted earlier the similarities in audience reaction to Cream's soloing and to jazz soloing, 'Spoonful' shows that the displacement of 'event' into the solo (as opposed to the song part) is misleading, as it replaces the jazz solo's purpose and progression, ironically, given its context as early progressive rock, with a refusal to progress dynamically.

But at another level, the 'exploration' within 'Spoonful' is looking forward, to acid rock and space rock jamming, where movement continually alternates with stasis, or is caught up with it. This is not exclusive to rock; it can be heard in Sun Ra as it can in AMM, or Steve Reich, but I think the alternation is most clearly signalled in the blues-rock improvisations that lead to more group-based versions. The use of repetition and slow progression attempts to effect a change in the way music is experienced, such that you are 'taken out of yourself' as points of reference; the presence of you as an individual, the music as a discrete thing, the band as producers of that, all get tangled up in a form of ecstasy and/or immanence. So the meandering improvisation is a crucial part of that, and the use of blues or jazz figures or patterns works as means to an end that get lost as the ending comes, and is withheld at the same time. For the performer, the prolonged instrumental leads to reflection being lost. Rather than imagine this to mean some sort of communion with the instrument or the music, what is occurring is that the physical, material part of playing takes over, and the performing body is suddenly caught within that rather than mastering it. The electric guitar (but all amplified instruments to some extent) allows individual notes to get lost, or to be prolonged, distorted, blurred. This is the micro level to the extended instrumental's macro level (which is in turn micro to the macro of 'progression' in rock). There is no causal determinacy here, but parallel alterations in the time of music, where something like progress occurs, while at the same time, it is made messy, lost in its construction. The electric guitar is an intervention in time. It is more than punctuation—or if you like, punctuation in its fullest sense. With electricity, music moves from occurring or unfolding in time to being an occurrence of time. This is a major part of the strangeness of music to 'lose yourself in'. But this loss is not just a hippy nirvana, nor is it an easy posture of nothingness; this loss is actually a proximity to a sense of self, as fleeting, coming in and out of time and presence.

At Woodstock, then, Hendrix is able to 'harness' this to the point where the contortions of his 'Star-spangled Banner' become political, there, because of the loss of mastery (not loss of technical control) of the music is the music, medium and message. It shows a political alternance otherwise absent from the relentless positivity of the anthem, not only because it veers between the 'correct notes' and bent, feedback or distorted sounds, but because it cuts between crisply played, discrete notes and the noise implications of those notes. It also alternates between drift and cutting, further enhanced by Mitch Mitchell's interventions on drums, including a parodic marching moment. Mitchell does not so much join in with Hendrix as musically fight him, or ignore what is going on, so we also have dissonant types of free playing.

Elsewhere in the concert, almost all the tracks are extended by what have to be described as 'work-outs' or jams, Hendrix telling the audience at one point in 'Voodoo Child (Slight Return)' that they can leave if they want—'we're only jamming' (10.35 in). The tracks 'Jam Back at the House' and 'Woodstock Jam' do not simply drift, or exhaust melodic variation, as they cut harshly into different sections, announced by Hendrix (like Coltrane on *Ascension*). The 'only jamming' reference is disingenuous: at a really obvious level, many want to hear Hendrix pushing beyond songs, so the jams are crucial parts of the concert. Jamming itself has moved from the rehearsal or post-concert session (this latter being the typical jazz jam session), where there is little or no audience, only participants or potential participants. Now it is the moment where individual and/or group invention is supposed to bring a community with the audience into being. With 'Voodoo Child', Hendrix solos into an ecstatic warping of the sound—notes bent to extremes, flurries of sound displacing individually picked sounds. The soloist is not just being an individual here, but, when improvising, setting up an endlessly mobile relation with the most proximate community (Hendrix's band), in order to pass this community by contagion to the rest of the audience. While this is perfectly possible with slightly less solo emphasis, with a soloist who is nearly always the one performing the solos (as opposed to moving around the band), the philosophical and political drama of the individual and community forming each other is played out.

The crescendo of 'Voodoo Child' leads to the 'Star-Spangled Banner', now drawn in as material for the developing of a new elective community in and around the concert. In an extension of the drawing-in of jams to the centre of the performance, here what would normally precede or close ceremonies or events loses its external, policing quality. The distinction between inside and outside (of the concert) is momentarily disrupted by this move, and this, just as much as the overt (if unconsciously summoned, according to Hendrix) symbolism of distorting the anthem, that is the political value of the performance. Woodstock and the State drift into one another, signalling the potential for the community Woodstock saw itself as being able to spread.

Hendrix's solos, like Woodstock, end up as representations of spontaneity; like many rock improvisers, a pattern solidifies around which solos are built, a structure in addition to the song skeleton. Rather than take this as a limitation, we should think of it as a clear refusal to draw the line between authentic performance and improvisation on the one hand, and substandard, mediated recordings. The jams become hyperjams: mediating, in an apparently unmediated live setting, the jam the band would actually have had at some other time. 'Jam Back at the House' is striking in this respect, as it works around set riffs, but riffs that are abruptly swapped for new ones at points indicated by Hendrix. The jam is most inventive when it solidifies into a syncopated band riff that almost doesn't move for two minutes, with Hendrix occasionally drifting off it, and in so doing, emphasizing the curious repetition that tries to hold off time while drawing attention closer to its passing (or not).

The Grateful Dead offer a simple combination of 'difference and repetition', where a song would be structurally repetitive, time-suspending, while over the course of a tour, or lifetime of concerts, the outcomes would not be known in advance. The Grateful Dead are renowned for this variation in live performance as well as the sheer amount of live playing, per concert, or in general. Derek Bailey frames interview comments from guitarist Jerry Garcia with a keen interest in this, and how the audience reacts and contributes to it, writing that 'they are the only rock band whose performances are based on the idea of improvisation and, unusual in any area, whose reputation is based on the expectation of change' (Bailey, *Improvisation*, 42). He also says to Garcia that 'you have a very special audience in that many of them come to see you over and over again and they don't come to hear what they've heard before' (46), to which Garcia agrees. Bailey is interested in this audience, but even though relatively positive, the overall sections on 'audience' are sceptical as to the valuing of an audience. The boldest playing cannot think of its audience, but it can hope to allow them in, knowing that they are going to get something uncompromising. For all Bailey's reticence, I think his hope for an ideal audience is revealed in his comments to Garcia, whose own thoughts are not so far from Bailey's (even if the musical outcomes are very different): 'the audience has a great night listening to us struggle [. . .] they're very involved and they feel in fact as responsible in some ways as we do' (Garcia, quoted in Bailey, *Improvisation*, 46). The audience is as interested in the production of a musical moment that at some level can only exist in that 'here and now'. This is to see the same sort of unalienated production as Watson sees claimed in free music. But, perhaps more significantly, the Grateful Dead offer, at the same time, a spuriously harmonious community, 'one big family'.[12] The drawback for that view is that it is a wilful ignoring of the power relations at play. Not everyone is equal in the setting of a concert by a band, and the community constructed in relatively improvised rock music *needs* or even *is* that playing out of power differentials. Like monarchs, the band might be 'ours', but the conditions on which that is based is that they are sovereign. The best, noisiest and truly experimental music tries to turn that power into failing, always potentially weak sovereignty.

Since Garcia's death, recordings of Grateful Dead concerts have proliferated. As with many dead rock stars, this is excused as being the only way people can hear their idols, but it also questions, as literally as possible, the supposed value of a live event further. The recordings circulate not only in your and the band's absence from the actual concert (as indicated by the 'knowing' reference to this on albums marked 'live'), but in the permanent absence of the key player. Death does not only add commercial value, but also a relation to the music unbundled from the spurious belief in the proximity that might be possible with the source of music (as opposed to the person outside of their music). The existence of the recordings undermines the 'purity' of the live event, but also the volume of releases threatens the individual importance of a specific gig, even as they are all taken seriously as individual moments.

The Grateful Dead had always had a healthy lack of purism in this regard, culling elements from many recordings (NB they were always recording performances) on the seminal meanders of *Live/Dead* (1970), and also combining concert and studio elements on the earlier *Anthem of the Sun* (1968).[13] Edwin Pouncey argues that the Grateful Dead brought considerable awareness of experimental musics, such as *musique concrète*, into their work, noting this particularly on *Anthem of the Sun* (Pouncey, 'Rock Concrète: Counterculture Plugs into the Academy', 155–6).[14] I don't disagree with this, but I think it is overstated, perhaps even in the case of Zappa, and that 'countercultural' rock used devices from outside quite casually, or in ways not fully explored by the 'academic' experimental musicians. Apart from that, the tape editing is weak (not in a good way) on this album, and the 'strange sounds' of *Live/Dead* are penned in to the imaginatively titled 'Feedback'. Pouncey goes on to highlight the connection between the Grateful Dead's tape experiments and John Oswald's *Grayfolded* (1995), which samples hundreds of hours of Grateful Dead concerts, creating restructured versions of key tracks such as 'Dark Star' (which opens *Live/Dead*, and ambles in at 23.15) ('Rock Concrète', 162). Oswald goes further: just as the band's own recordings flood out, losing the specificity of any one concert in a chaotic mapping of all possibilities of those tracks, so *Grayfolded* replicates the suspension of time in a particular performance and/or track, and it does so *fractally*. The same structures proliferate, but with almost infinite (possible) variation.

Deleuze bit

When Gilles Deleuze writes of repetition, he is careful to distinguish it from the usual understanding of the word. The implication of his book's title, *Difference and Repetition*, is that the two are entwined, and at some fundamental level, each does more or less the opposite to what we expect of the terms.[15] I think that this 'essential' repetition is going on in repetitive music, whether jamming, or mechanical style, circular rhythms. *Difference and Repetition* rarely addresses music, favouring literature and painting. This is because the 'repetition' initially being argued for is not simple repeating, but a sort of recall. Deleuze estimates that to recall in a way that genuinely repeats makes the repetition an event in its own right, always for the first time, which, in turn, brings the 'original' to be (so he writes about psychoanalysis and Proust, in this context). The implication for music is that it would not be a sequence of same or similar notes, patterns or whatever, but something endlessly changing, while repeating 'something' at a deeper level:

> the totality of circles and series is thus a formless *ungrounded* chaos which has no law other than its own repetition, its own reproduction in the development of that which diverges and decentres. We know how these conditions are satisfied in such works as Mallarmé's *Book* or Joyce's *Finnegans Wake*. The identity of the object read really dissolves into divergent series defined by esoteric words, just as the identity of the reading subject is dissolved into the decentred circles of possible multiple readings. (*Difference and Repetition*, 69)

Joyce and Mallarmé are there not just as exponents of experimental literature, but as writers in whose works we see a fundamental repetition of the working of literature, showing the repetition that is literature, through a differentiation of style. In musical terms, we might think of Derek Bailey as a good example here. His music is continually moving, purposely trying to stay away from generic gestures, and in so doing, he would highlight the kind of repetition Deleuze has in mind, where the artwork shows us a repetition that is always only occurring the first time.[16]

Deleuze justifies this shift in the working of both difference and repetition at some length, and centres it on the subject, a subject lost in time, because placed in it, and placed in it through his or her own perceptions. The subject is the repetition of itself and its construction, even as it asserts its identity/individuality (i.e. difference). In other words, it is a version of Nietzsche's eternal return, where the subject individual consists of moments, all of which exist throughout time, and none of which is accessible to a self-present individual, and moments are only ever (and always) returned to. The return is not performed by a subject, but is the way in which a subject comes to be. The subject only imagines any other form of time or being because the eternal return hides itself in the returning. Deleuze's take on this is as follows:

> Eternal return is the unlimited of the finished itself, the univocal being which is said of difference. With eternal return, chao-errancy is opposed to the coherence of a subject which represents itself and that of an object represented. *Re*-petition opposes *re*-presentation: the prefix changes its meaning, since in the one case difference is said only in relation to the identical, while in the other it is the univocal which is said of the different. Repetition is the formless being of all differences, the formless power of the ground which carries every object to that 'extreme' form in which its representation comes undone. (57)

This version of the eternal return is the fundamental 'repetition' (one that loses itself), but also occurs at other more visible or audible levels: 'perhaps this repetition at the level of external conduct echoes, for its own part, a more secret vibration which animates it, a more profound, internal repetition within the singular' (1), writes Deleuze at the outset of the book. Difference is filled with repetition (17)—so variation within an improvisation, even when very 'free' can be thought of as operating as the kind of difference that lets repetition through at an almost conscious level. Similarly, 'bare, material repetition (repetition of the Same) appears only in the sense that another repetition is disguised within it, constituting it and constituting itself in disguising itself' (21). This is not to say that very repetitive sounds are literally doing anything else, and in fact the less they do, the nearer the music would approach the explosive excess Deleuze finds in repetition.

The repetition does not reside within the music, but across the experience of it. Why not just say in the experience? Because the 'bare' repetition only comes to us as such when encountered, and the listening subject is brought to a certain kind of being (all the time), and we cannot simply set subject on one side, object on the other. Deleuze argues that 'repetition displays identical elements which necessarily refer back to a latent subject which repeats itself through these elements, forming an "other" repetition at the heart of the first' (25). This is not just another layer of repetition, but an 'othering' caused by it. This comes about as repetition happens 'only by virtue of the change or difference that it introduces into the mind which contemplates it' (70).

Repetition has to be thought of as such for it to be happening. Each repeated chord, motif, sound, and so on, is heard as part of a narrative where meaning is being withheld, but Deleuze argues that what is going on is exactly the opposite; in the experience of repetition, sense is lost in a way which is meaningful: 'the role of the imagination, or the mind which contemplates in this multiple and fragmented state, is to draw something new from repetition, to draw difference from it' (76), and this, I would argue, both as a whole and of every moment as it is repeated (the repeating making every moment).[17] The two levels of repetition are drawn together by difference, and make difference through occurring at two levels: 'between a repetition which never ceases to unravel itself [the eternal return level] and a repetition which is deployed and conserved for us in the space of representation [such as an artistic version] there was difference, the for-itself of repetition, the imaginary' (76).

Permanent insufficiency of repetition

But the jamming was too much for some. MC5 proposed to 'kick out the jams', a pre-punk display of disgust at hippy self-indulgence. They, the Stooges and the Velvet Underground stand not only as precursors of punk in sound and spirit, but also as an extension of the noise made possible through electricity, the noise that came from repetition, and the noise from the extension of sound in time and also away from 'musicality'. Jamming was not repetitive enough—too much skill implied that you couldn't just riff. The late 1960s saw an impatience with hippy ideals in general, and the version of nirvanic timelessness offered in, say, the Grateful Dead, seemed a rejection of *now*! Critics concur with the musicians of the Velvet Underground et al. that they represented a return to the authentic spirit of rock, but as I mentioned earlier in this chapter, the 'history of rock' is a continual managing of oppositions, rejections and conflicts, while, at the same time, not offering as clear-cut a distinction between 'good' rockers and 'bad' noodlers as critics would like (see next chapter of this volume on 'progression' for further illustration).

I want to argue that at all levels, from the superficial (length of songs) to the philosophical, groups like the Stooges were working with the same materials as those they challenged. Neither they, nor the MC5 nor the Velvet Underground was shy of extended tracks, either in the studio or live, and they would also extend album tracks in concert. The difference was that not only was very little happening, but it was also happening loud and fast. Tired of the torpor of extended soloing and polite blues riffing, these bands reintroduced aggression and transgression, both in lyrical content and musical form. In terms of physical noise, they followed on from The Who and mirrored what was going in early metal, but added a continual critique of the worth of what they were doing and themselves as performers. If the 'deadhead' community is an organic, harmonious one, the community summoned here is a threatening one where we can all blur into each other but in so doing, we can assert our agency in the world.

Walter Benjamin talks of 'nowtime' (*Jetztzeit*), which breaks up the linear illusion of time that structures the everyday world. It also goes against 'monumental' time, which is the time of conservation and conservatism. 'The awareness that they are about to make the continuum of history explode is characteristic of the revolutionary classes at the moment of their action', writes Benjamin ('Theses on the Philosophy of History', 253). All noise, all breaks in musical continuity contain something of this time (as attack on simply unfolding time), and it is cyclical, like Nietzsche's eternal return—its fleetingness means it always hovers in and out of existence. A new 'now' can recall previous moments where a simply accretive time was threatened and/or dismantled, so, for example, 'to Robespierre ancient Rome was a past charged with the time of the now which he blasted out of the continuum of history' ('Theses on the Philosophy of History', 253). Tracks like the 17-minute 'Sister Ray' are the first harnessing of that time as strategy. That is not to say we couldn't find precedents in Satie, Cage or Schwitters, or parallels with Morton Feldman, Lamonte Young, Fluxus. 'Sister Ray' does something else, because there is no danger of it enlightening us, teaching us anything, not even to listen better. It's not about understanding, either. It (as exemplar of their work, and that of the Stooges, the MC5) makes music physical to the point of being visceral. If we did think in terms of linear progression in rock, we could even say that it is the extension of the principle at play in jamming: Jerry Garcia thought the following of his music: 'when we're playing very open with no structure, sometimes the sound level can speed a sensory overload of a kind which starts to become a physical experience rather than a musical one' (in Bailey, *Improvisation*, 42).[18]

The long tracks of proto-punk are a direct erasing of the meandering 'expressions' musicians were doing more and more, live and on album. It is not enough to just reject the long form (as the Ramones would do); it is far more effective to wreck the purpose of it through the form itself.[19] Despite this attack on the newly serious rock music, the Velvet Underground, in particular, sought to get beyond the expectations of what pop or rock was supposed to do. They were not aiming to return to anything. As well as their connection to Andy Warhol, through John Cale, they had a direct link to experimental composer Lamonte Young. Such connections (many will go on to claim links of differing levels to Stockhausen) are an unfortunate mirror-image of the progressive musician's claim to be 'classically trained' or having a 'jazz drummer' in a rock band.[20]

Electronics, the studio, extending or cutting up performances all suggested another way out of the organic individual either spuriously free in consumer society, or apparently free in drug and/or hippy communality. Dub was developed into an avant-gardism by Lee 'Scratch' Perry, and arguably works in ways similar to *musique concrète*. Original sounds (in this case, mostly musical) are taken to be readymades, to be extrapolated from. In the case of dub, the result is a simplification, but one that is often harsher than the original. Dominated by percussion and bass, the physically powerful throb of the sound system is also shot through with other sound events, alterations in echo, and occasional editing effects (effectively like sampled loops). Dub is also, at a social level, something of a privatization of music production (or more accurately, a cooperativization) with DJs, producers and musicians remaining part of the audience. This was a result of official gigs not really being the prime source of dub (even if recordings still were)—as it was the sound systems that literally mobilized the music. This has been made more obvious and definitely more privatized, individualized, in the form of bass-heavy cars booming slowly through cities.

Dub implies incompletion—the studio can always be brought into play again—and records become documents of process rather than outcomes, which is helped rather than hindered by the often clichéd sounds in the music. Nobody is in charge of the music, or the products—the records are there to be manipulated—with the line between live, recorded and processed always unclear. Dub is based in machinery, but needs also to be seen as machine, much like the rhizome Deleuze and Guattari envisaged as the form made by interactions of wasps and flowers (*A Thousand Plateaus*, 10).[21] This is what, slightly tenuously, links it to the 'kosmische musik' or 'krautrock' of the late 1960s up to the mid 1970s. I do not wish to suggest these forms really have much to do with each other, but work here as further prolongations of the combination among electric amplification, repetition, the studio, and extended (aspiring to endlessness) forms of the music produced.

Around 1970, a form of music took off in Germany, with Faust, Can, Neu! and Kraftwerk at its centre. This 'kosmische' music aspired, just as psychedelic music, space rock and a fair amount of 1960s jazz had, to escape the everyday world. The groups cited here are the most well known, but are also linked through exploration of repetition, stasis and a machinic quality exemplified in the 'motorik' beat. The qualities of the programmed drums were pre-empted through a style of playing that refused blatant virtuosity (this applies to all the instrumentation, one of the reasons for this style of music to come through the anti-prog backlash of the late 1970s). Linear beats in bars and the possibility of expressive climaxes are lost, in a 'circular' drumming where each beat is both singularity and presence of the whole: in short, little changed, and if it did, it did on glacial time scales compared with either classical or rock expectations. The result is a driving beat that manages to convey total movement *and* stasis. The lack of accents and emphasis cool rock's individualism in favour of an objective rather than subjective community, existing to move (Hawkwind's 'Born to Go'). Guitars too would offer simple, often processed variation—if there is to be exploration in this music, it is not the single-minded adventurer ignoring all else, but part of a system working out its potentials. Instead of jamming, we have a slowly morphing programming. Keyboards, flutes, noises, tape cutting and splicing all take 'krautrock' out of the teleologies of virtuosic rock. Ultimately, 'krautrock' musicians mobilize Deleuze's sense of repetition and restructure the listener's subjectivity, away from a linear time of means and ends, and endings, to a timeless, often featureless, but shared terrain. Neu!'s albums all contain one signature instrumental of about ten minutes, with a 'motorik' core ('Hallogallo' on *Neu!*, 'Für Immer' on *Neu! 2*, 'E-Musik' on *Neu! 75*). Resolution is withheld—'Hallogallo' hints at a rock climax, but this is faded out, emphasizing its irrelevance. 'Für Immer' of course directly indicates eternity, and although more aggressive than its equivalent on the first album, still travels to no destination.

Kraftwerk are the apotheosis of 'machine music', their albums offering a series of models of the impending future, alongside futures already lost, or imagined. They share the 'motorik' beat with Neu!, not least because the drummer of the latter feature on Kraftwerk's first, eponymous, album, notably in the track 'Ruckzuck', which combines amplified flute with driving percussion, washed with synths. Kraftwerk claim to want a purely machine music, using robots to 'play' 'The Robots' at concerts, making extensive use of prerecorded elements in live settings. As well as a rejection of a humanism that is complicit with consumer capitalism, Kraftwerk would find the rock critique of that world still too limited. To reveal the mechanistic society in which we live, or are heading toward, they would have to risk aridity, 'soullessness', and use only electronic sound (by the mid-1970s). Not exactly critical, Kraftwerk offer a subtle and ambiguous look at technology. Their 'Autobahn' celebrates the road network devised by Hitler, in a move that returns the roads to being roads, and locations of pleasure. The track potters along with little change, the synth passages joined occasionally by vocals or car effects, in meaningful contrast to the ultra-purposiveness of Hitler's road imaginary. For Biba Kopf, the music of Neu! and Kraftwerk does something other than critique—in losing itself in the world of mechanized movement and speed. Of Kraftwerk's 'Autobahn' he writes: 'as empty as the open road stretching out before it, its most remarkable characteristic is its blankness, its neutrality ('The Autobahn Goes on Forever', 144–5); as for Neu!: 'Neu!'s is a driving music constructed by Dromo-maniacs driven to greater and greater excesses of speed in a frantic effort to escape the strictures of civic training, it has no discernible goal except to get lost in speed' (*ibid*., 146).[22] This is another way of thinking the loss in and of time that repetition structures.

The repetitive, cold soundscapes made by Neu! and Kraftwerk suggest a complicity with the technologized world, too much proximity to the machine, and surely to become a machine is to be alienated, to be someone else's tool? Such a reading is too literal—the machines at work here are organic as well as machinic in the everyday sense, and not just in the sense that there are human operators. The cyclical forms approach that of the raga's attempt to suspend standard (imag-ined, human) time through not only repetition and circularity, but also through over-tones. The 'motorik' drumming is always through effects, reverbing and flanging making the drum less of a tool for human expression, and more the thing that does the expressing (as much or as little of that as there is), like the talking drum. The repeated beats, recurring keyboard patterns and/or the guitar interventions all set up a system where machine and organism combine, reminding us that the distinc-tion is not really an opposition anyway. The animal is a collection of many machines, gathered, so we imagine, in the *soma*, body etc., with possibly one machine, the brain, as master, or regulator. Even Kraftwerk's machine continually evokes the non-machinic, or organic machinery, in the warm production of the 1970s and 1980s, or the direct use and evocation of bodily processes in 2004's *Tour de France*. Their tracks and albums sprawl, spread, stretch, but never attain, never reach satiation. They are flora to rock's fauna, rather than machine to human. So there are two levels to this subversion: firstly, in the rejection, through use of processing, synths, and so on, of rock's claim to authentically represent the individual,[23] second, that machine and human are intertwined, not as a result of industrial society, but as a *natural* necessity. In the end, having made this explicit, Kraftwerk proposed conscious merging, as a sort of *Aufhebung* or realization of machine society and organic machine, as suggested in their 1977 album *The Man Machine*.

This album seems to hope for a cyborg society where we are harmoniously mechanical, but the title recalls La Mettrie's '*L'Homme machine*, translated in English as *Man a Machine*.[24] In this 1748 book, La Mettrie works out a materialist explanation for humanity's existence, demystifying any possible God, and humani-ty's apparent transcendence of the material, organic world, through his emphasis on processes, and how everything that exists is a gathering of processes, rather than a uniquely endowed spiritualized or animated being. His purpose, or conclu-sion, though, was to try to renew ethics and politics in light of those thoughts. The noise of the 'kosmische' music is tied up in this layering and cross-fertilization of ideas about the mechanical and organic, and succinctly put into play through strategies of repetition, use of electronics and a sense that the music did not exist as animate, self-contained objects, but could continue to exist as processes (i.e. in the early days, be worked on in the studio, in later days remixing, restructuring, in the case of Kraftwerk). While the music from early 1970s Germany, and elsewhere in Europe, was very experimental, and cases could be made for the 'noisiness' of Popol Vuh, or Amon Düül, Amon Düül II, Tangerine Dream and the more rock-based groups, mention here, in the context of repetition, must be made of Faust, who also provide a link from *musique concrète* to industrial experiments.[25] From the first album, *Faust*, Faust operate a collage aesthetic, something we could almost say was inherently noise. The apotheosis of this exists in the form (form-less) of *The Faust Tapes*, where they literally spliced and repositioned tracks they had recorded. Their willingness to use songs from the outset (other bands men-tioned here came to that gradually, reluctantly even) makes their music odder (as with Can's songs), the proximity to norms offering an uncanny noise at the edge of rock. 'It's a Rainy Day, Sunshine Girl', the opening track on the second album, *So Far*, combines a surfy cheeriness with a thumping, mesmeric drumming that eventually suggests menace. As with Neu!'s flanging and reverb on the drums, here the drum's 'organic' nature is denied, as the range of sounds is not used, replaced instead by a monotonous and essentially unvarying rhythm. The drums can then stop being a tool to work the world, and no longer offer a way of the human subject to interact with the object. Instead, through the initial denial of the organic, the drumming gets out of being 'just' mechanical, and emerges as a machinic process that goes beyond the opposition of organic and machine as well as that of human-world.[26] With Faust, we see the play of repetition (many tracks offer relentless, metronomic drumming) and exception, or difference, as the col-lages, cut-ups and other tape experiments flicker in and out of songs, joining them, but only perversely, in an example of an exceeding of the album format. The attempt to maximize and/or get out of the constraints of forms both musical and material is where noise and 'progression' merge, sometimes.

NOTES

1. See Glenn C. Altschuler, *All Shook Up: How Rock 'n' Roll Shaped America* (New York: Oxford University Press, 2005), 3–23.
2. What was Bob Dylan betraying in 1966 by going electric? It would seem a logical and practical step, and completely consistent with his wish to innovate. Dylan's listenership sought a lost utopia, where the expression of dissent could prove itself to be pure, better than the world around it. This fatuous belief may not be as limited as it seems: the change in machinery could not be simply separated off from the form, which could stay intact. This would have consequences for content, too, as the music would become a more integral part of a song, possibly overriding the vocal part. Or they just didn't like it, because fundamentally, they were reactionaries, and saw no message, ironically, in Dylan's songs, only in the lyrics. Bruce Springsteen has, temporarily, at least, headed in the other direction (*The Pete Seeger Sessions*), but instead of this being a drive to authenticity, it is the change in approach, in the largely acoustic, massed folk band he has assembled, that is of interest.
3. There is also a discourse about 'electric' performances, which, consciously or other-wise, plays out the same sense of connection. 'Elvis Presley electrified teenage fans with his rockabilly tunes and his stage presence' (Altschuler, *All Shook Up*, 28). In a different context, Altschuler cites a particularly nasty review of Elvis Presley: 'Is it a sausage? [. . .] Is it a corpse? The face just hangs there, limp and white with its little drop-seat mouth, rather like

Lord Byron in a wax museum. But suddenly the figure comes to life' (88). While the rest of the extract prefigures abject Elvis, this seems to suggest Frankenstein's monster.

4. Even for the performers mentioned, these acts quickly turn into cliché, or at least come to be expected. It goes without saying that many have ended up making parodic versions of these moments.

5. Gilroy, 'Soundscapes of the Black Atlantic', in Michael Bull and Les Back (eds), *The Auditory Culture Reader* (Oxford and New York: Berg, 2003), 381–95.

6. It is hardly a revelation to associate Hendrix with noise, but Gilroy opens up a useful perspective, not only in clearly stating the different types of noise in his music, but also in noting that he was 'prepared to damage the superficial integrity of the traditions in which he positioned himself' ('Soundscapes of the Black Atlantic', 383). He does have his own Adorno moment in the conclusion of the article, bemoaning the lack of any possible 'electric church' in 'computerized dance music' (394).

7. See Kevin Holm-Hudson, 'Introduction', and John J. Sheinbaum, 'Progressive Rock and the Inversion of Musical Values', in Hudson (ed), *Progressive Rock Reconsidered* (New York and London: Routledge, 2002), 1–18 and 21–42, respectively.

8. Charles Hamm argues that the drive to provide a narrative for popular music is a classical modernist wish (*Putting Popular Music in Its Place* [Cambridge: Cambridge University Press, 1995], 1–40). I. Chambers conceives of a linear history for rock up until punk, at which point 'a sequential version of pop's history has been transgressed, violated' (Chambers, *Urban Rhythms, Pop Music and Popular Culture* [London: Macmillan, 1985], cited in Keith Negus, *Popular Music in Theory: An Introduction* [Cambridge: Polity, 1996]).

9. This can never fully be realized, but it can be messy. This is the low modernism to pit against what Hamm identifies as the spread of the modern notion of 'the classic' from 'classical' music to other genres (*Putting Popular Music in its Place*, 19–20).

10. Whiteley, *The Space Between the Notes: Rock and the Counter-culture* (London and New York: Routledge, 1992).

11. Whiteley also points out that Cream, Pink Floyd and Hendrix rejected the single altogether (37–8). This didn't stop record companies from finding tracks to issue as singles, though. This rejection is significant, as it accompanies the rise of the album, and therefore adds a level to the idea that the album format drove bands to extended tracks, concept albums, and so on. The concentration on albums was a rejection of the culture industry's attempt to commodify music. This 'backfired' as albums became an even more effective and profitable way of working this commodification. The progressive rock single of the 1960s or 1970s now seems like the oddity, the pleasing deviation from expected commercial norms.

12. Jim DeRogatis is suspicious of the 'community' represented by the fans of the Grateful Dead. He refers to Michael Weinstein's criticism that the 'Deadheads' are actually a safe reference point for those who gradually age while hanging on to wisps of 1960s rebellion, as well as his own criticism that the Dead's idealized psychedelic community was sort of like Sixties world at Disneyland' (*Turn On Your Mind: Four Decades of Great Psychedelic Rock* [Milwaukee, WI: Hal Leonard, 2003], 382–3).

13. This combination was designed to replicate the 'live performance', even as it merged studio with live, and used several performances as source material (see notes to *Anthem of the Sun* and *Live/Dead*, both of which refer to the process at work in *Anthem of the Sun*).

14. Pouncey, 'Rock Concrète: Counterculture Plugs into the Academy', in Rob Young (ed), *Undercurrents: The Hidden Wiring of Modern Music* (London and New York: Continuum, 2002), 154–62.

15. Deleuze, *Difference and Repetition* (London: Athlone, 1994), originally published in 1969.

16. The French word 'répétition' also suggests practice, rehearsal, further complicating the sense of time of 'repetition'.

17. I am not sure whether drone music would have the same effect, although I do not think Deleuze would. Indian 'ragas' would seem to offer something like difference and repetition in a very similar way to here, in their combination of improvisation and pre-existing elements (see Bailey, *Improvisation*, 1–11), and also in the sense that the music can only exist when repeated, always for the first time, as a new performance.

18. Agamben has the following to offer on this idea: 'Rhythm grants men both the ecstatic dwelling in a more original dimension and the fall into the flight of measurable time' (*The Man without Content* (Stanford, CA: Stanford University Press, 1999), 100.

19. This is central to Public Image Limited's first two albums, particularly the opening 'Theme' on the first album.

20. As rock diversified, other elements rejected the humanism of the hippy 'rebellion'. Satanism, and its presence particularly in heavy metal, rejected not only normal, Christian society, but also the utopian festival future. Satanic content is usually pretty risible; even the musically challenging Black Widow suffer in this regard on their album *Sacrifice* (1970). Early Black Sabbath managed to do more than throw in some references to the devil, and were more in the spirit of the miserable nastiness of *Witchfinder General* than the drama of *The Exorcist* (which used part of Mike Oldfield's *Tubular Bells* as its theme). In their hands, Satanism was just one more antisocial tool. Black Sabbath's menace relies on what are maybe quite obvious signifiers of doom and darkness—slowness, deep sounds, screams, unusual sounds—but these were put into service at high volume, and used riffs and highly developed bass lines, along with percussion that marked events, not time (as in the track 'Black Sabbath'). Later variants—the blackmetal of the early 1980s, or its extension found in Scandinavia in the early 1990s —all followed a low aesthetic, getting ever messier, musically. Gradually, members of the 'black metal' scene took it all very literally, but the music was getting odder. While Venom offered a type of Satanic pub meets punk rock, Burzum, early Mayhem and Darkthrone used feedback to the point where it often completely overtook the sound of guitars. Vocals became more throaty everywhere in metal, and this was very quickly clichéd, but Burzum's Varg Vikernes still stands out here with more of a moaning, non-musical and not overtly 'threatening' vocal.

The Satanic rejection of the present is combined with a review of the past that has led to now, in terms of its hypocrisy (Vikernes has since rejected Satanism, too). A harsher worldview and aesthetic experience will be able to shake the audience free of some of its presumptions and brainwashing. In this, it ties in with the rejections of polite rebellion offered by the Velvet Underground and others, in being more visceral, in trying to bring ideas out (however simple) through physical force (of performance, of sound, of unexpected spectacle), like a more interesting alternative to the performance art of the same time. Both metal and protopunk sought to remind audiences of the animal, and of the earth—again, like the more hippyminded, but not in the same way. Communion would be rejected in favour of an erotic, sacrificial community. If rock could aspire to being an electric church, here were the people who would deconsecrate it.

For an overview of the development of black metal, see Michael Moynihan and Didrick Søderlind, *Lords of Chaos: The Bloody Rise of the Satanic Metal Underground* (Los Angeles: Feral House, 2003), second edition.

21. Deleuze and Guattari, *A Thousand Plateaus* (London: Athlone, 1988).

22. Kopf, 'The Autobahn Goes on Forever', in Young (ed) *Undercurrents*, 142–52. 'Dromomaniac' is a term used by Paul Virilio in *Speed and Power* (New York: Semiotext[e], 1986). It refers to people and cultures that are obsessed with speed to the point of mania, and who must keep moving, keep accelerating. When acceleration does occur in 'kosmische' music, it is never to get anywhere, let alone get there faster. It is more of a heightening of the movement.

23. For a lot of rock musicians, this was not just a rejection, but an abdication. Until the conversion moment of 1980's *Flash Gordon*, Queen proudly insisted there were no synths used in the making of their albums, thus claiming a moral high ground not just for virtuosity, but for usage of instruments in itself. It also emphasizes the creativity in use of effects and studio techniques.

24. La Mettrie, *Man a Machine and Man a Plant* (Indianapolis, IN: Hackett, 1994).

25. Can also offer a connection, from Stockhausen to rock, and out again, but this has become as clichéd as the 'classically trained' assertions about, for example, Rick Wakeman. Can took the repetitive beat into a perverse funkiness, arguably making it closer to George Clinton's Parliament and Funkadelic. They combined this side with intricate and epic tracks that, like group-based jamming and other 'kosmische' music, avoided the narcissism of brilliance signifying itself. Their early vocalists, Malcolm Mooney and Damo Suzuki (the latter in particular), took singing away from rock, away from song, and toward instrumentation.

26. The same could be said of Mo Tucker's drumming in the Velvet Underground, and possibly even that of Bobby Gillespie in the early Jesus and Mary Chain, but despite its inflexibility, it still offers a stability, rather than an obstacle, to more usual musical expressions. The Velvet Underground was ultimately a rock group whose noise was more literal than relational.

5
PROGRESS

Across the range of new musics from the 1950s on, the studio had played a part—as laboratory in the case of *musique concrète*, or in the case of much popular music, as the location of commodification of 'authentic' music. Even in jazz, studio techniques intervened—in the form of separate takes, selection among those, and in positioning of a band to simulate a concert performance. The studio was not just about the preparation of high-quality commodities—the range of music was being expanded, and in ways that go further than Cage (after Plato and Pythagoras) it allowed imagining a world where all can become musical. The studio (and electronic instruments) were in excess to the natural soundworld—a challenge to the naturalism of humanity's 'musical impulse' and the musicality of the universe alike. Parallel to these changes was the move away from 78 rpm records, 'albums' of which required many changes of disc, toward the 45 rpm 7-inch single, the 'microgroove' 10-inch (played at 33), and ultimately for the generation of musicians active from the mid 1960s on, the 12-inch, 33 rpm 'album'.

All technologies play a role in moulding the content of artistic form, but this had never seemed so pronounced with the combination of the use of the studio and the LP record in the rock music of the late 1960s. Critics have consistently maintained that these two developments led to progressive rock, encouraging self-indulgent art music, or for considerably fewer critics, a chance for musicians to expand the limits of what rock could do. Key moments are Brian Wilson's production of his Beach Boys album *Pet Sounds* (1965), which did more than shape the record, as the studio's possibilities worked in a feedback loop with the material, each transforming the other, and the Beatles (with George Martin), with *Sgt. Pepper's* (but really all their albums from *Revolver* on). Ability to use the studio, in that now over-familiar phrase, as an instrument, rather than as passive recorder/documenter of the real stuff, expanded the possibilities for record albums.[1] Authentic performance and its capture could be dismissed as the purpose of the album. Similarly, it did not have to be a collection of singles, with some leftovers on the second side. The album could be conceived of as something like a novel or a film, or, and we have to admit that some thought like this, a symphony. For Wilson and Martin alike, the studio actually brought the world closer—the world of 'non-musical' sounds, which, even if only as backdrop, could imply either a self-contained world (as opposed to some songs isolated in a room) or the everyday world. While a vast number of what would come to be known as concept albums inhabit imaginary worlds (not very well imagined either), a possibly equal number are either set in mundane surroundings (The Kinks' *Village Green Preservation Society* one of these, but also most of Genesis' *Selling England by the Pound*), or try to evoke sensations through an imagined but not fantastical setting.

Many concept albums are barely that; they are, rather, collections of songs loosely tied together, thin ideas spread even thinner (The Pretty Things musically innovative and excellent *SF Sorrow*, is, unfortunately, one of these), or albums where the cover seems to unify the music. While the concept album was the height of innovation and, later (say, 1972 on), popularity, it was widely reviled as punk, disco and metal came along, and has only recently resurfaced, often a long way from the original progressive rock genres or approaches. Its intellectualism came to offend, its mimicry of classical music meant it seemed to have no meaning for the young (especially outside the middle class), and its length set up a barrier for all listeners. Overall, progressive rock, through its weapon of choice, the concept album, showed rock's will to become an accepted bourgeois art.

Sgt. Pepper's, a slightly more coherent collection than *Pet Sounds*, introduces the notion of rock as progression. Progressive rock was also connected to political, social or at least individual rebellion, and arguably there was a period (before its success of the mid 1970s) where it really was something different. Many would doubt, though, that progressive rock as a practice was or could ever be a type or vector of noise, even if we can come up with a list of 'acceptable' bands. So any band that was experimental and/or subversive or transgressive would be removed from progressive rock, just as J. G. Ballard would later be 'saved' from science fiction. So Henry Cow, 'rock in opposition' bands, selected more successful bands—perhaps a period of King Crimson, krautrock, are all recast as something else, and prog is left to define the too-successful, the overdramatic, the virtuosic, or groups like Yes and Genesis. Progressive rock, though, is an incredibly messy genre, and in its heyday of the early 1970s, it spanned most if not all other genres. So while this chapter will largely focus on those that need little or no critical assistance, bands who definitely obstruct and intervene in music through noise, I will also spend some time on more mainstream material too, if briefly. This is because, until the recent revival of a prog rock inflected by a rejection of what was wrong with it the first time, progressive rock had itself become noise, that which is pushed outside by musical critique, popular and academic, rejected because it is somehow wrong.[2] This chapter works through such presumptions and starts by crossing the line between what is critically acceptable and what has not been. So I will approach noisiness in, for example Yes, as a way of getting to the more obviously dissonant groups.

For the purpose of this book, there is a simplistic distinction to be made between mainstream progressive bands that harness noise and noises, bringing them into musicality as either background, moments of dramatic tension or linking strategy, and on the other hand, those who let noise be itself to some extent. These latter are the more blatantly dissonant, even if in terms of a teleology of rock, they now sit more comfortably in that story than the more melodic progressive material. There might be less emphasis on skill, and certainly little in the way of solos. This second category is consciously more socially subversive, and/or perceived as such. The integration of noise into harmonious structures also signals another distinction, between groups that resolve dissonances and those that offer them without fulfilling a promise of completion. So, Yes would be Hegelian to King Crimson's Batailleans.

Even a song-oriented, successful, acclaimed album like *Sgt. Pepper's* offers much in the way of noise: crossing of genre (music hall, Indian form and instrumentation, psychedelia, blues, brass band and classical), presumably troubling the expectations of listeners on first encounter; dissonance—'Day in the Life' cutting between essentially different songs, collaging lyrics, ending in the non-resolved massed orchestral finale, the integration of songs into a whole, using crowd sounds, effects, editing. All of this can now be read as smoothness but was a resistance to the prevalent 'album as collection' model. And yet, it does not really work as an example of noise; it is not dissonant enough, musically or socially. Its insistence on melody softens out what could have been generic stand-off and contrast. The dissonance and long piano chord at the end of 'Day in the Life' are still an ending, suggesting a society that heads in the same direction, despite its individualist components, and it does settle eventually, even if extended beyond expectation (this extension is the more noisy element, I think).

The concept album supplies a cohesive narrative, even when applied vaguely, as in *Sgt. Pepper's*, so that any divergence is sanctioned by its position in the whole. As it develops in the 1970s, via sidelong tracks, it does this at the musical thematic level as well as in the vocal narration. Yes's *Close to the Edge* is a clear example of a rock band aspiring to sonata form, as different sections pursue different musical and thematic tasks around a central idea of two world visions: of stress and rapidity on the one hand and a more pastoral critique of this on the other. Edward Macan argues strongly for progressive rock's 'roots' being in classical music and that what it is is a realization of the classical in rock.[3] Macan insists too strongly on this, though, to the detriment of rock's contribution to 'progressive rock'. Groups like Yes were able to trade on both types of music for cultural capital: for the 'serious listener', their rock was validated by the classical, and for those who were wary of traditional, orchestral music, the rock side would compensate. Where Yes are in tune with (nineteenth-century) classical music is also where they are in tune with the epic narrative novel of the nineteenth century. Even if the lyrics are often too obscure to allow easy understanding, the music and the presentation of lyrics always move tidily, even if through patches of dissonance, to a conclusion. This applies equally, even in an exemplary way, to the harsh 'Gates of Delirium' of *Relayer*. An opening section that is more or less heavy metal is succeeded by harsh interplay at high speed between the band, for several minutes, but this waywardness is brought to a close by a surging band climax, announced by the prog staple (or what would become one) of the slow, emphatic journey around the drum set. After this is the gentle, hopefully nostalgic coda. Despite the literal appearance of noisiness and dissonance, narrative never goes away, as a battle is being 'represented' in even the harsh central movement. Noisiness is not to be found at this level in Yes.

Their double concept album *Tales from Topographic Oceans* (1974) is widely reviled as the prime example of superstar, elitist excess. It outlines an obscurist pantheistic mysticism, with a sort of elemental bait. The lead singer, Jon Anderson, cobbled this together on half-digested extracts from Swami Paramahansa Yogananda's *Autobiography of a Yogi*. I would argue that there is genuine excess in and around the album as a whole. We can take the lyrical conceit as being noisy to some extent, as it is resistant to interpretation, almost Joycean at points, and often to do with tonalities and timbre rather than meaning, but we don't need to insist too much on that. Similarly, there are many hints at noise in the playing, particularly on sides 3 and 4, but in an exact opposition to the relentless non-endings of Neu!, there are continuous, softly ecstatic resolutions.[4] From a class analysis perspective, this would mean that Yes can never offer a critique, as formally this sense of completion hides alienation (both personal and economic), with the promise of solutions from within (the individual, current society). In fact, their gestures toward dissonance would emphasize this complicity.[5]

I would assert that *Tales of Topographic Oceans* actually troubles because of its noisiness. In retrospect, it was dubbed an unacceptable album by a generation of critics and musicians who generalize their experience of 1976–7 to the world as a whole, and this unacceptability is the first way in which it becomes a site of resistance, retrospectively rather than at the time of its making, or because of something inherent in it. Internally, it attempts to attain dissonance, playing it off against returns (even from one sidelong piece to the next),[6] melodies, conclusions and microtunes, even if always moderated or 'sublated' into an ending 'nous sommes du soleil' ('we are of the sun') the summoning of our true selves through the ritual of 'Ritual' (side 4). This is its Hegelianism, a progress that encapsulates the genre metonymically. Therefore, there is a playing out of the individual as historically situated, of being defined through negativity (the alternation between self and other, master and slave, historical time and personal being).

The project as a whole is excessive, though, and not just in a 'rock excess' kind of way. The album is, for the time, a long double album, over 80 minutes long.[7] Its musical themes need to be tracked over long stretches, and it offers a messily utopian, vacuous mysticism as an implicit critique of materialism. It cannot be simply taken in, let alone on first listening—and yet Yes played the entire album to audiences unfamiliar with it. The audience might feel threatened by this, accustomed as it is to being pandered to, but Yes were not attempting to awe the audiences (maybe a bit), but to get them lost in the progression of music unfolding, as avant-garde jazz audiences might. Punk saw this kind of behaviour as elitist, domineering and plainly setting a wall up between the masters (performers) and their victims or servants. Could it be, though, that listeners critical of such an approach felt their mastery threatened, and were not prepared to accept music until mastered? As with all albums that are experimental or testing, it is only a matter of (not much) time before the audience is prepared, so such an effect of loss could only be temporary.

While the spirit of progressive rock was to challenge its audiences, and experiment, in fact this experimentation was limited to albums and early performances of them (in the case of Yes, or ELP, for example). Robert Fripp, of King Crimson, who took a very different approach, featuring genuine improvisation in every concert, to the point where some of these became 'album tracks', argued that most of the groups labelled progressive were no such thing.[8] The concerts would be formalized, and one overlooked element of Yes—that they are not really a soloists' band, as the whole group plays the instrumental passages—would be destroyed by the formalization of the 'solo spot'. These are the nadir of 1970s self-importance, and even a perverse noising-up of Yes cannot save the solo.[9]

King Crimson might feature an ever-changing array of 'great musicians', but not even central figure Fripp is really a soloist in that way. The key to King Crimson is the group dynamic, and in theory, the mutual creation of a creative moment with the audience. Operating more like an avant-garde jazz band, King Crimson only occasionally offered a sense of conclusion, notably on *Lizard* (1970), and its main early tracks such as '21st Century Schizoid Man' or 'Catfood' are marked by steely guitar and sax blasts. The sound is often harsh, especially in its mid 1970s incarnation, and could better be thought of as jazz meeting metal. In addition, the band continually changes direction, and renounces its past. Audience and band cannot settle into a 69 of virtuous appreciation. That is not to say it did not or does not happen. As with all music, transgression is only fleeting, but the attempt is worth making; a key part of noise is to imagine noise is possible, to behave as if noise *is*. The title track of *Larks' Tongues in Aspic* illustrates this well. Occupying 13+ minutes, it develops over 7 sections, building from clatters, drones, repeated simple phrases, and eventually crashing into a rock climax, which is then undone by the mournful decline and gradual disappearance of that elegiac section—continual change is not rewarded, but dissipated.[10] 'Larks' Tongues in Aspic pt II' (a rare example of a track that has survived in the King Crimson concert repertoire) does not so much conclude the album as overpower it.[11]

While I would personally rescue much of progressive rock, there are swathes of it whose only hope is the comedic or ironic. In terms of absence of noisiness, the polite electronica of Tangerine Dream, Vangelis, Jean-Michel Jarre and Mike Oldfield seem absolutely opposed to social, formal, critical transgression or subversion, but that is to forget how these records were consumed—as part of a continuum with psychedelia, 'krautrock', prog of all kinds, jazz-rock. At a push, Vangelis produced some mildly challenging music (notably in Aphrodite's Child), and *Tubular Bells* was generically unusual, but that's as far as one could go. Worse, though, and devoid of any 'noise potential' is the still bluesy rock that could make no claim to progression, where groups (Argent, Uriah Heep, Golden Earring) took the simplest bits of extended form ('long tracks') and extended songs through meandering and soloing around a restricted range of tonal manoeuvres (Love's 1967 album *Da Capo* seems guilty of this, but is more interesting, as it condenses jamming that occurred live, while seeming to be elongated in a contrived way).

Can we judge the phenomenon of the extended track? Clearly after a while, it is not at all radical: live, it became an obligatory part of the 'uniqueness' of an event; on record an expectation that at least one or two tracks would 'stretch out'. There is nothing interesting, radical, or conservative about the length of a track (although a long single challenges the conventions of length built up around radio and/or TV music channel conventions). The multi-sectioned long track tries to mirror classical music forms, and just like them, can be more or less radical, setting problems and solving them, or making itself an extended awkwardness of dissonance and failure to resolve. Longer tracks would be less likely to feature on an album as played live in the studio, so multitracking is a crucial component, and came to be used as a tool to expand, rather than 'enhance' the music recorded. Punk mostly eschewed the long track, or the extended version, but Public Image Limited offer a critical take on the long track. 'Theme', which opens *Public Image Limited*, is PiL's statement of intent, an anti-progression; in a murky overall sound, bass slides, guitars clang and scrape, over taut, repetitively explosive drums, while John Lydon harangues. From a progressive point of view, this all seems wrong, but it is so in an uncanny, proximate way: it is over 9 minutes long, it rises and falls, seemingly a narrative of despair, ending with 'I just died' amid bass, guitar and drums disuniting in a parodic take on the rock crescendo finale, and so doing, in concluding it falls away; 'Theme' suggests not only classical music, and perhaps the opening of a narrative or concept album, but there is no 'theme', only, or nearly only, 'I wish I could die' over and over. The track is a commentary on the epic, on virtuosity, clarity. An endless 'no no no' to even 'krautrock's upward motion.

Dissidence appeared before that, though, sometimes formally, in the music of the 'Canterbury Scene', or Magma, but also with political intent in the shape of

Henry Cow, Slapp Happy and 'rock in opposition' (RIO). Within what sometimes can seem a similarity of purpose and stylistic intent (complexity, extension of pop and rock formats, genre combinations and clashes) in 'progressive rock', ideological choices led to many subgenres and approaches, and certainly many 'progressive' musicians not only resisted the name, but associated it with what post 1976 critics would claim of it—that it was overblown, fanciful and dishonestly difficult, a display of complication rather than complexity. The 'Canterbury groups' offered a jazz-ish take on rock, not like fusion, which sought to blend them into a seamless pap, but a collision of the thinking within those styles, in a bid to break musical boundaries. Soft Machine and Egg (and later, Hatfield and the North, in particular) brought together polytonality and awkward time signatures, cutting tracks instead of allowing them to merge. This is a music of disruption, which Henry Cow took further still. But despite Robert Wyatt's avowal of ordinariness,[12] Soft Machine did pose a critique in the shape of a challenging, unpredictable musical form. Even side long tracks such as Wyatt's 'Moon in June' on *Third* do not settle, even if Wyatt is the noise to the impending 'jazzy' sloth of the rest of the album. They were also explicitly outside mainstream society and music, and therefore implicitly criticizing it. Henry Cow were following on from composers like Cardew, who resisted not only capitalist society, but music that turned away from that society rather than criticizing it. The riots and revolutionary potential of 1968 were still present for many, and needed to be brought out (for some):

> the Situationist project of disruption, danger and chance which flitted within and without the grasp of the masses in 1968, remained embryonically embedded in Progressive even after its corporatization between 1969 and 1971. There were those, in short, who felt that society, or at least individual consciousness, could be changed through rock 'n' roll, both its performance and its ethics. (Stump, *The Music's All That Matters*, 142)

Henry Cow's music is dissonant, harsh and seemingly contradictory, its players apparently free (but largely scored) and independently operating within a larger structure that never quite solidifies easily for the listener. A music of permanent cultural revolution, it is overtly didactic too. Like early Soft Machine, they make something like rock, but through experimental jazz (or vice-versa). Henry Cow works as noise at many levels, with its dissonance, its political dissidence, its refusal of art for art's sake, or vague utopianism. The future would be crafted out of the ruins of bourgeois culture and (musical) conventions, and the first stage is to make the ruin audible. Their music is noisy within progressive rock, ironically, for being progressive in an older sense. This strain of experimentation never had the influence of avant-garde 1960s jazz, but its aim is the same—to formally invoke resistance and creativity despite society's constraints and temptation ('rock in opposition' has a bit of a puritanical side—despite this, there were differences in levels of commitment to specific political ideals, with Univers Zéro more or less non-ideologically minded).

This raises the question as to whether music with a purpose can be considered noise. Surely whatever way noise is defined (as it varies according to context), it cannot accept utilitarianism, being a means to an end. If noise is disruption, though, that can be critique, and if actualized as highly fragmented music, almost lurching between its disjointments, then noise has not been banished. Noise, even as it alters, disappears, becomes non-noise and still carries the charge of having been noise. Bataille writes that the momentary sovereignty attainable in eroticism, sacrifice, 'little deaths' etc. can be brought back as a kind of perpetual incorporation of that which cannot be incorporated. More than a memory, it acts as a breach that is never closed. Leslie Boldt-Irons, writing of Bataille's positing of art as a way of accessing excess, says

> The energy which is released from the notion reverberates within the reader as a simulacrum of death, and what reverberates is a sense of transgression, in the return to continuity, in the fading of the notion. The limit of the notion does not, therefore, disappear altogether, for, as Foucault writes in his 'Preface to Transgression', the limit is annihilated by transgression, but remains to heighten the sense of transgression. ('Sacrifice and Violence in Bataille's Fiction', 95)[13]

Henry Cow and 'rock in opposition' produced such disjunction, as would This Heat.[14] Alan Freeman notes that rock in opposition (RIO) has become an identifiable style, essentially with the outlook of Henry Cow ('Rock in Opposition, part 2', 19),[15] but it was firstly a grouping for concerts and possible recording. Freeman comments on this, highlighting the non-specific nature of 'opposition':

> RIO wasn't tied down to a particular style of music, as it was more of an attitude, a creative outlook without concessions to the general media or popular trends, whether motivated politically, socially or musically, in opposition to the 'lowest common denominator' attitude of the record industry. ('Rock in Opposition, part 1', 7)[16]

The groups did share a sense of crossing musical boundaries, and that this would not result in fusional musicality, but continual dissonance, fragmentation and disruption. Univers Zéro's early sound is almost medieval, with folk and classical, as well as electric instrumentation. Samla Mammas Manna shared their fractured style with their fellow RIO groups, but they are a cross between Faust, Zappaishness and very fast jazz progressive rock, much favoured also by Italian progressive bands of the 1970s. RIO musicians saw themselves as being apart from the commercially successful progressive rock, and would influence 'no wave' and lead to the more recent category of 'avant' (a counter-productive term, which solidifies what was an awkwardly oppositional practice into a tidy new genre), but while Yes and Genesis could seem to be the opposite of Henry Cow and King Crimson, what we have is more of a continuum, joined by experimentation, awareness and mobilization of non-rock sounds, styles, timings, structures. This is more where progressive rock's noisiness lies, and also with its rejection.

Although positive use of the term as a marker of influence was waning in art theory, rock music, from psychedelia on, sought to claim Surrealism as forebear. The more interesting might favour the messier, more inventive dada, but Surrealism's more direct version appealed to musicians and fed their whims until they became whimsy. British progressive rock of the 1970s is rarely far from what can accurately be described as Surrealist humour (for good and bad). The worst of this occurs in scatological 'crazy' titles as favoured by Dave Stewart's bands (Egg, Hatfield and the North, National Health), Robert Wyatt and Caravan. The silliness of titles belies the complexity of the music (its first function), but also mirrors its 'quirkiness'. The titles then go on to signal the lack of importance of content (or at least content as more significant than form). Humour in general provided an anti-dote to an increasingly self-satisfied rock elite in the late 1960s, and the Surrealist element tied in neatly with drug consumption (to be slightly reductive). But other than the Bonzo Dog Doo Dah Band, who, despite playing and playing with many musical genres, are a bit too firmly in the genre of comic music, it is Frank Zappa that pushes humour to (beyond?) its limits.

Zappa could, arguably, feature in many places in this book, his eclecticism a constant, his musical experimentation covering not only all genres that exist but also some that probably do not. But it is not enough to praise him for his use of *musique concrète*, or a transformation of the guitar, or his satire on American soci-ety. It is how these combine with humour that gives us the way into Zappa's noisi-ness, as it does more than comment, or sit back and chuckle (though sometimes it does just that). For Michel Delville and Andrew Norris, Zappa's music is a 'maxi-malist' meltdown of music into a joyous festival. Maximalism conveys the excess of his music (they approvingly note that Zappa's music has been accused of being 'far too noisy and of containing too many notes', *Frank Zappa, Captain Beefheart and the Secret History of Maximalism*, 1).[17] The content and purpose of the lowly humorous albums is a further component of his 'maximalism'. They do not allow that Zappa is postmodern, as he is not doing pastiche (26), instead, along with Captain Beefheart, he reintroduces the body, through a multiple excess, similar to Artaud's theatre of cruelty. Zappa's humour is extravagantly physical, and the instructive nature of the vocabulary of *200 Motels* would seem to take Zappa into punk's territory of shock and base humour. But largely, it is an exaggerated version of 'crazy' elements in British progressive rock. What saves it, then? I am not sure it is saved all the time, but the 'too much' is what counts, the relentless scatologi-cal, sexual or vegetable humour is more troubling than 'well placed' humour (Steely Dan's dry humour might be better, but it is not noisier). Despite their claim that Zappa is not a pasticher, Delville and Norris essentially conclude the book with a similar claim, arguing that Zappa's laughter toward the end of 'The Chrome Plated Megaphone of Destiny' on *We're Only in It for the Money* is a 'forced hilarity which is not laughter, but the *sound* of laughter' (159)—an ironic distancing, a metacommentary—an indication that the preceding humour has purpose, critical intent. Both Delville and Norris and Zappa want everything here: a humour that is too low to be ironic, and then a knowing ironic sense that not all the preceding humour might be that funny.

The casualness of Soft Machine and Robert Wyatt's humour is perhaps closer to dada (and Soft Machine specifically refer to dada and pataphysics throughout side 1 of their album *Volume Two*, for example). Wyatt's lyrics are forever returning to the question of what is being sung, whether on *Volume Two* or Matching Mole's 'Oh Caroline'. One of the reasons for this is, I presume, that a lot of these lyrics were improvised, and the most obvious material is to refer to what is going on at that moment. So these songs become not just commentary on the song form, but also on improvisation. But Wyatt adds a more interesting subversion, in altering the tone of his voice, often against the grain of the song's inconsequential words, pouring in a yearning emotional feel. In the case of 'Oh Caroline', 'sung with Wyatt's ambivalent timbre, it's especially hard to know what Wyatt exactly *feels* about the words he's singing, thereby upending the cosy rock listener–artist relationship' (Stump, *The Music's All That Matters*, 126). Wyatt is not ambivalent at any specific point; it is more the change in registers that creates the overall ambiguity. To return to Delville and Norris, it is in Captain Beefheart, specifically the troubling difference of 'Dachau Blues' from the rest of *Trout Mask Replica*, that we see this same effect: 'the avant-gardism of its formal and generic deformations combines with its apparently misplaced humour, to suggest a rewriting of the rules of popular music, a musical victimisation of the listener who isn't in the know' (*Frank Zappa, Captain Beefheart*, 93). In other words, however challenging the album is as a whole, elsewhere its humour is swampy, genital, anal. Its music is consistently disjointed, jerky, scratchy, but it needs the inappropriateness of Dachau as dada or Surrealist material for comic avant-gardism.

Linking these 'progressive' musics is a reliance on expert musicianship and studio work. Some might have flaunted this, but all, and none more so than either Zappa or Beefheart, sought to control the material, or at least let go through skill (in improvisation, seemingly casual songs written in awkward time signatures). Forgetting the pomposity of some groups at the peak of their success, it was this musicianship (rightly or wrongly, musicianship as a whole, not just drum solos, or 'guitarist of the year') that punk railed against, and the way into 'anyone can do it' is through 'I can't do it, but I'm doing it anyway'.

NOTES

1. Outside of the newly forming rock genre, the artist/producer also worked in popular music, film music and easy listening exotica. Individuals like Martin Denny, Bob Lind and Joe Meek and teams such as BBC's Radiophonic Workshop, featuring Delia Derbyshire and Ron Grainer, were part of this move to harness the experimental possibilities of the studio.

2. Progressive rock is almost alone in such vilification, and this must have something to do with the influence of the first generation of writers to cross from popular to academic music writing (and also to music journalism outside of dedicated music periodicals), a generation that will always divide the world into pre-punk and after, with goodness defined in relation to its distance from progressive rock.

3. Macan, *Rocking the Classics: English Progressive Rock and the Counterculture* (New York and Oxford: Oxford University Press, 1997). Macan has a lot more to say about the track 'Close to the Edge', arguing for an unfolding mystical quest at its core (95–105).

4. Jennifer Rycenga makes an excellent case for the strangeness and experimentation of *Tales from Topographic Oceans*, her case, for me, hinging on the following argument: 'the form remains definitively formal without becoming a closed system. But, as is true of the lyrics, the form does not play out a standard narrative pattern. The uncoupling of form from both lyric narrative and formal expectations established open temporal space', 'Tales of Change within the Sound: Form, Lyrics and Philosophy in the Music of Yes', in Holm-Hudson (ed), *Progressive Rock Reconsidered* (143–66), 154.

5. This is simplistic, of course, and trades on the plainly false claim that the people in progressive rock were middle class and punks were working class. In some high-profile cases (Genesis, Pink Floyd on one side, Sex Pistols on the other), this might be true, but it falls down in most other cases.

6. At one point in the closing track 'Ritual', Anderson says, 'We alter our returning', suggesting a Nietzschean eternal return, where the return is one of perpetual change, before, beneath and around fixed subjectivity.

7. As mentioned earlier, it is almost a truism that albums spawned progressive rock, but here is a striking example of the album form being both used and exceeded: the length of sides plays a substantial role—all tracks are between 18 and 22 minutes, but even this is being played with: one long track might be okay, an album with two at a push, but here were four. At the same time, these tracks are not uniform, so many different elements feature—each track is structured differently, and they all combine in the closing 'Ritual'. This album pushes at the limit of the LP form. The same has happened with CDs featuring one track only. It is also worth noting that the new-ish format of 8-track tapes was very demanding on the album format, with considerable rearrangement needed to balance the 4 sections an 8 track would divide into. The exception being double albums.

8. See Eric Tamm, *Robert Fripp: From King Crimson to Guitar Craft* (Winchester, MA and London: Faber & Faber, 1990), 23, for a number of such remarks by Fripp.

9. The solo spot might annoy, and be musically unpleasant, and it also disrupts the procession of a concert, but these are not enough for noise to be occurring. The solo spot presumes an audience expectation, an acceptance of skill and assertion of individuality. It controls noisiness, and as with all sounds that impose themselves, we might initially conceive of them as noise, but the interference, limited as it is, is a heroic reassertion of a subject in control, didactic and demagogic.

10. Gregory Karl proposes a more clearly narrative reading. Arguing that many of King Crimson's songs are about alienation and trauma, he claims, through a very approximate use of 'convergent evolution', that 'Larks' Tongues in Aspic, pt 1' brings this together. The track is the progress of a traumatised individual through a set of encounters or experiences ('King Crimson's *Larks' Tongues in Aspic*. A Case of convergent Evolution' in Holm-Hudson [ed.], *Progressive Rock Reconsidered*, 121–42). This is interesting, and even feasible, but once we get to the forced reading of 'Larks' Tongues in Aspic, pt 2', as continuing the idea it seems reductive and literalist.

11. 'In the early 1980s, King Crimson annoyed many with repetitive, mantric music mixed with effects-laden noodling. Arguments could be made about how the whole idea of a rock group made up of creating individuals was formally removed, to be replaced by an operational unit working with processes. It would consider the cyclical structure of many of the tracks on *Discipline*, the anti-solo in Brötzmann or Coltrane mode of 'Epitaph' on *Beat*, and maybe the endless frustration of the refused termination or expansion of '*Larks' Tongues in Aspic* pt 3'. Tamm also argues for the diversely experimental nature of 1980s King Crimson (Robert Fripp, 141–2).

12. See Paul Stump, *The Music's All That Matters: A History of Progressive Rock* (London: Quartet, 1997), 123.

13. Boldt-Irons, 'Sacrifice and Violence in Bataille's Fiction', in Carolyn Bailey Gill (ed), *Bataille: Writing the Sacred* (London: Routledge, 1995), 91–104. Bataille makes this argument in *The Accursed Share*, vol. II (New York: Zone, 1991), 106–9. Douglas Kahn introduces a similar idea in his discussion of the line noise crosses and brings into being, in *Noise Water Meat* (72–9, 99–100).

14. This Heat sit somewhere between progressive rock and punk outlook: improvisation meshing with composition, tapes and found objects featuring strongly, including in live settings. They also shifted between songs (which never followed pop structures, but shadowed them) and experimental instrumentalism, sometimes at more or less the same time. Their critique of consumerist capitalism gives them a political positioning between prog and post-punk (e.g. Scritti Politti), which is precisely where Simon Reynolds locates them (*Rip It Up and Start Again: Postpunk, 1978–1984* [London: Faber & Faber, 2005], 211–12).

15. Freeman, 'Rock in Opposition, part 2', *Audion* 31 (winter 1995), 19–25.

16. Freeman, 'Rock in Opposition, part 1', *Audion* 30 (spring 1995), 7–13.

17. Delville and Norris, *Frank Zappa, Captain Beefheart and the Secret History of Maximalism* (Cambridge: Salt, 2005).

6
INEPT

In a linear account of experimentation, or of new developments and genres in music, punk follows prog as night follows day. From Attali, we have the Bataillean sense of a dialectical history where disruption is always present, noise always coming in, then dissipating. From the recent revival of both post-punk and prog, it has become clearer that the story of a year zero moment in 1976–7 is false. Sales figures have always shown this, and beyond Britain and the USA, the divide was never so sharp, possibly because, even if relatively obscure, groups like Magma and the messy experimentation of Rock in Opposition showed that avant-garde rock did not have to be about self-aggrandizement through either solos or validation through an approximation of classical forms. However, the idea within punk itself was very often that a new start was being made, that an older generation of (apparently) middle-class musos were being made to make way for the new breed. A key part of punk, and what even on reflection for those involved at the time, many years later, seems to have been the driving creative element, is the seemingly simple thought that 'anyone can do it', quickly followed by 'so go and do it'.[1] Years of polls for 'best bass player of the year' and the like had consolidated a smugness among listeners and musicians alike that many found not only annoying, but a betrayal of music and youth. It seemed particularly offensive to see the lifestyle of wealthy rock stars and the excess consumed even in making their music, at a time of serious economic difficulty after the 1973 oil crisis. Britain had a specific mix of class awareness and class-based politics in the 1970s, and according to Jon Savage, this is what is distinct about British punk and the explanation for punk's success.[2] The mainstream rock of the 1970s, whether progressive rock (now seen as regressive) or heavy rock, seemed to be predicated on an unbreakable elitism, based on virtuosity. Essential to crossing the divide between passive worship and making music, or being close to and involved in the music, was the idea that creativity was not determined by skill. Skill would in fact be a hindrance.

Many punk bands made a virtue of an actual lack of skill. In the case of the Sex Pistols, this lack was overstated (while hardly virtuosos, the original musicians were all competent, with pub rock's earnest chug never far away). This would gradually be forgotten if and when they did improve, but the message for others remained. Ineptitude is a strong, fundamentally noisy anti-cultural statement, and, pleasingly, comes in many forms (believers in the importance of technical mastery might imagine that only such a skill can permit variation, the emergence of personal styles, and so on, but just as there are many 'wrong notes', so ineptness is an opening of sound). To many, ineptness is very directly noise: the playing of incorrect notes, or the wrong kind of playing maybe even offending the delicate sensibilies of the elite listener/performer. The inept player will make many mistakes, or what are perceived as such. He or she will make choices and create combinations that are 'wrong', and this is what has led to the belief in the creativity that comes from a lack of preconceptions and a willingness to try out anything, even if badly. The results can be taken (and in punk, were) as more authentic, the lack of preconceptions allowing a greater creativity and personal expression to emerge.

inept • 89

The limits of skill themselves would also drive resourcefulness (that and the cheap equipment).

My use of the word 'inept' is not to be taken as a criticism, it has been chosen precisely because it has been *presented* as a criticism of punk and related musics. Neither is this chapter going to consist of blanket approval for badness. Bad music or playing can be fun, but what I am interested in here is how lack of ability becomes a source of musical experimentation, full with noise, how it overcomes itself without ever succeeding, and how seeming ineptitude attacks presumptions about 'good music', including of the various experimental types. For all the initial radicality of *musique concrète*, it has become institutionalized. Even now, with the widespread usage of computers in music, skill of an operational kind is still valorized. Punk raises the question of competence and goodness. Whether that lesson has been incorporated or essentially and slyly rejected by many experimental musicians and audiences is unclear to me. I tend to think that for all its virtues, the dominant avant-garde music magazine *The Wire* actually falls into the latter camp. Even when we can 'accept' lack of skill, as long as the product is deemed good, there is still the question of 'bad music'. The inept are split into good and forgotten, and new canons formed. Can music be bad and listened to? Bad music in the form of people not being able to play together in a band, or based on laziness and contempt for audiences, is just shit. Bad music as that which is *wrong*, though, is interesting. It is common to play something that is 'so bad it's good', or to reimagine something as actually good, while before it was not heard that way (the smug 'guilty pleasures' listener), but what about something that is just rubbish? Or: music that manages to be heard as both good and bad, through either purposeful and self-hindering messiness (as in some no-wave music, perhaps, especially DNA).

What punk was about and where it came from is a question that occupies many a writer, not surprisingly, as this was the generation where analytical writing about non-classical music was normalized, even if begun earlier. Statistically, the most popular answer as to musical origins is to look back to garage music of the 1960s, the Velvet Underground, the MC5, and a New York radicality channelled through the New York Dolls, via the visual daring of David Bowie, and Malcolm McLaren. It was he who initially made the claim for the Sex Pistols and punk as realization of the Situationist cultural revolution (plotted in a purposefully aimless way in 1960s France, for the most part). This is not exactly wrong, even if it can easily be partially countered with the much more eclectic listening of, say, John Lydon, with his interest in Van Der Graaf Generator and reggae. Stewart Home, in *Cranked Up Really High*, makes a forceful counter-argument for punk being unimportant and shallow, and that these are its strengths.[3] Instead of a reconstruction of punk, though, what I aim to present here is a repositioning of punk as a quantitative moment in noise, where the scale of ineptness made it audible noise. Historically, there has always been noise through incapacity (or unsuitability, in cultures where there are limits on who is to produce music and of which kind). Some of that noisiness ties in to Attali's account of the wandering musicians of the late European middle ages. Also, there is always a limit on what is acceptable, however widely an individual or a culture listens, and this is connected to judgements of ability. But I want to claim that ineptitude as a mobilized negativity spreads, consciously and not, within and around the music of modernism and since. This happens in line with changes in the visual arts, where the emphasis on manual skill is increasingly replaced (within avant-garde art) by conceptual creativity. So, ineptitude is not simply an authentic move, nor is it an improvement, or a 'contribution' as such; the imagination in those terms, about the creative untrained person, is also part of the acceptance of a lack of skill. In short, ineptitude is a problematic challenge, as will be seen in the 'precursors' of the ineptitude of punk.

In reimagining music as organized sound, John Cage alters the parameters of what can be considered musical, and also changes the role of the musician. The prime requirement of the musician is to be good at listening. So the infamous 4' 33", and other silent pieces, are not just about the sounds forming music in the absence of purposeful, directed sound; they are also a mobilization of the audience, with listening the construction of the piece. Other works attack the idea of musical skill, or more accurately address it head on. The prepared piano uses hindrance of the 'proper' sounds to expand the musicality of the piano as whole object. Improvisers in and after free jazz have extended this principle to the 'non-musical' areas of instruments. Cage used radios, turntables, metals, recordings, tapes, and of course, sounds of the world. Musical skill is minimized, but of course there are skills involved. Cage is moving the location of skill from the hand to the mind (just as conceptual visual artists do). While he is interested in chance (another way of sidestepping skill, this time of arrangement), the resultant works are not random, or just any old sounds thrown together. The non-musical has become musical, the non-musician a musician. Cage is not interested in lack or absence of skill, even if the strategies he uses offer that prospect. Instead we are all made skilful, through *fiat*.

But there are still composers, not least Cage himself, for all his renunciations of music in favour of 'organized sound'. At one level, all become composers, while engaging in a silent piece, where all you do is set the duration (or follow one of Cage's timings), whether alone or as performer or audience in a concert setting. The composer figure will never go away, though, and the composer is set tasks by Cage: 'one may give up the desire to control sound, clear his head of music, and set about discovering means to let sounds be themselves rather than vehicles for man-made theories or expression of human sentiments' (Cage, *Silence*, 10). This composer is an appropriator, following on from Duchamp's 'readymades', and the appropriator, while making what is very often an interesting statement, or work, *is* making the object part of his or her art. The artist/composer has 'let' the sound or object occur in the context of the making of an artpiece.

In parallel to Cage's reconceptualization of music, Jean Dubuffet wants to deconceptualize all art. Where Cage disturbed the art institution from within, Dubuffet sought to get outside it, both in his own art and through championing the work of what would now be labelled outsider artists, but were first labelled 'naïve', then, by Dubuffet, as makers of 'art brut' (raw art). In his writings, Dubuffet constantly attacks what he calls 'cultural art', which insists on limiting art to what the insitutions of art and 'official' artists deem artistically valid. Having only recently begun painting, Dubuffet writes and presents copious argument on this point in the late 1940s. Now that we are accustomed to consuming modernity as a triumphant succession of avant-gardes, we can forget how even experimental art was corralled into 'right' and 'wrong' forms, schools, styles, and so on. Certainly in Europe, music was still seen as the preserve of a talented group of producers and a slightly extended élite audience. Jazz, which Dubuffet features in his art in the 1940s, was still far from accepted, and popular song was deemed acceptable only as entertainment for the musically illiterate. Dubuffet targets the 'classically trained' musician thirty years before punk, describing the conservatoire trained musician as a 'chien savant' (a dog that has been trained to perform tricks and gives the appearance of intelligence in so doing), and an 'ass', faithfully and ploddingly following its instruction (*Prospectus*, 34).[4] Music is supposed to be open to everyone, as performer or listener, but somehow modern society has lost this idea, he argues. The opera singer might be skilful, but what we want is singers who are like us, or at least more recognizable. Opera singers are like 'five-legged sheep' (35). Dubuffet's writings are shot through with an incessant sub-Rousseauian vision of a lost (but reattainable) authentic artistic expression. We are all artists, claims Dubuffet (48). When he says this, as with Beuys, there is something more direct compared with Cage's didactic approach, where we are all made (or remade) as artists. For Dubuffet and Beuys, humanity is about creativity, and to deny the latter to anyone is to deny the former. Dubuffet praises the work of the insane, the obsessive, the primitive, the 'failed' artists. To him, these categories embody the creative moment more than the constrained 'normal' people or trained artists. For him, their expression is unmediated, pure by virtue of not having to consider and follow standard rules about the production, reception and consumption of art (176 and *passim*).

Dubuffet is aware of the contradictions in what he is espousing, particularly in his own art, where he consciously aims to re-create the art of children, the insane, and so on. The contradictory view of skill is instructive. He begins by asserting the skilfulness of popular singers and so-called primitive artists (45), but later on he is highly enthusiastic about lack of skill ('long live ungifted painters!' [85]). This contradiction is the playing out of the question of something ostensibly bad or wrong turning out to be good, in a novel way. Dubuffet's own answer to the question is to focus on the undesirability of training in the production of art. Since the fifteenth century, we have had the category of 'professional artist' (47), as a result of valorizing the 'great painter' over painters in general. The belief in genius carries with it exclusion, as we know that even if there is such a thing, it will by definition be a monstrous talent, reserved for the very few. Thus, arbiters, purchasers and critics of art continually limit the world of art to those deemed great. Dubuffet's different positions on skill can be seen as the assertion of unrecognized skill, or of 'other skills'. Those other skills are not only perceived as lack of skill; they could well involve or require a genuine absence of relevant abilities. With Dubuffet, then, only the produced artwork can be assessed (judged?), mostly on the basis of interestingness or of authenticity of expression. Unlike Cage, for whom the musicianliness is improved, with Dubuffet, the musicianship or painting skill becomes irrelevant.[5]

In his own work (in all formats) and in his recommendations, Dubuffet is clear that the world of art will expand dramatically if we can lose our prejudices about talent and its role in the production of good or acceptable art (and he put this into practice with numerous forays into music using 'exotic' instruments and playing others he clearly had not been trained to play). We might untrain ourselves, not use the skills we have acquired, or mess them up. Using non-standard material, avoiding standard settings, making ephemeral, unpleasant or otherwise uncommercial work could all be part of this. Contrary to those who build new skills out of that, Dubuffet is in favour of work that is not careful, and says we need to ditch an over-emphasis on care ('rejetons les travaux fastidieux' [*Prospectus*, 66]). Only then can the artist restore his or her relation to humanity and then communicate it.[6]

There have been outsider musicians similar to the artists championed by Dubuffet, and today's interest in Daniel Johnston and Jandek confirms the persistence of the model of the tortured and/or completely individual creativity. Even something as simple as a frail, emotive voice can be enough to suggest art that is coming from somewhere far removed from the artworld, and the sense that the music 'had' to come out one way or another. Slightly different is the more purposeful lack of ability that we see in a few groups of the mid to late 1960s. Both Cornelius Cardew (with the Scratch Orchestra) and Gavin Bryars (Portsmouth Sinfonia) established groups (in 1969) made up of 'real' musicians, non-musicians and musicians who would play unfamiliar instruments. While the presence of a named composer hints at a simple shift from the mobilization of notes or a score to that of people and instruments in their own right, these groups could not be contained as they would be in the situations set up by the artist Phil Collins (parties, an office, getting people to mime to Smiths songs). Noise is inevitable, especially in the case of the Portsmouth Sinfonia, which looked to the collisions of different 'interpretations' or styles within a piece. It did not necessarily consist of purposeful bad playing—although as such was inevitable—noise and the humorousness of failure against the seriousness of skill were being aimed for. The location of badness would not be known at the beginning, so a chaotically structured unpredictability, fractal meat on spongy bone, would result. One of many renowned musicians that featured in the Sinfonia was Brian Eno, who would continue to describe himself as a non-musician musician, on the grounds that all sound, all manipulation of sound, was of interest, as was silence, quietness and self-generating not-quite-repetition. Free improvizing groups would also be open to the untrained or the seemingly unmusical, but it seems to me, in this case, that non-musicians are undergoing an initiation ritual where their innate musicality is to be brought out. If not, or if they seemed incapable of following the implied rules of a band's working, they would be shuffled back into the ranks of the non-musical. Many of Derek Bailey's collaborations or championed performers were felt by many to not be appropriate for 'true' free improvisation. This seemed only to encourage Bailey.

Other ensembles are often lumped together—AMM, Musica Elettronica Viva, the Nihilist Spasm Band, possibly the Red Krayola. The first two operate somewhere beyond free jazz and aleatory compositional music (in sound terms, if not compositionally); the last is a genuinely avant-garde psychedelic band, but the Nihilist Spasm Band epitomize an early version of music that combines absence of standard musical competence, 'DIY attitude', actual straightforward noisiness, and the inconvenience of not really fitting any of the established avant-garde categories and subworlds. They formed in 1965, and still play. They make their own instruments (the drumsets apart, which are fairly standard items, even if assembled oddly), which resemble guitars, violins, and so on: 'our instruments are mockeries of conventional instruments', says member John Boyle.[7] Kazoos feature strongly; the drumming is mostly fierce and fast. The volume is high. It sounds like focused if untuned improvisation, but the music is imagined differently: 'The Spasm Band, in contrast, does not improvise. We make noise and sometimes patterns form from it' (Murray Favro, interviewed by Rui Eduardo Paes).[8] Free of avant-gardist rhetoric, they can be consumed as 'improv', but sit outside of genres.

Like punk later on, there is a carelessness and slackness that makes up a key part of what they do, especially in combination with a purposeful sense of simply going ahead. If not overtly political as a group, there are tracks like 'Destroy America' on 1968's *No Record* where the idea of nationhood is attacked, with an emphasis on the U.S. and Canada. We should not take the Nihilist Spasm Band as a group 'that just wanna play'—they are a parodic version of that, through the combination of their playing, instrumentation, insistence on not limiting notes to be used and anti-musicianship. 'Destroy America' starts with shouted lyrics, then shifts through atonal chords, kazoo and pounding drumming. The reprise at the end of the album sees the seriousness of the anti-American, anti-nationalist 'message' undermined by coughing and phrasing the words through kazoo. Where free jazz soars ecstatically, *No Record* flounders merrily.

That the results are often not far from free jazz tells us about a shared noisiness (or continuum of noisiness?) at points where 'acceptable' musics are broken down or are being dismantled. Of course, many who hear unfamiliar, atonal, loud or messy music of any sort assert that it's not music, and they might be more right than those who say 'it's all music'. There is also a meeting point where the inventiveness that comes from lack of skill (no presumptions, but also having to maximize limited resources) joins up with those who would break out of technique (possibly in the same person—like the mucousy saxophone playing of Charles Gayle). All levels of skill can be evened out with the use of untuned instruments, or objects not usually considered musical, or instruments you are not used to. As with Cage, other values do emerge, notably listening, but also the need for collaboration in order to do so. This kind of listening can be more or less didactic, but an offer is nonetheless being made. Those who listen will be part of a community; they are invited in. Punk and post-punk might offer this to a few, but essentially it is a bid to make you listen. They are not afraid to tell others to shut up either. It is a different kind of taking charge of listening. Not the first provocation ever, but in music it was the most significant movement to combine aggression, popular appeal outside art audiences and a vindication of whatever you wanted to vindicate, no matter how good or bad it was and you were.

Punk groups appear in droves in Britain after the Sex Pistols had started out (although punk spread so quickly by the time they were having hit singles, others already existed). In stark contrast to the professionalized virtuosos of rock, these were largely bands that were either competent (a key virtue of pub rock) or more or less incompetent. While they would not be ashamed of this, neither was it purposeful, and many bands improve in terms of musicianship, and if they lasted, would quite often leave punk behind entirely. Stewart Home notes that punk listeners praise amateurishness (*Cranked Up Really High*, 88), and he himself thinks Lydon's voice too arty for the Sex Pistols to be truly punk. Is amateurishness the same as ineptitude though? It is certainly a more positive take on absence of standard talent. It indicates the willingness to accept whatever level you have, a refusal to play the 'corporate game' being played by over-commercialized rock, a genuine love of music, self-reliance; it is an admirable quality because you are still willing to try and play music despite limitations, so it shows bravery and intent. Amateurishness can also be the refusal to 'improve', 'conform', play safe. Ineptitude as a resource in itself is limited, without access to large quantities of different instruments to not be able to play, but the limited can be the pursuit of the inept by other means—so Oi! bands and Crass-related bands alike would have to rely on limited musical possibilities for variation, and work with textures, speed, disruptions.

At the insistence of Malcolm McLaren, the Sex Pistols were portrayed as musical naifs, barely able to hold their instruments ('make sure they can't play', McLaren intones on 'God Save the Queen (Symphony)' on *The Great Rock 'n' Roll Swindle*). Their power was to lie in a lack of concern about talent and ability because the message was one of authenticity, albeit in a highly and always already mediated way. McLaren certainly overstates his role in manipulating the group, but much of their significance and impact derived from impressions of their attitude beyond music, or that they brought to the music. Following Stewart Home, it is clear that the Sex Pistols had too much going on, even before you consider the images generated around and by them. Lydon is too dramatic, the lyrics nowhere near as vacant as could be. The musicians, particularly Glen Matlock, are perfectly capable of decent, effective pub rock. The noise of the music did shock, however (whether it would have done without the non-musical elements of punk is debatable), the lyrically nihilistic and provocative songs drawing attention to the overall 'punk aesthetic', because once you have drawn in listeners that would despise all rock music, you have your ready-to-be-offended constituency, and they dutifully declared the music a racket, or that it was not music. But the noise of the Sex Pistols is in and through the mass media: their noise is the social disruption pointed out by Attali (without reference to punk), where social and political authorities reject a troublesome, popular entertainment because it could spill over into outright rebellion. The Sex Pistols were an advertisement for 'unacceptable' behaviour, anti-role models, and the mass media feared contagion, a contagion it would fuel. Other forms of rebellious music (with the possible exception of the early heavy metal that portrayed itself as Satanist) looked to move outside of 'straight society', but the punk generation had noticed that you were not going to be allowed to 'do your own thing', or that to try to meant facing conservative society head on, hence the success of message-driven rock like the Clash, which not only enacted the rebellion, but spelt it out, *represented* it as lyrical content.[9]

The Sex Pistols, though, were close enough to nihilism, first in the hands of Lydon's lyrics, where everything is to be demolished, then in the capering form of McLaren's manipulable Pistols of Cook, Jones, Vicious and assorted lags, like Ronnie Biggs. This second format of the group can be taken as a logical outcome of the first: having broken down initial resistance, and shown the emptiness of society, and reflected it back, what else was there to do but wallow in the exposed spectacle of collapse (at the risk of ventriloquizing McLaren)? The arrival of Sid Vicious brought the musical level down, and faced with actually improving, Vicious managed to stall skill though drug intake and a concentration on aggressive performance. Like dada, the Sex Pistols were not 'doomed to fail' but lived on in failure (including posthumously, and in comeback form), our future, our no future is their no future too.

Home argues that the essence of punk is novelty, as in novelty records, not avantgardist insistence on the new (*Cranked Up Really High*, 13), and on that basis, *The Great Rock 'n' roll Swindle* would be more punk than *Never Mind the Bollocks*, and that is probably true. However, what Home is also highlighting is the endless insistence on authenticity in punk discourse—who is toughest/most dangerous/worst/best/more working class/stupidest/challenging/revolutionary. Punk raises the question of authenticity in ways it cannot fully close off; in other words, while it is at stake, the answer in the shape of a particular band or brand of punk could never be final. The same rhetoric of the 'early days authenticity' flows through punk—the origins must be best. Why is punk not allowed to be derivative? A strange turnaround occurs where new versions of stadium rock could more or less replicate the styles and values of precursors, but the only thing you could repeat in punk for it to be valid was 'attitude'—not much to be going on. Punk, then, operates (i.e. acts as a centre for, without directly causing) the Nietzschean transvaluation of values, where ideas of what is of value in music become so open it is no longer possible to assert 'x is the true thing we must value in music' without being immediately contradicted. The Sex Pistols, as well as being at the forefront of punk and the foreground of its discourse, seem to offer a sense of this from the start and through their 'decline'. Arguably they return us to the 'true' values of rock 'n' roll, in a return to the importance of the single, and of live performance. The Sex Pistols' concerts brought the state of exception of Altamont into a permanent condition: violence among the crowd, and toward musicians, being the literalist interpretation of the music made by many spectators. This was a largely consensual violence, even if bands got tired of it, and the outpouring of aggression along with being part of an elective community is a form of the erotic, ecstatic community of loss of self suggested by Bataille.[10] In terms of recordings, singles were affordable and immediately set punk apart from older rock music, which on occasion had scorned the format almost entirely. *Flogging a Dead Horse* works less as a 'best of' the Sex Pistols and more as a clear representation of their intent, compared to the lumpier *Never Mind the Bollocks*.

It is only on albums and b-sides that swearing could be found, and nowhere better than on 'Bodies': 'Fuck this and fuck that, fuck it all and fuck a fucking brat'. The song is about the messy physical outcomes of abortion, and offensive to the traditional for talking of it, and to pro-abortionists, who take it as anti-abortion in intent (which Lydon denies).[11] The album is permeated by direct critique of a Britain both fossilized and decaying, and the noise value of 'God Save the Queen' as a single in 1977 is obvious. There is also a signal of punk's flirtation with Nazi imagery, with reference to 'the new Belsen' a trivialization of the death camps as much as a critique of the package holiday or 'holiday camp'. 'Belsen was a gas', which finally surfaces in *The Great Rock 'n' roll Swindle*, seems to minimize what occurred there. Both Siouxsie Sioux and Sid Vicious used the Nazi swastika, and Siouxsie also suggested a decadence that owed more to a sexualization of Nazism rather than a Weimar decadence. Nazi imagery was a vital resource for transgressing accepted values, and would spread widely in industrial music, often to the point of unwitting caricature (unlike Laibach's 'witting' caricature).[12]

Is the *Rock 'n' roll Swindle* noise on account of badness? Its messiness, ineptitude, laziness all add up to making it more of a punk realization of an album/film (albeit skewed through McLaren) than the formulaic structure of *Never Mind the Bollocks*. So here, by numbers, is how to find noise in the *Swindle*:

1. First, isolate what is wrong with the album (as it is the music that is the object here): the songs, the structure, how little a buyer gets.
2. Take the various elements of the album and point out how they disturb or disappoint expectations: there is not much Lydon, there is not much punk.

3. Look at how the album caricatures punk: the Sex Pistols without Lydon are reduced to covers of rock 'n' roll hits, comedy songs with Ronnie Biggs.
4. Think about how the image takes over, at the expense of authenticity, the key selling point of punk.
5. Take Sid Vicious, iconic, taking apart 'My Way' and actually reminding us of Las Vegas Elvis. Build him up, remind people that he is nothing but image, and can barely play bass.
6. Or 'Johnny Rotten' reduced to covering songs he does not like, which he tells us, and which is retained on the recording.
7. Make something of the variety of musical styles used, the orchestral moments, the funk medley of 'Black Arabs', the music hall feel of large chunks.
8. Point out the irony of where the noise is in the *Swindle*, i.e. not in the aggressiveness or messiness of any specific bits of music, but in the failing and failings of the whole.
9. Note that noise can go wherever you want if you want to sell it to its full potential.

Public Image Limited (PiL) finally transpose Lydon's ire into the music and the forms, and even the production (large but also tinny) of the songs. As well as the 'anti-prog' of 'Theme', PiL deconstruct the Sex Pistols through an ostensible attack on McLaren, combined with musings on the public perception of what the Sex Pistols and Lydon himself, as Johnny Rotten, were up to (in 'Public Image'). But while Lydon rails against miscasting and misconception, he is also undoing his own persona, and self-referentially addressing the very statements he is making at that time in the song (e.g. when referring to himself as performer leaving the stage), and the multiple irony of those multiple positions is summed up in the finale: 'public image, you got what you wanted/the public image belongs to me/my entrance, my own creation/my grand finale, my goodbye'. Musically, the introduction of dub (to be expanded on *Metal Box*), while not exclusive to PiL, was still something punk audiences could well reject, and for a few albums (up to the ironic *This Is What You Want This Is What You Get*), the sound changes, with the core audience the ones being unsettled rather than some notional 'establishment'. The smart dress, the corporate-style name, the long tracks—all of these feature already on the first album—acknowledge and try to drive punk's purpose on through a punk rejection of punk.

Crass proposed a more direct confrontation with capitalism, based on an initial separatism, i.e. they founded an anarchist collective and commune, and would release records that would appear in the capitalist marketplace but criticize it both in terms of business practice and in the songs themselves. Crass were (and in different form, are) an extension of 1960s anarchist ideals, while not wanting to be seen as part of the generation of hippies, who had failed to effect change. So if the Sex Pistols were at the centre of a social noise, Crass were the social noise itself—an alternative lifestyle, predicated on equality, responsibility for society along with individual rights being the message that could seem noise next to the mainstream signal. Crass released regularly, copiously and cheaply, generally specifying a maximum price for the record (which unfortunately was not always adhered to, and is uncontrollable second hand). The records sold tens of thousands of copies but somehow never dented the charts. The conspiracy-minded noted that the highly aggressive and often funny attacks on Margaret Thatcher's government might have led to this, just as the Sex Pistols' 'God Save the Queen' stopped at no. 2 in the charts in Britain, despite seemingly selling more than the no. 1 at the time.

Crass actualized notions of self-reliance, autonomy, DIY, and set a counter-cultural model in place that would persevere through festivals in the 1980s and raves in the 1990s. As well as the commune, the record label and the political sub-version, they also tie in with a tradition of instrument-makers like the Nihilist Spasm Band, notably in the use of tape samples. These would usually feature political speeches by the governing Conservative party (and also before they got into power), and, more formally interestingly, self-referential recordings, for example of discussions with politicians that sought to censor Crass. Even the live part of Christ—The Album splices bits of talking and very poor recordings into the straight concert material.[13] On occasion, they stretched beyond the palate of punk—'Reality Asylum', their expression of disgust with organized religion and Christian-ity in particular, features tapes of choral singing, screams, burning. Such tracks link them to the nascent 'industrial' music, made of tapes, cheap synths, non-musical instruments and a lo-fi 'studio as instrument' aesthetic. Crass, New York no wave and industrial music alike involve many non-musicians, and this as a purposeful statement. The subversions on offer were harsher for subverting the rules of 'proper' music. The political purpose of Crass might militate against their noisi-ness, but their view on activism is more subtle than we might at first think:

> Rock can not be politicized, despite what followers of Oi, or Marx, might say. Rock is about all of us, it is the collective voice of the people, not a platform for working-class mythology or socialist ideology. In rock 'n' roll, there aren't any workers to 'wot' about. Rock is about freedom, not slavery [. . .] Punk is a voice of dissent, an all-out attack on the whole system'. (Penny Rimbaud, sleeve notes for Christ—The Album).

This is a political position, an anarchist one—but anarchism itself is a messy non-ideology, even when committedly idealist.

Nonetheless, a more forthright, simplistic take could be seen as better. While right-wing punk and skinhead bands were proudly anti-intellectual and pro-vio-lence, this 'thinking' is not restricted to them alone. Home quotes The Oppressed as a classical example of leftist skinhead music (Cranked Up Really High, 84), and that this did not at all mean rising above skinhead concerns, as the emphasis on violence, simplicity and aggressive and offensive political outlooks is how Oi! transgressed the expectations of rock critics keen to drag punk into acceptability and worthiness (83–4). It is clear that it was not only anarchist intellectuals who were 'above' the interests of The Oppressed, as even mainstream punk was unnecessarily literate. In response, for example, to anyone for or against chaos 'in the streets', The Oppressed say, 'chaos chaos chaos, don't give a toss' ('Chaos', written by the 4-Skins. All tracks referred to are from The Oppressed, Oi! Oi! Music!).[14] They complain about Margaret Thatcher's government, but it is all gov-ernments that must pay: 'hear the people scream and shout/ we want government, government out' ('Government Out'), and anyone outside your immediate group might need to be fought: 'who's to blame the rich or the poor/fight the enemy fight the law/we'll stick together, we'll see it thro'/we're gonna riot, me and you' ('Riot'). Many right-wing skinhead bands back institutions of power, but here all power is subject to the control of the boot. The group (of skinheads) is a microcosm of working class/youth society—highly social and bonded in its self-reliance. The Oppressed display this with near-harmonious multi-track choruses—an expression of how 'the enemy' brings us together. So in 'Magistrate', it is this social voice that intones, 'Magistrate, magistrate/you're the cunt we all hate' (New Model Army would base their notion of an anarchist, autonomous community on this formal strategy). The Oppressed are a complex bringing together of many of punk's musical 'failings', which are nothing to do, here, with musical inability as such, but a refusal to play along with the expectations of politically committed music. So there would not be any outwardly directed message to society as a whole, and such message as there is is for the existing group alone. They do not try to interest the listener musically (even with the oddity of a drum machine) but try to make the songs assertions without form or content, purposefully reducible to slogans, often self-referential, or with gratuitous obscenity, or fighting, all of which would play out in gigs, and not just theirs. This masculine aggressiveness (not restricted to men, but a valorized male attitude) replaces the (would-be) sexual masculinity of virtuosity.

Home identifies skill as a 'male attribute' (*Cranked Up Really High*, 107), i.e. it is something males possess and do, and something that is imagined as inherently masculine. Similarly, Mavis Bayton argues, 'rock is associated with technology, which is itself strongly categorized as "masculine"' ('Women and the Electric Guitar', 42).[15] More than a philosophical or political position, it directly impacted on women's involvement in rock. Home claims that although not many women could be identified as punk, it liberated many to produce music, without having to pay those required dues. We might also note that male musicians were adopting a 'feminine' attribute in refusing skill, or at least in minimizing it. New York spawned 'no wave', something that sought to prolong punk without falling into new wave, which was much more palatable to the music industry. Key no wave participants are Lydia Lunch, coming from performance art, Ikue Mori, with her most unfeminine but also unmasculine thrash and pulse drumming. All-female bands such as the Slits, LiLiPUT, the Raincoats, Y Pants, the Bush Tetras and mixed bands like DNA, Contortions, Teenage Jesus and the Jerks moved women away from their traditionally accepted role as singers. While no wave brought funk into collision with punk, it is the messier end that ties in with the noise of the inept.

Much of the lack of skill was only apparent, and the line between purposely playing 'against' skill and without is blurred. For Savage, already 'the CBGBs groups had wiped out the previous generation's belief in musical skill' (*England's Dreaming*, 98).[16] Bands such as DNA, Mars and (elsewhere) This Heat purposely combined a range of non-musical practices, whether lack of skill, playing against virtuosity, playing 'badly' or in ways that punk and new wave audiences would have found challenging. The inept becomes a more interesting term, as once it is allowed (or sought, perhaps), then the importance of skill is diminished, but also, ineptitude of any sort undermines the notion of skill itself. Skill becomes a judgement, not a craft. Lack of skill is the judging of that judgement, and the ending of that judgement (as it loses relevance).

inept • **99**

No Wave also played with the notion of precursors, imagining they were some sort of primal music while also being a reference to primal music, or, as Reynolds has it, 'the No Wave groups *acted* as if they had no ancestors at all' (*Rip It Up*, 51). This combines with playing as if devoid of any ability, and the groups try to step out of avant-garde and rebellious lineages alike, *as if* it were possible. No wave such as DNA is music of the failure to escape, but which virally feeds back into what it is trying to avoid to undermine it. Among the puzzled contributors to the sleeve notes to *DNA on DNA*, Byron Coley puts it this way: '[DNA's music] transmuted from inarticulation to expression and back again'. DNA are still quite unusual in that they raise the possibility of a noise song: while it might be tautologous to say this, noise music largely avoids song structure, or noise elements become background. Shouting or pushing the voice is not quite enough for a noise song, but DNA (at first, especially), with their short condensations of punk and free jazz collisions, the antimusicality of the singing, the anti-song approach of the guitar and the endless (so non-punctuating) drumming, at least raise the prospect.

To claim ineptitude as a method, even if incidental, for attaining noise is paradoxical, even disappointing—and if the latter, that is an appopriate outcome. The problem lies in redeeming the inept, while not reframing them as 'differently talented', which it is hard not to do. This difficulty also replays the near-dialectic of the non-musical and the anti-musical, where both can be thought of as purposeful and the product of an apparent lack of appropriate skill. So to empty out the inept a bit more, I will conclude this chapter with a brief section on the value of ineptitude in the Germs, John the Postman and Alternative TV.

The Germs sit high in punk mythology, helped by the death at a young age of singer Darby Crash. At the beginning they were strikingly unable to play, but something held the songs together. Such improvement as there was as time went on was marked by the undermining or incompletion of any new ability that had come along, so not rising to the unwanted high-stool of 'talent'. The aggression of their performance, the rawness of the sound, including on record, gives them the authenticity that the punk fan has bought into. This is not to say there is nothing to that, but it is a value, an ideological construct of purity that would be almost impossible to either attain or maintain. The Germs tried hard to fail in either, and this will to failure plays out in the opening to 'No God', which is a moderately, rather than comically, rendered copy of Steve Howe's acoustic guitar intro to the Yes track 'Roundabout', and whose falling away into the song neatly parodies the smooth transition in 'Roundabout' between the different sections. The first single, 'Forming'/'Sex Boy' highlights the band's ineptitude to the literal point of telling us about it, with 'Forming' ending with these lines: 'whoever would buy this shit is a fucking jerk; it's played all wrong, the drums are too slow, the bass is too fast, the chords are wrong, it's making the ending too long' (later song lyrics, the equal of Lydon's, would also trouble believers in the purity of badness). 'Sex Boy' is badly ranted and played (in concert), but the real noise element here is in releasing it as a finished song, when it is worse than most bootlegs, and the song is often lost in ambient sound.

John the Postman, it would be tempting to say, pushed the envelope of terribleness. Not in a band at all, he would jump onto stage and lead unrousing, long, versions of 'Louie Louie' (for the most part) with improvized lyrics and occasional return to the phrase 'Louie Louie'. This was formalized in the shape of John the

Postman's Puerile (band and album title), where the band shamble along, with breakdowns, and an aimless, random (*not* aleatory) improvised middle section, announced as the 'Sister Ray bit'—and so going even further in pointlessness in both repetition and jamming than the Velvet Underground. Home places John the Postman within a history of ineptitude that feeds on 'Louie Louie': 'Louie Louie (version)' takes the amateurism of the Kingsmen to its logical conclusion with grossly incompetent musicianship and a drummer who seems to be experiencing extreme difficulty simply keeping time' (*Cranked Up Really High*, 40). Like the Germs, John also refers to the song and the fact it is going nowhere and is not very good. Unlike the Germs, there is no redeeming creativity in either the planned or improvized sections. This is what blunts its chance of authenticity, and turns it into something else: an expression of alienation. John the Postman is outside musical norms and, more importantly, values, and wants to stay there; this is a genuinely apathetic alienation (more active than Durkheim's notion of anomie). Instead of an expression of a pure musicality or even of a self, John the Postman is the assertion of refusal to no other purpose, even 'nihilistic'. It just circles in on itself as the listener tries to make it mean, make it express or signify.

Alternative TV offer the same distanced amateurishness where it is the ineptitude that maintains the separation from society, and, particularly with the album *Vibing Up the Senile Man, part one*, this forms the bridge into 'industrial music'. Alternative TV manage, on this album at least, to make a transgressive music through an ineptness that is nothing to do with the attitude of 'just do it', but comes across as more of an enforced action, resisting the action and society at the same time, through a refusal of musical value, even in established experimental forms (many of which involved either a high degree of musical skill, or at least knowledge, or, as today where this has become heightened, access to expensive electronic machinery).

NOTES

1. As the fanzine *Sniffin' Glue* put it, roughly: 'here's a chord, here's another, here's one more, go form a band'.
2. Savage, *England's Dreaming: Sex Pistols and Punk Rock* (London: Faber & Faber, 1991).
3. Home, *Cranked Up Really High: An Inside Account of Punk Rock* (Hove: CodeX, 1995).
4. Dubuffet, *Prospectus et tous écrits suivants, vol. I* (Paris: Gallimard, 1967).
5. This still leaves him with the problem of judging. If the purpose of art brut is to evade censure of creativity, what would bad art brut look like? Are we to judge on the criteria usually applied to 'official art'? Should we just say 'it's all good', which would patronize the artists? Dubuffet is clear that we should analyse and compare art brut productions—as it is not therapy but creativity, and there is no specific 'art of the mad', any more than there is art by people with knee problems, or the dyspeptic (*Prospectus*, 202).
6. We should be clear that Dubuffet is not some kind of social worker. He is strictly against 'utility' in art. It must not serve a higher purpose, or else it will necessarily be ruined. So the choice of words in the statement about carefulness is important, with 'travaux' suggesting 'works' in the sense of 'building works'.
7. 'The Nihilist Spasm Band: "Godfathers of Noise"' (interview with Rui Eduardo Paes), www3.sympatico.ca/pratten/NSB/
8. *Ibid.*

9. The distinction is not so much between those who have and express a political view-point in their music and those who do not, but between lyrically critical music and music where critique is combined with a formal critique. The Clash are mentioned simply as short-hand here, and this reference is as much to the reception of the Clash as their intent or prac-tice. What I have in mind is the attack (rather than critique) on Christianity in Siouxsie and the Banshees' 'Lord's Prayer', the interpretation of which combines vocal cynicism with sim-plistic, repetitive and lengthy riffing and drumming, or PiL's 'Religion', the first part of which is delivered sermonically.

10. Unlike football violence, also prevalent at the time, the enemy was not present at the concert, so, at the risk of psychoanalysing, the group would end up being projected as such—or, the aggression would turn inward, into the crowd, in a form of narcissistic masoch-ism. Really? Marginally, maybe.

11. On the song, Lydon has said 'I'm not anti- or pro-abortion. Every woman should have the choice when they face it. [. . .] And if you construe ['Bodies'] as being anti-abortion, then you're a silly cu-- sausage' (interview with *Q* magazine, www.johnlydon.com/q05.html).

12. Important precursors are Mel Brooks' 1968 film *The Producers* and Serge Gains-bourg's jaunty concept album about Nazis, *Rock around the Bunker*, of 1975.

13. The inclusion of residual sounds is a familiar practice in punk, and perhaps reaches some sort of sublime Alternative TV-inspired nadir in the 'noise' band Cock. ESP's album *We Mean It This Time* (with badly edited arguments, small bursts of noise music and sounds too extraneous to be musicalized) The parody of progressive rock formats—the double or triple album, the live album (instead of virtuoso solos extending the pieces, songs crumbling and played well below the minimal levels set in the studio), the long track—these occur on a rea-sonable number of occasions within and around punk, but *Christ—The Album* is a pleasing example nonetheless; parodying the packaging of epic 1970s albums, it comes in a box, but this is decorated only with a tiny version of Crass' 'insignia'. Inside is the double album, a crappy poster and a wordy pamphlet made out of rough paper and devoid of Hipgnosis-style 'artistic inspiration'. Other records came only in card sleeves, or with photocopied mono-chrome sleeves. Scritti Politti made even rougher covers, including all kinds of debris, and material that became debris in the cover, such as the cost of manufacture or arbitrary political statements.

14. The 4-Skins close with 'chaos, chaos, chaos/don't give a toss'—giving it the tone of a threat about to be carried out. The Oppressed alter this, repeating the phrase, and repeating the now two-line chorus at the end. This heightens our immersion in violence, as well as signalling the centrality of it to 'our' community. The return to the opening verse after the first chorus (referring to skinheads in 1969) shows the Oppressed build a historically grounded community.

15. Bayton, 'Women and the Electric Guitar', in Whiteley (ed), *Sexing the Groove: Popular Music and Gender* (New York: Routledge, 1997), 37–49.

16. The Ramones play a big part in that scene, and the incredibly short, loud, repetitive tracks could work as a kind of noise, but I think the formula makes it too easy for an audience, even live, to settle in. On the other hand, maybe after the 'variations on themes' of prog, especially live, a formula was in itself a radical statement.

7
INDUSTRY

In the shadow of punk, something that would come to be called industrial music was being made. Like punk, industrial music was suspicious of musicality, but its hatred of contemporary art and society went deeper, its critique harsher as a result. Like dada, it offers an anti-aesthetic, using the tools of art to undo art. Unlike punk, the answer was not change, but awareness of the fetid state of capitalist society. Like punk, the individual was the target—he or she would be thrown out of their standard socialized patterns of thinking and behaving, but the extremity of what was on offer would make it difficult to have the instrumentalist inspirational effect of punk ('just do it'). Like Derrida, industrial music knows there is no outside to escape to that is not already consumed by the inside. Industrial music plays out the accursed share of modern society, staging sacrificial performances and making music that offers momentary collapse of rational thought in the shape of a listening that would *know* in advance what it would be listening to.

As a genre, industrial music is highly flexible, with the shared element of the use of all that had mostly hitherto been seen as peripheral to music, and to modern(ist) thought. Stylistically, it often combines objects not usually thought of as belonging to music, notably in the form of percussion. There is a heavy use of what were not yet called samples and cut and splicing of same. There is a mostly transgressive content to songs and imagery, and a subversive use of existing musical conventions in 'experimental music'. Despite Cage's accurate misgivings about the notion of experimental music, groups like Throbbing Gristle and Cabaret Voltaire consciously adopted the thought-form of the experiment, testing their strategies on those attending events, and also on listening, where records are concerned. The music aimed to be both primal and at the cutting edge of contemporary culture. This combination would allow a hyperrationalist critique of rationalist society (in the same vein as key inspirations William Burroughs and J. G. Ballard).

Early industrial music has an ambivalent relation to technology and industrial society, which it mobilizes in various forms of parody. At a time (mid-1970s on) of dramatic industrial decline in the west, it seems to industrial music groups that the west is entering its own form of decadence, as its rationalism festers. Industrial music is music for the end of industry, the end of dreams of liberal softening of the capitalist machine. Or, as Biba Kopf puts it,

> they did not, as sometimes supposed, celebrate industrialism. Britain's industrial age was over well before TG and CV began operations. In effect, the pair bridged the gap between its end and the beginning of the coming computer age. Though it was already dead, TG sniffed a potential energy source in the gases given off in the chemical reactions within the decay of the corpse. ('Introduction: Bacillus Culture', 11)[1]

The Futurists had proclaimed the music of the future to be one of machines that could not only represent but be part of industrial society, but it is only from the mid-1970s on that anything like this music exists. *Musique concrète* had advanced the Futurist notion of synthetic sound, and sampling of the world, but its politeness meant academization, a newly professionalized sub-genre of official programme music made by composers. Industrial music shares many superficial similarities with that music, with Stockhausen, with Cage's gestures, with 'krautrock', but brought together elements from many avant-gardes, many noise moments, to structure and de-structure a new noise. This noise would be made of non-musician ship, non-musicality, a refusal of all norms (in theory) in the interest of pushing experience as far as possible. In this, it shows its connection to art practice, art schools, performance art. This music would not 'change your ideas through art', but threaten you, expose your limits, so that even if as a listener you did not agree with the new vision, it would still have been inflicted on you. As discussed below, this hardens into a style rather than a shared practice, the same tools over-circulating. At that point, a second phase of industrial music appears (often produced by the same people), where the music is made with much more advanced technology, rather than the DIY splicing of the late 1970s. This is a much more beat-driven music, and a more aestheticized take on the playing out of power in music.

Industrial music shares an overall belief in autonomous art production, in terms of the music itself, and its production on independent labels, often with low-quality sound and self-produced art (recalling *samizdat* anti-propaganda in Communist Eastern Europe). The term 'industrial music' is mostly thought to have come from Throbbing Gristle's label Industrial Records, rather than from an assessment or even assertion about the attitude of players to industrial society. It operated on the outside of accepted music industry structures, taking its music outside of concert venues, and being perverse in the musical objects it made (Non's records with multiple centre holes, to be played at any speed, sometimes, as with *Pagan Muzak*, just offering locked grooves instead of tracks; Throbbing Gristle's twenty-four-cassette box of concert recordings; very limited editions).

Industrial music is almost the polar opposite of Crass, in that it was too late for a new society, and in this, they shadowed Margaret Thatcher's declaration that there is no such thing as society, while laying the blame at her door and that of capitalism. While Thatcherism 'offered' individualism, and punk tried to claim it too, industrial music is very often antisocial, isolationist. In Heideggerian terms, it looks for a dwelling in industrial society, rather than the thrownness of acceptance *or* denial of that world. While this contains a hint of authentic being, it is only despite and against society, despite and against hopes of authenticity. Industrial music aspires to live in unresolved negativity, like Bataille's idea of sovereignty, hence its insistence on transgression rather than revolution, momentary if multiple moments of revolt rather than a change of society into something better.

Nonetheless, it is a musical 'movement', making records, playing concerts and so on. It is not just a utilitarian mobilization of strange sounds in order to make something happen—it has form, or, more accurately, a 'formless', where the forms (e.g. albums) exist as deformations. Its content/subject matter and its situating itself as nihilistically oppositional (nothing is true, so *as a result*, everything and anything is possible) take it away from official avant-gardism which would produce objects clearly delineated as aesthetic. Central to industrial music's position is its refusal of the Kantian separation made by capitalist, rationalist, industrial society, where art or industry could be autonomous, as this has led to a profound alienation. Far from making music that would relieve this alienation, Throbbing Gristle and others dwelt in it, arguably to the point of wallowing in it.

Let's not imagine there was much in the way of irony in industrial music, when it is there, it is in straight-faced parody, not playing with the ideas that oppress in such a way that leaves them intact, as could be said to be the case with, say, ZTT/Trevor Horn/Paul Morley's approach in the mid-1980s, inventive as it was. Industrial music does not accept the language of rationalist culture, but, knowing it cannot get out, acts as if it can, and posits endless alternative cultural positions often neglected in avant-garde culture (usually violent, sacrifical forms). Heavily dependent on Burroughs, industrial music would not just tell you what was wrong, but reconfigure communication in ways consistent with breaking free of social control. In this it recalls the anarchist idea from the early 1900s of 'propaganda by the deed', of giving an example that would not only expose social power, but force it to act, exposing its practice behind its façade of tolerance. Kopf argues that 'even if no new truth was revealed, CV's applications of Burroughs' cut-up theories were stimulating in themselves' ('Introduction: Bacillus Culture', 11)

Burroughs argued that society is a network of control mechanisms, and that the only ways out (even if provisional) involved taking language apart, taking apart the disciplined 'Cartesian' bodies we are placed in. His notion of 'the word' or language as a virus is one where our division into two has been enforced, but the virus that made this happen can be harnessed, used as inoculation or even as weapon. The division into mental self, soul or spirit on one hand and body on the other is not dismissed by Burroughs but historicized, made contingent, and as with Bataille and Throbbing Gristle, the dismantling of this duality would not bring monadic, hamonious fun, but an exacerbation of existence, of an excessive cycling back and forward between what seemed opposites. This is what is behind the insistence on sadomasochism, violence and physical ecstasies in this music. Also from Burroughs comes the idea of how to criticize rationalist society in a way that gets beyond the analytical. In 'The Electronic Revolution', and many places beside, Burroughs offers ways of intervening in society, through noise, to disrupt it, as opposed to offering an alternative, using and distorting the literal, linear communication used by institutions. Playing tapes at the wrong speed, cutting up and recombining texts and tapes, playing sound recordings in odd public settings for subliminal effect—all were taken up by industrial musicians.[2]

Throbbing Gristle and transgression

Jon Savage outlines five aspects of the first few years of industrial music: 'organizational autonomy' 'access to information', 'use of synthesizers, and *anti-music*', 'extra-musical elements' and 'shock tactics' ('Introduction, *Industrial Culture*, 5).[3] These are not just shared characteristics, elements of style; rather they are essential components of a thoroughgoing critique or even attack on conventional modern, Christian, artistic, moral, capitalist thought and living. Another way of characterizing the industrial music of the late 1970s and early 1980s is in terms of transgression and perversion. All the above strategies listed by Savage aspire to subvert to the point where subversion is no longer tenable, as we do not know on what grounds we could still subvert, or break free, or even whether we wanted to, 'confronting ALL assumptions in ALL aspects of that particular genre of culture' [i.e. music] (Genesis P-Orridge, sleeve notes to Throbbing Gristle, *Second Annual Report* CD). Confrontation, degradation, mutual abjection, shared violence, unlimited expression of taboo subjects and acts: all work across Throbbing Gristle's music in vocal content, musical form, performance and cover design.

According to Throbbing Gristle and Cabaret Voltaire, modern, technologized industrial society controls our minds, acting as a limiter on expression and attainment of potential. Both aim to disrupt our standard thought patterns and break down our acceptance of taboo: harsh electronics, loud volume, tape cut-ups, badly played instruments and non-instruments begin as a wall, distancing an audience, to slowly draw in listeners, this time dismantling walls of prejudice. Visuals, often of extreme violence, or pornographic scenes, threatening or disturbing in vaguer ways, would interact with the sound elements (this both on covers and in performance). So far, so utilitarian: the music is there to serve a purpose, an instruction, or what scientologists call 'deprogramming'. Also, the imagery, physicality and aggressively poor performance/recording quickly become expected moves. Throbbing Gristle had various strategies to get around this, of which more below, and with them, a strong parallel with Bataille emerges, and crucially, in the move from explicit trangression to philosophical, nihilist transgression that plays with authenticity rather than trying to salvage it.

Throbbing Gristle emerged from performance group COUM Transmissions, using extreme physical actions—sex, excretions, violence, cutting, restriction, liquids, solids . . . unlike Paul McCarthy, very little was stage blood (this is not a value judgement). Unlike the Austrian *Aktionists*, there seemed little overriding purpose. Instead of being a comment on taboos on physicality and a testing of the limits of the body as exploration, here there was little comment. As with Throbbing Gristle, the resulting 'artwork' was left to its own devices, free of comment as such, which was replaced by sloganeering, which, even if meant to convey messages about bourgeois morality, offered something more like a disconnect than an explanation. Both COUM and Throbbing Gristle pursued a mission without an agenda, endlessly preventing their own ideas being functional, clear oppositional stances. COUM's show *Prostitution* (London, ICA, October 1976) saw P-Orridge and Cosey Fani Tutti physically abusing themselves with abandon, while the gallery displayed pictures Cosey had made working for porn magazines. Throbbing Gristle would use transcripts from Ian Brady and Myra Hindley, more on murderers in general, Holocaust imagery, violence retold as jaunty fairy tales. Both groups carry messages, *and* withhold them. *Prostitution* is about exploitation, commercialism, and how a capitalist commodity aesthetic has replaced a more sacrificial ethic of physical and mental liberation, but it stages sex and violence unquestioningly; no matter how far into an ecstatic experience the participants get, the audience is still at an aesthetic distance, even if this is being disturbed. Throbbing Gristle named their studio the death factory, and talked of a 'death factory society' of late capitalism (in Simon Ford, *Wreckers of Civilization*, 6.17);[4] so the use of Auschwitz pictures, or of a canister of the poison gas Zyklon B, is telling us about a society that has rationalized its production to the point where death is industrialized, and as well as the actual victims of death camps, most of society is doomed to a living death. P-Orridge, introducing their 'Music from the Death Factory', at *Prostitution*, states

> it's basically about the post-breakdown of civilization. You know, you walk
> down the street and there's a lot of ruined factories and bits of old newspapers
> with stories about pornography and page three pin-ups, blowing down the

street, and you turn a corner past the dead dog and you see old dustbins. And then over the ruined factory there's a funny noise. (in Ford, *Wreckers*, 6.28)

The link to Romanticism's rejection of rationalizing society is clear, an aesthetics of decay replacing the heroic symbolism of the ruined tower or the crushing sublime power of violent nature. Industrial society had come a long way since the early nineteenth century, largely backwards, according to 'industrial musicians', turning away from harsher but vibrant realities of danger, eroticism and sacrifice, as well as the liberating potential of technology, in favour of a rigid, coercive outlook that was seeping around the world. As Baudrillard put it, at much the same time (1976) as Throbbing Gristle set out, 'society as a whole takes on the appearance of a factory' (*Symbolic Exchange and Death*, 18).

The presentation of those 'challenging' materials was highly ambiguous, though. While Genesis P-Orridge has criticized Whitehouse in particular for using violent imagery and stories in an exploitative, comment-free way (Ford, *Wreckers*, 11.16), the *success* of the particular mission of taboo-breaking and exposing the brutality of rationalized society at one and the same time is precisely in the banalisation of those images, and the absence of judgement. On that basis, listeners and readers should be wary of claims made by P-Orridge about presentation of 'extreme' imagery as critique. He says, for example, that 'Zyklon B Zombie' is about stupid glue-sniffing punks, taking it a step further (*Wreckers*, 8.16), but he also notes the strikingness of a description he encountered of queuing for the gas chambers, rather than telling us anything more about it, which we might have imagined 'useful' with regard to a song whose verses are flatly about Jewish girls on their way to die.

Throbbing Gristle's view is that the institutions that have held power have sought to control our thinking and behaviour, and that only a complete rejection of taboo can break through this. This does run the risk of titillation or shock without purpose, except that of drawing attention to the 'boldness' of the artist. Incredibly, art critics still use this line of attack (for example, with Jake and Dinos Chapman), which I am sure is, on many occasions, valid, but it is also a defence mechanism, one that helps the viewer/listener to not admit to being shocked. Much of the shock value would be more obvious in performance, where even (what is now) clichéd performance art can be effective because physical barriers are being crossed, in the presence of others, even if, in terms of originality, there is little going on. In any case, the audience is being made complicit with the sounds (and/or visuals or content), which is in itself uncomfortable, and more so for liberal and 'avant-garde' consumers, who imagine themselves always 'open' (it is a double discomfort: first from the 'trangressive' acts', second by the breakdown of liberal tolerance).

Beyond dubious lyrical and taped materials, the recordings try to disrupt the listener's expectations—they are often atrocious—both out of necessity and choice. The date of the first Throbbing Gristle album, 1977, is an era still in the grip of hi-fi dreams filtered through quadrophonic sound, where rock musicians over-dubbed endlessly to bring a crisp and rich sound universe where ears could live in peace (1980s tinniness would be even worse), and theirs was an album where you can rarely make out the lyrics, where all the musical elements are excessively overdriven or murky. They also mix live and recorded elements, and edit blatantly, audibly, messily.

The tracks 'United' and 'Zyklon B Zombie', originally a single, illustrate well what Throbbing Gristle knew soon—the need to move on—and this, they, like Cabaret Voltaire, Non, and slightly later groups such as Severed Heads, would do, and this is why industrial music is the first music to offer the possibility of all-engulfing noise, and is also capable of recognizing the fleetingness of noise. 'United' is melodic if incredibly simple, and seems a parodic attempt at community, or an attempt at community that would parody the society inhabited by the disciplined. 'Zyklon B Zombie' is also more or less tuneful, with a proper chorus, but very messy sound, the lyrics unclear, the tones of voice and music both getting lost, losing shape. Throbbing Gristle would continue to 'confound expectations', with constant changing of sound for each release, while maintaining the looseness of recording live and/or with bad machinery. They would happily use irritation as a method, trying to test the uninitiate and fan alike (*Wreckers*, 8.24). This means that the encounter with their music is always process (hence their wish to document and release so much live work), always a work undoing itself.

This is where Bataille's sense of transgression comes in. For many, it is an easy comparison to pitch Bataille against any old odd, provocative music that may have explicit lyrical and visual elements, and is designed to shock, or use shock as a key. At the most obvious level, the concerns of Throbbing Gristle are similar: both they and Bataille are interested in breaking out of rationality, to what seems like a truer, if more threatening state. It is a mistake, though, to extend this to a recommendation of actually breaking out of society altogether, or that even if this were possible, that it would signal a return to a less corrupt society, able to deal with death, eroticism, violence, the lack of meaning of the universe, etc. Both Throbbing Gristle and Bataille are only interested in their 'transgressive' material as a way in, a means to unlock a living beyond means, an inhabiting, however brief, of an emptied silent world where the subject individual is lost. This is only ever fleeting, as a shocking picture cannot shock forever, nor can it elude meaning (Bataille *was* endlessly fascinated by pictures of a Chinese man, apparently in ecstasy, having his limbs cut off, but it was his fascination with it that gradually became the subject matter of his analysis of the phenomenon).

For Bataille, sacrifice, eroticism, the irruption of death, and, albeit at a remove, experiencing extreme art, all worked through contagion (*Eroticism*, 113). This contagion is possible because our individualized being contains (is the containing of) a lost continuity with others, or even everything that is not 'I'. Performance art and 'extreme' music are attempts at something like a Bataillean sacrifice, where aesthetics becomes something more (actually something less, as it is about loss of meaning, control, and so on). Aesthetics carries the hope of a project, of making something happen with outcomes, however ambiguous these might be. It is quite different to use art not only to critique art but to elude art altogether, while remaining in the space and time art or music should be occurring (e.g. the concert, the exhibition), and the essential tool here is the breaking of, or, sometimes the mere raising of, taboo:

> 'We were interested in taboos', P-Orridge told [Jon] Savage, 'what the boundaries were, where sound became noise and where noise became music and where entertainment became pain, and where pain became entertainment. All the contradictions of culture'. (in *Wreckers*, 6.10)

Such a practice is not going to work if it is a constant transgression—this would mean transgression had become law—a suitably Crowleyesque phrase we can imagine certain industrial musicians being happy with, but the law here is the return to reason, the permanence of a state making it the norm, and therefore losing any charge, any disruption it may have offered. Transgression requires taboo, and cannot do away with it; it 'suspends a taboo without suppressing it' (Bataille, *Eroticism*, 36). 1980s industrial music, with its interest in power, seems to wish to make violence, domination, sex and brutal 'honesty' the norm. Throbbing Gristle, like Bataille, aim to keep the taboo hovering nearby; what is the point of transgression if we are comfortable with it (in which case it isn't transgression, it being relative)? For Bataille, transgression is only interesting in the presence of fear and anguish at the prospect of breaking the taboo (*Eroticism*, 38). This should not lead us to the conclusion that because twenty-first-century culture is so immured to violence, nothing can shock, and that therefore to try would be to stage an anachronistic art gesture. At a really simple level, there are always audiences that will be offended, and we should also be wary of imagining the world as a steady Hegelian progression through avant-gardes, each surpassing the last, as this implies perfect knowledge of that history on the part of everyone, and that if 'it's been done', it can never be done again. The Hegelian mistake is to canonize the avant-gardes of the past, valorizing them *as* past. Bataille is on to this when he criticizes those who praise de Sade. Bataille's love of de Sade is reliant on the sense that we should think that there is something wrong about it. Once it is normal philosophy and literature, it is over, or has been domesticated (*Eroticism*, 179).[5] Taboo heightens our experience just as much as transgression, but only once transgression is being played out:

> If we observe the taboo, if we submit to it, we are no longer conscious of it. But in the act of violating it, we feel the anguish of mind without which the taboo could not exist: that is the experience of sin. That experience leads to the completed transgression, the successful transgression which, in maintaining the prohibition, maintains it in order to benefit by it. (*Eroticism*, 38)

So successful transgression can only ever aspire to be 'successful'—it is caught in a loop of alternating failures—in its mundane failure in not disposing of the taboo, its alternative failure in getting rid of it and thereby becoming the norm, and above (beneath) all, its failure to even fail properly, as it negotiates between various ways it does not come to be. Transgression is always potential, or always already lost, but this does not stop Bataille, or Throbbing Gristle, acting as if it were possible, and those moments are the moments of noise much more than the literal noise of 'Walls of Sound' (Throbbing Gristle, *DOA*). What remains is something Bataille thinks of as a wound (see his *Inner Experience*) where you have the sense something has changed, that you were somewhere outside of everything, even if you were never really present for your not being there. This wound is the sense that something lies beyond rationalist, capitalist, murderous society, even though this something is almost nothing, and that therefore something is wrong with existing culture. This sense of wrongness becomes almost more important than changing it (or the belief you will change it), more corrosive, perhaps, in addition.[6]

Debris

Industrial society entails a renunciation of 'symbolic exchange', a relation to death, nature, sacrifice, birth, etc., and all that is beyond rationalized parameters. Symbolic change is not a real utopia, but one always gone, and always in thrall to violence, but a violence nonetheless that comes to stand as the other to capitalism (as Baudrillard argues, in *Symbolic Exchange and Death*). Late capitalism uses people as resources even though it largely could dispense with them, presenting them with the unanswerable 'gift' of living death through industry (*Symbolic Exchange and Death*, 39–41). Symbolic exchange is the kind of hyperbolic excess industrial music offers, at least at the outset, when it represented a noise as well as representing or presenting it in the art itself. In parodying industry without directly satirizing it, Throbbing Gristle is work away from productivity (ineptitude, non-musicality, bad recording, suspect content, which fails to even deliver itself as it is lost thanks to ineptitude, and so on), an excessive return of music commodities so that they cannot work as business.

Humans are superfluous to industry—either cheap substitutes for machines, or removed from the workforce—either way, harnessed or not, a 'man must die to become labour power' (*Symbolic Exchange and Death*, 39).[7] They are debris just as much as the deserted areas, 'terrains vagues' and empty quarters of modern cities, the abandoned machines. The end of labour has not brought freedom, only redundancy, and this being-as-debris is continually at stake in Throbbing Gristle, even in the name: 'Gristle, reject matter, unwanted, separated from good' (in Ford, *Wreckers*, 5.16) making it clear that the name is more than just a genital reference. Humans and objects built by humans would rot alike, the ripe meatiness of 'Hamburger Lady' (*DOA*) vying with the failings of tape machines, the inbuilt obsolescence of technology ('IBM', on *DOA*).

So industry has always created its own residue, and with obsolescence, programmed or not, machines and objects are discarded once enough surplus value has been extracted. The ultimate end of the industrial object is failure, its very force making it into waste-to-be, just as oxygen-breathing bodies are storing up their own death through growing numbers of free radicals. A paradox never fully addressed by the 'excessive' critiques of capitalist rationality offered by Bataille or Baudrillard is that capitalism is incredibly wasteful and destructive, even if missing the sense of the need for sacrifice, claiming that the usefulness or desirability of an object will never fade, despite awareness it will. Utility itself can come undone, in obsolescence, non-utilitarian or inappopriate usage, in decay, in function being surpassed by displays of functionality or technology. Duchamp's readymades—where an already constructed object would be turned from its purpose, and made into art—opens the way for industrial music's use of superfluous or deviated machinery and things.

Duchamp took everyday objects, whether a typewriter case or a urinal, and displaced them, by signing them, giving them a title and putting them on display. Duchamp's own statements on the point of this move are highly and purposefully contradictory, but clearly the readymade challenges the 'ordinariness' of the object and the artfulness of the artwork. Anything could in theory become a readymade. Similarly, any machinic sound outside of industrial music could be reheard as musical, as the Futurists had suggested. Beyond the conceptual input, little of traditional artistic *work* occurs (even in 'readymades aided', such as *LHOOQ*, a cheap reproduction of the *Mona Lisa*, with added facial hair), bypassing the question of acquired skill—the same as with the introduction of tapes, percussions and cheap, droning synths. Like Duchamp, and Warhol after him, industrial music's relation to a world where rational thought, and pre-existing categories of human activity, is not straightforward. For every critical element, there is also complicity, and this dual nature is a key component of 'early industrial music'. In the case of materials of industrial provenance, there are intimations of alienation—through machinery, away from music, away from organic sounds, but there is also joyous use of those materials. Percussion, for example, might use found metals, and offer little in the way of fixed rhythm, but can also re-create consistent pulsing reminiscent of industry itself. One way of conceiving this is to think of the materials being turned on themselves, the institutions and the society that made them (and in place of sadistic control of the workforce, the consensual masochism of repetition and intensity). Alternatively, the use of metals/debris/non-musicality could be read as a wallowing in alienation.

The materials are being removed from the restricted economy of usefulness—and put to other uses—what Denis Hollier terms the 'use-value of the impossible'.[8] These are uses which do not serve higher endpoints, but involve being consumed: in the case of already residual machines and objects, they are offered a semblance of purpose, but this purpose is a destruction of purpose, of goal-oriented action, and can involve literal destruction.[9] This appropriation is a form of taking control, but it is control of the residual, the inappropriate, the low or abject of technology. To an extent, this has been sanctioned in sound installations that, in general, consider that simply displacing an object or refocusing our attention is worthy of attention, but there will always be other residues (the real residue lurking in what seems beyond revaluing). Sound art takes its cue from Cage and Fluxus, but even Fluxus cannot match the oppositional stance of industrial music at its outset. For Cage, the use of the non-musical opened up an ideal world of sound, where the possibilities of musicality were endless. For Throbbing Gristle, it is limits and boundaries that provide initial impetus. Industrial music does not seek musicality but the effect of sounds in the space musicality is supposed to be conjured. These sounds will not improve your listening or your awareness of the world as soundworld, but try to address your listening's limits. The post-industrial objects that serve as instrumentation, even enhanced by effects or processing, draw attention to the undoing of musicality, the destruction of a harmonic oneness with the world. This is achieved simply: 'unpleasant' sounds, high volume, unexpected and harsh changes, jarring non-musicianship, poor sound quality, turning what might have been a rich sonic live experience into mush. Industrial music aims for Bataille's sense of continuity, of a community formed through initial distancing through violence, eroticism, breaking or staging of taboos. A sense of harmony is exposed as the true alienation.[10]

Bands such as Einstürzende Neubauten, SPK and Test Department reintroduce rhythm, albeit from non-standard percussion devices (recalling that percussion is an act, above and before being a collective noun for a set of instruments). The combination of machine debris and machinic percussion can first be seen as a replacing of the industrial component, as it becomes its own trace, overlaying its first meaning with a new usage that creates a second meaning, but this meaning is only of the first. It is not a reinterpretation, but a bringing out of what was already there, but not present. The combination also proposes a 'modern primitivism', as, like early twentieth-century art, industrial music and 'culture' circa 1980 saw a value in musics defined as primitive (whether non-Western, archaic, or by the insane). Early period Einstürzende Neubauten (and SPK) make music composed almost entirely of metal objects. These are not only hit, but scraped, scratched, broken, etc. Amplification, effects and playing in non-standard locations augment that sound. The rock band is reconfigured as it gathers around various metal objects, the instrumentation completed with power tools (SPK were very keen on these latter). Electronics represent the machine's creativity surpassing that of the human. The results are surprisingly musical, especially with many years' delay, but that does not mean it has become only a gesture, nor that we should just accept it as part of an expanded musicality, since part of its purpose is an improperly anarchistic democratization of revolt (in the case of Einstürzende Neubauten).

Machine

Electronics, tape collages and fragments, industrial, scientific and medical machines are a central part of early industrial music, and come to dominate as the music clumps into becoming a genre, in a return to the rhythmicality of Kraftwerk and Neu!, admittedly with a core or veneer of aggressivity. The machine is part of humanity's alienation, but, as noted above, this alienation is not lived as such by many industrial musicians. If anything, the alienation is a dwelling location, because it cannot be disposed of. An increased emphasis on pre-prepared machine sounds (and on found sounds and objects) is a clear rejection of the rock aesthetic as filtered through Romanticism, where the artist channels the world, subjectivity etc., through individualized creative genius. The terms of reference for this might have altered for punk, but not enough. Like Joy Division, industrial music cultivated a collectivist, anonymous aesthetic. Like Warhol, there was nothing necessarily wrong with becoming a machine.

Industrial music itself acts as a machine within which artist and audience are activated, in ways that claim to 'deprogramme' our cultural conditioning. As Burroughs had illustrated, the choice of form, a form that would deform itself and spread that deformation through contagion, could impact as much as content, when trying to reveal the hidden workings of modern society. Industrial music creates a rhizomatic structure of interlocked practices, where a machine of chaotic possibilities forms itself. But couldn't we say this of all, or at least many, musics? Feasibly, but what makes it of interest here, what makes it noise, is that it turns objects, ideas and power structures into music, while also not respecting the expectations of musical audiences, including that of the avant-garde of either music or art. For the first time, volume drives the sound (rock volume and feedback *convey* the music). Noise that is actually 'just' noise is introduced, with SPK's 'Emanatiön Machine R. Gie 1916' (on *Information Overload Unit*) being an important example. Unlike Throbbing Gristle, SPK want their noises recorded with precision, emphasizing the noisiness in a different way (as with early CDs 'capturing' faults like hiss and exaggerating them, or indeed the high mastering of Japanese noise musicians like Merzbow). As well as bursts of piercing noise and clusters of hissing noise, we get layers of machine pulsations. As the layers separate out, they do not so much complement each other as interfere with each other. SPK's first album is a machine that is not operating harmoniously, and in not doing so, works against machinery as an essential part of industrial mass society. A new perverse machine is made, complementing the interest in taboo and transgression.

Beyond the sometimes very literal relation industrial music has to modern machinery, there is the machinery of ritual: part of the machinic wish of industrial music is to free thinking through rhythm as well as arrhythmia (hence Psychic TV and the Psychick Warriors ov Gaia heading in the direction of trance music in the late 1980s, early 1990s, and 23 Skidoo also moving in the direction of funk). As well as the valorization of some sort of repressed primitive culture, there is the aspect of actual ritual. Esoteric knowledge represented something that had been hidden, shunned or banned by proper-thinking society, and anything outside norms provided material for industrial music. While many actually believe or believed in the worth of specific arcana being dealt with (Aleister Crowley, sacrifi-cal and/or sexual practices from outside modern society, alchemy, and so on), or the power of consensual violence in sex, or the thoughts and actions of serial kill-ers, these are also to be thought of as machines or technologies, just one enabling element in a comprehensive rethink of the world. It is their unpalatability that makes these ideas interesting and capable of conveying new patterns of thought and/or aesthetics (where aesthetics would lose its autonomy as a realm, without becoming a 'way of life', as what was on offer was to continue as disruptions).

The music itself could work as ritual, as on 23 Skidoo's *The Culling Is Coming*, Coil's *How to Destroy Angels*, the instrumental parts of Psychic TV's first album, notably *Themes*. The possibility of a non-ascetic, non-religious meditation was what was sought, not just for the participants, but also for audiences, whether live or listening to recordings. This music was even more of a machine than that which used oscillators and the like. Coil's piece, subtitled *Ritual Music for the Accumula-tion of Male Sexual Energy*, is clear about its having a purpose:

> The many varieties of religious music from around the world contain a vast quantity of clues to the way in which sound can affect the physical and mental state of the serious listener, yet many find their associations with the religion itself—the dogmatism of churches and the obvious shortsightedness of many cult leaders and their followers—too great a stigma to overlook in their appreciation of the sound and its potential, for its own sake. [. . .] On this record [. . .], we have tried to produce sound which has a real, practical and beneficial power in this modern Era. (*How to Destroy Angels*, sleeve notes)

The 'music in itself' to be retrieved is not at all a statement about the listenability or the aesthetic value of religious or other music, rather of its potential to affect the listener. Coil use percussion extensively on this record, and seem to be aiming for a primal music, and the other side, a continuous oscillation, might also work as a noise-induced meditative state. This meditation is not about improvement or enlightenment. Like Bataille's meditation in *Inner Experience*, transgression and eroticism take the individual out of isolation, but to no purpose. This is a goal that undoes itself, even as it substitutes a more powerful 'jouissance' instead of the goal-orientation of orgasm.

Industrial music makes noise explicit, acting as cultural noise at many levels, and making sure these layers collide in collage. Beyond the earnestness of much improv, art or 'classical' mobilization of the non-musical, or of noise, or of machines, industrial music combines content and form to challenge not only prevailing aesthetics, but the notion of aesthetics being its own domain, and also the notions of what is normal, rational, desirable or true in modern society. It echoes the anti-modernism of dada, of primitivism, of 'outsider' art, and does so in order not to leave existing society behind, not even to subvert it, but to pervert it, to encourage continual transgression and rebellion, in the form of interferences.

NOTES

1. Kopf, 'Introduction: Bacillus Culture', in Charles Neal (ed), *Tape Delay: Confessions from the Eighties Underground* (London: SAF, 1987), 10–15.
2. Many were interested in the use of frequencies that would disturb human bodies, taking sound away from the control of hearing, and also subliminal messages. They would soon realize this latter was very much less interesting than imagined (see Neal [ed.], *Tape Delay*, 120). Tipper Gore's Parents' Music Resource Center (PMRC) would imagine all kinds of messages hidden in rock music, often by being played backwards. This is a classic example of music being made noise through aggressive reaction to it. The defining moment of the absurdity of their approach was in a trial where Judas Priest were being held responsible for a suicide due to hidden messages in the song 'Better by You, Better Than Me'. Singer Rob Halford sung the lyrics in court, which were played backwards, and the case was thrown out.
3. Savage, 'Introduction', *Re:Search 6/7: Industrial Culture Handbook* (San Francisco: Re:Search, 1983) (eds V. Vale and Andrea Juno), 4–5.
4. Ford, *Wreckers of Civilization: The Story of COUM Transmissions and Throbbing Gristle* (London: Black Dog, 1999).
5. See also Bataille, 'The Use Value of D.A.F. de Sade', *Visions of Excess*, 105–15.
6. This might lead us to a more therapeutic view of a culture letting off steam. Bataille's idea of the 'accursed share', where excess must be squandered, and a sacrificial economy present or else greater disaster will follow, appears to be one such model, like that of Freud. Bataille, though, has excess as primary; everything that exists is a residue of excess.
7. The workers can be harnessed through Throbbing Gristle's 'Discipline', where the call to order is matched with mechanical, repetitive machine percussion. Like most of their work, it is quite possible that 'discipline', possibly in the context of eroticism, is a recommendation.
8. Hollier, 'The Use-Value of the Impossible', in Carolyn Bailey Gill (ed), *Bataille: Writing the Sacred*, 133–53.
9. In the early 1980s, Mark Pauline's 'Survival Research Laboratories' staged events where hybrid machines would fight, destroy, be destroyed, make explosions, and so on. These futile and strangely anachronistic performances look to a parallel universe of deviated technology, like the earlier experiments of Jean Tinguely, or the Watts towers. This has long since moved terrain into the Burning Man festivals and Robot Wars.
10. To be fair, industrial music's general isolationism is different to alienation or exposure of same. As Boyd Rice puts it, 'I never understood alienation. Alienation from what? You have to want to be part of something in order to feel alienated from it' (in *Industrial Culture Handbook*, 52).

8
POWER

From Throbbing Gristle to the industrial music of the late 1980s (Skinny Puppy, Ministry, Consolidated), power is an essential part of the content and/or 'message' of industrial music—the use of samples from politicians or religious fundamentalists supplying the key, within either jarring noise music or powerful rhythms overlaid with largely electronic instruments. Unlike subversive music of the 1960s and 1970s, industrial music is formally complicit with power—replicating some of its structures (e.g. aggression, control, propaganda). Its critiques then, while far from being nuanced, are ambiguous, often suspect or seemingly absent. Very often it could seem to be captivated by power. At its best, industrial music also deals with this complicity—both in terms of content, drawing the listener into complicity, and in terms of form, where the listener is either distracted from the violent content or made to submit to it. Beyond the structure of the musical pieces themselves, the overall practice is also a playing out of power, through challenging institutions, the listeners' moral expectations, and in concert, often establishing a threatening ambience. Many of the famous instances of performance art/noise/industrial music took place in the ICA, London, thus reducing the expectation of a standard concert or event at that location. It is of course possible to argue that initial and excessive shock is a distraction—presumably one reason that all industrial music backed away from this in the long run, or adapted it to annoy core 'transgressive' lovers of violence (e.g. Whitehouse's joyous rocking out, almost karaoke version of themselves on recent tours).[1]

Throbbing Gristle used imagery from the Second World War, including a lightning flash as their logo, and at some stages wore camouflage uniforms. Their use of what was forbidden, as material, often involved Nazism or other abusive, violent power relations, such as stories of serial killers. Genesis P-Orridge, however, persistently claims that Throbbing Gristle offered a critique of our fascination with violence, how we repress that fascination, and how the media play on it. As seen in the previous chapter, he singles out Whitehouse as a group that was and is simply exploiting 'extreme' material (see Industrial Culture Handbook, 12–13, for a general distancing from such in the content of TG's material). If industrial music is ambiguous about power, violence, extreme behaviour, exploitation, and so on, then we can also see that P-Orridge is disingenuous about this—there was no judgement on offer in Throbbing Gristle, but a set of subtle questionings disguised as violent and offensive valorizing of unacceptable imagery, movements and individuals. The strength was precisely in the uncertainty and the excitement that it generated (much more effective than the frisson some might get from 'transgressively' listening to groups that are oriented to the extreme right wing).

Industrial music is a Foucauldian take on power. In his Discipline and Punish (1975) and The History of Sexuality (1976),[2] Michel Foucault argued that modern western society is 'carceral'—a giant prison, where every structure and institution is there to tame and discipline us (the French title is Surveiller et punir—the visual control of surveillance is central). Power is internalized by individuals through endless micro-processes where the body is regulated, defined, identified as the means of controlling you. Many have taken this as a call to arms to bring down and challenge power, and Foucault occasionally suggests this, but as *History of Sexuality* emphasizes, it is not that easy, as the only imaginable paths to freedom are also caught up with power. Therefore, the 'sexual revolution' of the 1960s and 1970s was no such thing, but at most a new way of structuring power relations. Power relations can be worked on, and there are, briefly, the noises of 'counter-discourses' that resist dominant ideas and rules (even if these are then incorporated as renewals of norms). The implications for industrial music are significant: power is to be used, not wished away. Even a subversion of power must entail the resources of power—and not even an opposing one, but those of the dominant structures, hence the purpose of transgression—without taboo and belief in that taboo, there is no transgression. Powerful, mechanized and/or tribalistic drumming sought to reconfigure an audience's relation to what they were hearing—this would not be entertainment, ambience, sound track. Rhythm, volume, noises, harsh interferences and frequencies—all targetted the body as listening device so that the mind-body dualism the modern western listener has been disciplined into was undone, even—perhaps especially—if only momentarily. It is a given that the musicians in question believed that this was not something that could be suggested or offered politely—the work was too extreme to function except at maximum intensity (this applies equally to recordings, even if the listener is allowed considerable scope to refuse). This is neatly summarized by Test Department:

> There is death thrown into life. A deadness for those shackled to the familiar. A world lying cold and inactive, the movement of nature broken and over-whelmed, destroyed by blind faith in efficiency. People submerged by the commonplace, programmed by a technology whose language of command, analysis and control strangles the mind with a cold logic. Dislocated, the body greeds for the new, a release of power, the capacity for risk. From this need a huge sound emerges drowning everything, the redundant, the inflexible, the inevitable collapse, the old and the trivial are annihilated by a sheer and dia-bolical intensity. (sleeve notes, Test Department, *Beating the Retreat* [1982])

For Test Department, as for other mid-1980s industrial bands, this embrace of power was not defeatist, and only a misreading of Foucault could think he was either. Test Department engaged with actual politics, supporting the miners' strike, recording with the striking Welsh miner's choirs (*Shoulder to Shoulder*, 1985). They used Communist imagery in way that was provocative, but also pretty clearly symbolized their views. The difference beteween them and established Communist parties was that power could be harnessed at individual and micro-levels: 'all the power which stands against you is your potential power. You stand as the transformer, where power against weakness becomes power against power' (sleeve notes, *Beating the Retreat*).

The initial subversion proposed by industrial music is a total refusal of values and morally induced fear of phenomena and imagery. Ideology comes in, either as musicians clarify their perspective or as a specific tool for further confusion (Laibach). Many of the groups seem to favour right-wing thinking and events—to a large extent because this was taboo—note that it is not the valorization of anything indigenous, or of an authentic national working class, that is of interest. However, Boyd Rice, and, apparently at least, groups like Death in June and Der Blutharsch, have assumed views familiar from elitist if not race-based extreme right-wing thinking. Those who might imagine an easy collusion between right-wing ideas and aggressive performance that targets the audience should note that many of the overtly fascistic musicians moved away from experimental and/or industrial approaches, in favour of renovated folk music (precursor to the 'new folk' of the 2000s), true to actual fascism's mistrust of the new, and took an imagined heroic past as point of reference. Similarly, though, we could argue that the recuperation of fascism's own aesthetic preferences (rather than fascism as aesthetics) is also an interesting way of troubling preconceptions, in that statuary, European folk musics, epic architecture and events were all borrowed for industrial imagery from right-wing aesthetics while not being necessarily, and certainly not inherently, fascistic.[3]

Laibach are a particular case. What would briefly be known as 'electronic body music' did seem to be a fascistic mobilization of a newly ultra-disciplined body—whether in the politically neutral Nitzer Ebb or the overtly right-wing Front 242. Reductive, repetitive music combined with lyrical interests of earlier types of industrial music and, consciously or not, removed the gender trouble of Throbbing Gristle in favour of a muscled homo-eroticism. Laibach joined in with this style, creating pulverizing versions of major hits such as Opus' 'Life Is Life', Queen's 'One Vision' and the entirety of the Beatles' *Let It Be*. Often, they would declaim in German, exposing the previously unnoticed totalitarian moments of songs, with their demagogery there for all to hear. Such deconstruction extended beyond music, as they established the movement *Neue Slovenische Kunst*, an organization looking to restore Slovenia, and Slovenian culture (which has a substantial German component). Their use of fascist and Communist imagery and language, combined with a heroic agrarian aesthetic, made them seem to valorize a Volk-based 'renewal', but what they managed (and still do) to do was subvert the then still extant Communist regimes of Eastern Europe, liberals in the west, and presumably fascists, who would tire of their frivolity.

Other groups were or are more concerned with the practice and playing out of power between individuals, whether sexually, violently, abusively or in terms of other extreme behaviours. The logic is that this in some way represents a repressed and profound human reality. While there is not much happiness in, say, Whitehouse or the Swans, there is a great deal of black humour, for example in the very excess of the subject matter. So Whitehouse's obsession with sex is highly exaggerated, to the point of parody, in 'My Cock's on Fire', 'You Don't Have to Say Please' or in later albums like *Cruise*. Whitehouse represent a strand of industrial or noise music that has been called 'power electronics'. The terms covers a lot of noise music, but initially (c. 1980), it applies to music based on synths, electronic machinery, often with use of effects and samples, and connected to 'extreme' events, characters, obsessions. This can be done more or less suggestively, like Throbbing Gristle, or on Whitehouse's *Buchenwald* (1982). That album recalls the Nazi death camps, but largely without lyrical content. Instead, piercing electronics alternate with hums, oscillations and occasional screamed vocals. Is this aestheticizing mass murder (bearing in mind the many references they also make to serial killers)? Or is it something like the 'art after Auschwitz' Adorno thought nearly impossible? I think its noise lies in not telling us, but in trying to summon something of 'unspeakable' events. Musically, Whitehouse did not deviate much from the one sound palette until *Cruise*, where a more digitally constructed pulsing noise took over. Overall, the complexity and amount of text spoken or screamed has gone up, and the music acts as doubling of the text—i.e. performing in such a way as to physically create the effect the texts comment on. The music can variously be taken to be accompaniment, literalization, doubling, ambience, or in fact the central part, with the texts an attempt to match the physicality of the sounds (albums since 2001 see words battling with music, making the relation internally noisy).

Whitehouse raise the questions of misogyny and misanthropy perhaps more than anyone else, and are not particularly interested in justifying their purported outlook.[4] But the shocking elements are not necessarily where we expect them, so neither is the 'noise'. On *Quality Time* (1996), the strangest track is 'Baby', where splashing water mixes with laughter and other vocal sounds. It raises the spectre of child abuse (as the voice slows and goes from pleasure to pain) and recalls 'Incest 2' on *Buchenwald*, which also has bathing sounds (i.e. water being raised and let go). It could also be an 'adult baby' scenario, with the deeper, slower bits of the voice of the adult male, and the other, higher moments the vocal playing out of the fantasy. Or both possibilities together? Meanwhile 'Quality Time' insists on the female point of interest being a 'human toilet', and she ends, kneeling, eating a man's shit, as she is penetrated from behind (I think). The explicit degradation cannot be ignored, and William Bennett's vocals parallel the lyrical content, veering from commands, to wheedling to very high-pitched screaming, culminating in a screamed 'Quality Time!/Quality Time!', which seems to undermine the whole preceding tale, by making it seem ridiculous.[5] In this track, the synths brood and structure periods of silence where presumably initial reluctance is overcome, through the male's cajoling.

Is such an aesthetic oppressive? Looking away from the content of Whitehouse tracks, and even the harsh electronic 'soundscapes', there is still another level where power operates, and it is certainly totalitarian, in that it seeks to be a total experience that inflicts itself. The purpose of the approach varies: on the one hand, the volume and difficult sounds try to convey the affect suggested in the vocals; while on the other, the text of a track is part of an overall bringing of the listener into a shared abjection. There is power in the infliction of message and and sound—and it might well be that this, albeit not always in this form, is essential for noise to occur, to be brought to be. Between listener and performer there is a contract, akin to that outlined by Deleuze in his *Coldness and Cruelty*, on Leopold van Sacher-Masoch. The masochistic contract permits a temporary suspension of equality. Unlike the spurious contract of slavery (where a slave loses the capacity to contract through contracting), it is important to note the suspension of law, and its replacement by rules, guidelines, etc. Whitehouse seem a long way from the consenting sadomasochism/BDSM Deleuze proposes in his rethinking of the term 'masochism'. They praise sadistic inflicting of pain and humiliation. An early collaboration with Steven Stapleton, *The 150 Murderous Passions*, tries to bring out the closing section of de Sade's *120 Days of Sodom*, through electronics, Stapleton's graphics and a hint of the content of the book. These '150 passions' are extremely violent, and odd in that de Sade merely lists them, where generally he dwells lovingly on details. The album echoes this, a hint of perfunctoriness as we descend, conveying an inevitability of 'evil'. But it is not really sadistic. It might be Sadean, i.e. accepting of his philosophy and interests, but it is not really sadistic in practice, as not inflicted. Just as with de Sade, the listener/reader has put his- or herself in a position where 'infliction' will occur.

Whitehouse certainly aim to shock—like all avant-gardes, industrial and noise music expect to shock, and, just in case you weren't surprised, the content tries to be as offensive as possible. But it is also highly literary, a very self-aware 'shock-ingness', that quickly palls, at least as shock. Only after any outrage fades can listening happen. In terms of noise that raises a near-insurmountable problem—it has to keep the promise/threat of noise while suspending it, or even ignoring the possibility of noise in favour of message/signal. It also signals something important about the listener. As Bataille argued, in writing of the too-easy acceptance of de Sade as libertarian, a moralist and a political radical, de Sade receives an unwanted use-value, and loses the transgressiveness, and this is what needs to be maintained (see chapter 7). Similarly, is there much point to Whitehouse once we either accept or dismiss the content or get used to the form? Whitehouse did come to recognize the need to change, to at least temporarily shock or at least surprise, but the question doesn't go away. This failure to constantly shock is inevitable, rather than a fault, and Whitehouse continue to turn on themselves, and perceptions of their 'predelictions', constantly trying to get us *hearing* instead of securely listening, trying to break a masochistic contractual listening.

Superficially, Swans share the same concerns as Whitehouse, but despite titles like 'Raping a Slave' and details of abusive sexual and emotional situations, the content is not the same. Swans' music (in the early to mid-1980s) is a stripped-down brutalism. The lyrics are highly repetitive, simplistic anti-poetry. This gives a focus matched in the music. Where Whitehouse set up a spatialized experiential listening, Swans close off space in the repetition of riffs and unvarying percussion. Swans are interested in creating a visceral reaction. Michael Gira, mainstay of Swans, has no time for what was initially thought of as noise music—i.e. improvisation based on seemingly non-musical elements, saying that 'there are all these bands around New York, these noodling little artists who get together and improvise in some loft, invite their friends over, play Kazoos through pickups and beat up their guitars. That's a noise band' (in Neal [ed], *Tape Delay*, 145).

So Swans play at high volume to dispose of polite alertness. Away from the high volume of performance, this is achieved through the monotonous reiteration of violence musical and lyrical. The CD format has actually helped this go further, as where the record was divided up, or shorter, now there are full CDs' worth of insistence. Listening cannot settle into this particular repetition, unlike that of 'kraut-rock' or American minimalists (and I would include the ostensibly noisy, but actually only loud, Glenn Branca in this), as it is too simple. Where minimalism and rock repetition imply variation, Swans' reiterations are made mindless, coming close to machinic. What prevents this attaining a Kraftwerk-style purity is the dissonance achieved in even the oddly sparse arrangements. On recordings, this is abetted by abrupt editing, illustrating the arbitrariness of ending, as opposed to offering closure, either in glory or failure.

If Einstürzende Neubauten renconfigure the shape of a rock band or performance, Swans replicate it as lifeless, or as being killed. *Cop/Young God* (1984) or *Greed/Holy Money* (1985–6) suck the masculine vigour out of rock, excising the energy in slow, repetitive blocs where each moment reappears fractally as the bloc that is a song, then album. Any complexity there is being undone, as in the opening of 'Time Is Money (Bastard)', where rapid-fire electronic percussion gives way to relentless rhythm that drudges the listener through tedium and into a catatonic non-listening. Like Throbbing Gristle, but made much more explicit as subject matter, the key interest of Swans is power through physicality. For them, we are ruthlessly embodied, our entire thinking driven by it. While institutions have been able to exploit this, it seems a timeless and inevitable condition of humanity. This is played out through the relentless and lengthy non-exploration of almost static if violent music, and endless returning to the abject body, one rarely personified or 'subjectivized'. This is why it is important not to mitigate what seems to be (a mundanely) excessive dwelling on exploitation and harm, nor to vary the sound to 'shock' people. Here the 'problem' for the listener is what Agamben terms the normalization of the 'state of exception', where the exercise of sovereign (in his sense arbitrary and total) power is no longer occasional or transgressive, but made into a new law.

Noise is akin to the masochistic contract, but is it still forcing desire and pleasure into a situation where power dominates? Noise cannot want—it can put you into an unwanted liberation, force you to be free, somewhere between Rousseau and Sade. Noise might be the opening up of desire, or the erotic, but it has to suspend it—no release, just a sudden end when it does stop. Noise brings you to your body, your body without organs, perhaps, but also a body made ear. When noise occurs, listening gives way to hearing, giving way in turn to the loss of hearing—not literally, but in the sense of losing the ability to distinguish sounds, to keep sounds as a merely auditory input. The volume and the harshness of the sounds bring your body to be, in noise, even in the loss of awareness. In the case of the Swans or Hijokaidan, this would be in the unrelenting mass of sound. In the case of Merzbow, Masonna or Violent Onsen Geisha, harsh changes do not allow you to settle, however submissively.

Is noise fascistic? Noise cannot carry content, so not overtly. Many have misunderstood noise and industrial music's interest in extremes, and presumed that the use of certain imagery might imply advocacy of Nazism, for example, or violence, in general. Beyond the level of presumed content, though, there is still the question of noise itself being in some way fascistic (formally, or, alternatively, in its relation to the listener). Historically, we can point to the Futurists' love of the sounds of war as indicating fascist potential, but in practice the extreme right is not at all interested in noise. It seeks loudness, rather than noise, and the restriction of sounds into a monitored code: i.e. in the form of state-sponsored, pseudo-traditional music, clear transmission of 'the message' when in power, more ambiguous when 'subversive'. Noise is the outsider to be expelled. In this, as in most other areas, fascism is merely the extension of rationalized liberal society.

But if noise evokes anything, it is often not that far from phenomena that fascism, or totalitarianism in general, might praise: the non-rational, some form of sacred, giving yourself over into something beyond the individual, attaining some more authentic, lost sense of either body or mind, the notion of submitting, the control on the part of the noise producer, the power of a spectacle that is physically oppressive. Bataille had the same problem: in looking at phenomena outside the capitalist worldview, his theory seemed to tend toward fascism. His answer is relatively simple, and transferable to noise: fascism is part of what he calls the 'heterogeneous', but is specifically about the control of that realm.[6] It is ultra-profane rather than sacred. The sacred, here as noise, is at a different exit point from the rational, liberal, capitalist world, and the loss of that world's restrictions stays loss. Noise and other recent experimental musics run a risk in ambiguity: there is no judgement of good or bad—in the music or performances themselves. The imposition of high volume, for example, is masochistic, contractual (as Deleuze would say in *Coldness and Cruelty*),[7] whereas music in commercial city centre areas is not—so noise, even if it will not offer a 'positive' stance, can invoke resistance, can be it.

The noise of consumer society has to be jammed somehow—wearing a Walkman, listening to a noise music CD would not be enough—this individualizes revolt into a neatly controllable form. Listening to noise which confuses you, or prevents you from operating correctly in the city, would give you a radically broken perspective. Noise is always on the side of more—even if not always (or ever) good or bad noise. Noise is not just volume, but the spread, dissemination and dispersal of its non-message. Samizdat, CD-Rs, graffiti, shareware—all act as forms of noise in spreading themselves parasitically. A few years ago, there was a sense that this could lead to a form of future rebellion through hacking, but that has been surpassed by the Net's will to noise, which is self-creating, auto-reproductive, auto-destructive. Within noise, we might detect another proliferation: Deleuze and Guattari name it 'microproliferation', and this can lead to the destruction of sound from within itself (*A Thousand Plateaus*, 296), taking silence, music and noise with it.

Noise can be about confrontation, and this confrontation can, say, in the case of punk or hip-hop, mean that noise (often imposed negatively as a critique of that music) can become a means to ends: without descending to the level of music as message, some (few, in fact) have managed to combine ideas in words and ideas in sound, while remaining noise. For this to work, the message must be limited, self-reflective and only function in the confrontational encounter with the noise. Whitehouse, especially in recent albums, have merged the physical with the mental/psychological: the words and harsh sound *need* each other, *depend* on each other, risk being lost in each other. This dependence and mutual loss of identity occurs between performer and audience in all noise. The prime purpose of confrontation is confrontation itself. Those who are there when noise is occurring do not lose themselves in some sort of happy bonding, but are driven inward, too far, and therefore lose ready access to this inside. In its place, through what was initially staged as confrontation, there is now an immanent group, where we are neither individuals nor a community (except in the Bataillean sense of one based on the moments of sacrifice).

Does exclusion imply a catalyst for rebellion, through the creation of such a community? Noise is on the side of revolt rather than revolution (not that this can be said of all experimental music), as revolution implies a new order, and noise cannot be a message-bearer (other than of itself as message). A politics requires consciousness and agency, not present in noise itself. The use of noise, however, would not be in the way of politics. We could imagine a politically engaged use of noise, where the noise had purpose—and this could be minimal (creating a group, community and so on, as in Hakim Bey's notion of the temporary autonomous zone), or maximal (using noise to highlight issues or problems). Noise itself could serve a didactic end, and 'change the way we think' or perceive things. Any of these would disqualify the event or sounds from being noise as such, as the noise would now be drawn back into the realm of the useful, the realm of clearly assigned values, only with noise now as positive value. The values or the binary opposition would have been revalued, in a simple reversal, rather than being trans-valued. To counter this, or in the full knowledge of this, noise and noise music are not purist, and therefore cannot complain about being adulterated, without also losing their status as noise. Occupying this paradoxical space is what noise is (not) about. Then, noise has structured the space as a process, and we have something like Deleuze and Guattari's 'smooth space', a vague location full of intensities and noises (*A Thousand Plateaus*, 479), defined by what occurs in them, and then as them (482). Attali advocates 'composing' (see *Noise*, 133–48), which is a form of 'active listening' and participation. We can challenge power through 'conquest of the right to make noise, in other words, to create one's own code and work' (*Noise*, 132).[8] Ironically, it is the success of the 'music business' that could lead to its downfall, as 'no longer having to say anything in a specific language is a necessary condition for slavery, but also of the emergence of cultural subversion' (122).

While noise cannot remain message and still be noise, musicians can create other kinds of noise, such as the moral panic that seeks to disqualify NWA or Body Count on grounds of being a danger to society, or in terms of hip-hop not using much of music's canon of activities (instruments, 'tuneful' singing, original music). Groups can *mobilize* noise or the way they are defined negatively as social or musical noise. When noise catches on, it will no longer be any sort of avant-garde: uniquely, perhaps, if it were to become a movement or inspire one, it would already be failing. On the other hand, the artists are trying for something; there is an attempt at communication—an excessive one, even. Maybe noise will fail more prosaically, and always be marginal (which would allow 'noise practitioners' to be perceived as an unrecuperable force). Success, would, in any case signal the end of noise—and when assessing those who would challenge power in order to be redefined as not-noise (i.e. marginalized social groups), it must be borne in mind that they will often be trying to end noise, just as Cage sought to bring noises into organized sound.

Public Enemy encapsulate hip-hop's attack on power, in moving on from a moralistic critique of black oppression and exclusion that prevailed in the 1960s and 1970s, and on to an ultra-rationalistic attack. This is formed at the lyrical level by what principal lyricist Chuck D imagined as despatches from hidden black urban America, and at the musical level by samples, musical and otherwise, scratching, beats (often from the first two), all maintained intensely. It is not just in the explicitness and anger of the lyrics that this music differs from 'protest' music, but in its construction—the rhythm (at the forefront of tracks) and speed of it would create a different physical response and engagement, moving on from jazz, rap and funk, even while referring to them, often by incorporating samples (see Mark Dery, 'Public Enemy: Confrontation', 412).[9] According to Dery,

> Public Enemy's backing tracks are every bit as political as its lyrics. Part morality play, part *musique concrète*, part blueprint for the building of a mind-blowing bomb, the band's music is a noisy collage of sputtering Uzis, wailing sirens, fragments of radio and TV commentary about the band itself, and key phrases lifted from speeches by famous black leaders, all riding on rhythms

articulated by constantly changing drum voices. ('Public Enemy: Confrontation', 408)

Public Enemy's approach is not dramatically different from that of industrial music, although of course we can point to the different situatedness of black hip-hop artists compared with industrialists, but we should not determine outcomes and effects from that context. Power will be exposed by a competing display of power—adoption of uniforms, display of weaponry adding to the music (the evolution of gangsta rap will turn this rhetorical use into actual events, but centred on rival factions rather than targeting the police as, say, NWA would have suggested). Institutional power will be exposed lyrically, and the responses of dispossessed black America suggested likewise. The videoclip will add to this. 'Black Steel in the Hour of Chaos', from *It Takes a Nation of Millions to Hold Us Back* highlights conscription, the 'over-representation' of black men in U.S. prisons—and the narrator, innocent except for being a 'militant/Posing a threat, you bet it's fuckin' up the government', leads a breakout, killing a guard along the way. The video was widely perceived as advocating violence on law enforcement personnel (David L. Shabazz, *Public Enemy Number One*, 72, 86).[10]

Like the Burroughs-inspired experiments of industrial music, Public Enemy try to reveal the machinations of power and discrimination in a technologically reflexive way—i.e. how it is told is important; how it is framed is part of 'the message': 'our music is filled with bites, bits of information from the real world, a real world that's rarely exposed' (Chuck D, quoted in Dery, 'Public Enemy: Confrontation', 415). The exposure is only possible through a radically empirical component (sirens, chases, shots, speech fragments, etc.) and the abstracted, heightened 'realism' that would create proximity to the listeners, particularly a young black audience (e.g. the rap declamation of the state of excluded blacks, pounding rhythms suggesting the urban environment): 'from the beginning, [producer Hank] Shocklee and Chuck D conceived of Public Enemy as "a musician's nightmare". "We took whatever was annoying, threw it into a pot, and that's how we came out with this group", Shocklee recalls. "We believed that music is nothing but organized noise"' (Dery, 'Public Enemy: Confrontation', 418). This 'pot' is how the samples, lyrical approaches, volume, add to an evocation of the urban as well as a call to action. Without the 'pot', it is just a politics lecture.[11]

Public Enemy's use of volume does differ from industrial methods. While shows do play with the spectacle of power in a similar way, the recordings feed into car-dominated urban areas, where stereos get bigger and louder, and above all, bassier. The music is literally mobilized (see Chuck D on this, in 'Public Enemy: Confrontation', 413) and becomes noise for those even in the car, who now hear throughout their cyborg car-bodies, as opposed to via their ears alone. For others, the booming bass car is simply noise pollution. This noise undermines the physical integrity of the area it crosses, particularly if suburb or exurb, a perfect interference, compared with the oppressive power in inflicting music over long periods, which might be an interesting social intervention, but is not noise. It is organized, homogeneous aggression, akin to state displays of power (or, of course, its use of persistent music to annoy its enemies [Waco siege, Iraq]).

The materials that go into the music are themselves noisy—heterogeneous, often untuned, or, alternatively, 'borrowed', in the case of samples, and sometimes this would be heightened in the studio, contributing to the above-mentioned 'pot' ('Public Enemy: Confrontation', 411), but Public Enemy will always stop short of interrupting the message fatally. Chuck D notes, for example, that although fast rhythms are essential to Public Enemy, there is a limit to rapping speed, because it is important for the lyrics to be understood (414). Much of the actual noise 'of' Public Enemy rests in reactions to them, just as with NWA, whose provocative use of the word 'nigga', in name and title of their second album, their aggression toward the police, their acknowledgement of the violent life lived by many blacks in America were all perceived as advocacy of violence. (Tricia Rose argues that black rappers are kept marginalized, kept as threat, even after having commercial success [*Black Noise*, 184].)

Two techniques, far from unique to Public Enemy, although less widely accepted in the late 1980s than since, constitute noise in musical terms, or, more precisely, to what is deemed to 'properly' musical. These are, of course, sampling and DJing. Both are non-musical in that they do not involve a musical instrument and are not 'creating out of nothing' as is imagined on guitar or piano. So, as Susan McClary notes, 'the romantic search for authenticity is thus frustrated in advance by this music that foregrounds its own fundamental mediation' (*Conventional Wisdom*, 160).[12] Sampling is the Duchampian recognition that art can be made out of existing objects, and that once you do this, the status of art objects alters in turn (e.g. in this case, we stop imagining that playing the guitar involves a pure interaction of skill with musical creativity, and instead see a set of conventions playing out across a machine with finite [if huge] possibilities, further structured by tonalities and playing strategies). Sampling allows referencing as well as selecting elements to structure the new work. In Public Enemy's case, this includes references to black culture, to black protest, as well as samples highlighting oppression. The sample is noise in two, almost opposed, ways: if presented as is, its empiricism is radically non-musical; if altered or 'manipulated' (a slightly unpleasant term that to me seems to relegitimize practices under the aegis of skill), then their reality, presumably the purpose for including them, is disposed of. The musical sample seems to suggest lack of creativity, but is a rejection of isolated 'genius' musicians in favour of an intertextual music world. Even though the grafting of one track onto another, whether mainstream R&B or 'mash-up', is not of great interest in its own right, it carries its small noise in the unexpected encounter of often very different musical genres, and the listener's first moment of encounter. The sample is also legal noise, with copyright issues to the forefront in a corporatized music business. Over the years, the music industry worked out protocols of recognition, royalties, and so on, though John Oswald's whole career of 'plunderphonics' and Dangermouse's *Gray Album* have still managed to annoy copyright holders. The scratching of and use of beats from records is an extension of making music up from samples (in fact with the DJing coming first in the cases of Jamaican dancehall and late 1970s rap). The group format is radically altered, as now the machinery consists of record decks, mixers, drum machines and other samplers. The rest is essentially vocals. Hip-hop emphasizes the focus on the vocalists, but in the case of Public Enemy, the music is not just background—and this stresses the noise of replacing musicians with DJs—in a way, records are generally allowed to be background, even if we 'should' have instruments, but foregrounding them through 'bad'/inappropriate playing of records, and turning this into the musical element is not 'proper' music.[13]

Industrial music and hip-hop both address power, and do so via various noise strategies, principally in the mimicking and perversion of institutional power being exposed, criticized, and so on. Incorporation of noises, or playing at volume, is not enough to signify noise (actually, that is precisely what it does, *signifies* rather than being noise).[14] As with all noise, it turns into style, to paraphrase George Melly, and the evocations of power become clichéd. Industrial music is the exemplification of noise's relation to power, which is that it is other to power, but cannot overturn it. Hip-hop's mobilization of noise sets up a resistance, that if it works, the noise dissipates, but a more activist engagement can result. Lyrically, 1990s rap does go to extremes, and offensiveness, more or less purposely, but formally, an extreme simplification is increasingly the way rap is in opposition to musicality, which heightens the lyrical or vocal part. Commercially successful rap, gangsta or not, in its assertions of power, and a powerfully recentred subjectivity, fits neatly into corporate power, in a way that 1980s rap and hip-hop did not really envisage. Meanwhile, industrial music got closer to rock musics, which in the form of hardcore or grunge, had incorporated noisiness (volume, lo-fi, feedback, samples, and so on) without ever really bringing the interference of noise. As noted above, this allows others to assert their authenticity due to not being appropriated, or listened to as entertainment (one target of this thinking, Trent Reznor, addressed this in Nine Inch Nails' *Broken*). These incorporations should not be seen as a bad failure, but as the inevitability of noise in failing. That groups like Swans moved on from their early aesthetic to a psychologically and musically more varied approach is not a maturation or a stepping back, and neither is it any less interesting or challenging for not being noise in the way it attempted to be in the mid-1980s. The same can be said of hip-hop's move away from the confrontations of Public Enemy or of the Wu-Tang Clan's referencing of global popular culture. But the moment where noise directly addressed power was literally fleeting. With the noise music of Japan, power is not dismissed as such, or escaped, but exceeded.

NOTES

1. 'Industrial music' did not uniformly follow this path. Groups like Nurse with Wound and The New Blockaders would continue to push the limits of *musique concrète* and take it in ever noisier directions. We could imagine such highly influential 'bands' informing a more organic and teleological history with ease, as they lead into later types of explicit 'noise music'. Alternatively, they could be the noise to the current historicizing and theorizing of noise, a hidden spine, perhaps. Or maybe the lymphatic system within its arbitrary body.

2. Foucault, *Discipline and Punish* (London: Penguin, 1991) and *History of Sexuality*, vol. I (Harmondsworth: Penguin, 1978).

3. Giant stadia, concert halls, transport systems etc., might be fascistic but they do not belong to fascist regimes alone. Furthermore, as Bataille argues, all architecture disciplines and ultimately limits humanity ('Architecture' in Neil Leach [ed], *Rethinking Architecture* [London and New York: Routledge, 1997], 21).

4. See www.susanlawly.com

5. Bennett's voice has a major role in Whitehouse, as the initially maniacal or murderous voice comes apart in screaming. At one level, this signifies the arrival of protagonist and listener as some sort of culmination of abjection or 'shitfun', but it is not a voice of power—its variability suggests frailty and the high pitch a denial of masculinity and control. This is not a

voice that can carry a message—instead it is carried by the text and sound. Pete Best's voice offers a contrast, with its ranting, wheedling, spitting—this has become part of the rhythm of Whitehouse's sound since *Cruise*, as lengthy tales of exploitation accompany the pulsing electronics.

6. See 'The Psychological Structure of Fascism', *Visions of Excess*, 137–60.

7. Gilles Deleuze, 'Coldness and Cruelty', in *Masochism* (New York: Zone, 1991), 9–138.

8. Attali also refers favourably to pirate recordings, and to illegal radio stations (131). These certainly challenge the production system, but are they really outside consumerist consumption of goods?

9. Mark Dery, 'Public Enemy: Confrontation', in Murray Forman and Mark Anthony Neal (eds), *That's the Joint: The Hip-Hop Studies Reader* (New York and London: Routledge, 2004), 407–20.

10. David L. Shabazz, *Public Enemy Number One: A View Inside the World of Hip-Hop* (Clinton, SC: Awesome Records, 1999). The book contains a lengthy over-empiricist study of audience reactions to this video and that of 'Get the Fuck Outta Dodge', looking for gender and race differences (72–105).

11. Tricia Rose notes the connection forged by this complexity, as one of 'the tension between postmodern ruptures and the continuities of oppression' (*Black Noise: Rap Music and Black Culture in Contemporary America* [Middletown, CT: Wesleyan University Press, 1994]), 115.

12. Susan McClary, *Conventional Wisdom: The Content of Musical Form* (Berkeley and Los Angeles: University of California Press, 2000).

13. Recently, DJs playing sets of records have tried to move away from the organicist 'flow' achieved by mixing and matching tracks, and highlighting the sound of records being played (as was done in samples in both industrial music and hip-hop)—Miss Kitten, for example.

14. For subversive signifying, where the dispossessed, notably those from the African enforced diaspora, express their contextualized subjectivity in 'signifyin', and in doing so, begin a resistance to it, see Henry Louis Gates, *The Signifying Monkey: A Theory of Afro-American Literary Criticism* (New York: Oxford University Press, 1988).

9
JAPAN

In many ways it only makes sense to talk of noise music since the advent of the various types of noise produced in Japanese music, and in terms of quantity this is really to do with the 1990s onward. There is music we could identify as noise from as early as 1970, such as Masayuki Takayanagi's post–free jazz *Mass Projection*, Les Rallizes Desnudes in the 1970s. Many of the now reasonably well known performers such as Keiji Haino, Merzbow, Hijokaidan, Incapacitants and Masonna were active in the 1980s, but because what we have here is not a statement of purity and origins, I think we should prioritize by quantity, reception and, to some degree, self-perception by artists, at least to begin with. For me, a story of noise music that is not obsessed with 'being the first' as marker of achievement in its own right must construct a story where temporality is confused, merging with receptions, and how later constructions view or incorporate 'precursors' as precursors. Whichever way we approach noise in Japanese noise music, and allowing for latent chronologizing (i.e. not ignoring that we at least perceive time and influence in art to work in one direction), something new comes to 'noise', comes to 'experimental' music. There is, if you like, more noise in Japanese noise music, whether in terms of volume, distortion, non-musicality, non-musical elements, music against music and meaning.

Japanese noise music is a loose, pleasingly futile and facile genre, grouping together musicians with enormously varying styles (many of them varying immensely in their own recordings and performance, such as Keiji Haino or Otomo Yoshihide). With the vast growth of Japanese noise, finally, noise music becomes a genre—a genre that is not one, to paraphrase Luce Irigaray. In other words, it is not a genre, but it is also a genre that is multiple, and characterized by this very multiplicity. This means that as a genre, it is neither arbitrary or quasi-colonialist, nor do we gain much definition from it. Japanese noise music can come in all styles, referring to all other genres, like science fiction does, but crucially, asks the *question* of genre—what does it mean to be categorized, categorizable, definable? This is what ties it together as a genre.

But what exactly is Japanese about it? It can be taken as a resistance to conformity, a sort of extreme and messy combination of 1960s ideas and the more aggressive outlook of late 1970s and early 1980s music. Is it a misunderstanding of what these 'foreign' musics mean to a western listener? To some extent, yes, but cross-reception, continual creative misunderstanding across cultures, is another possible key to Japanese noise music itself.[1] Is it a reference to traditional musical forms? Largely it is more interested in western forms, while dismantling forms in general, but we could see the freedom it at least seems to offer as a reaction to the hierarchical apprentice-style learning of traditional musics, high and low, and close restriction of who would be qualified to play. Some do refer to traditional music, but not exclusively (Keiji Haino, Chie Mukai). Mason Jones rejects any such connection: 'Most Japanese bands that I know personally don't think there's much connection at all between their music and traditional Japanese culture' (*Japanese Independent Music*, 52). Do the musicians refer to Japanese philosophy, or is a zen aesthetic played out in ways that address modern subjectivities? It can certainly very often be read that way, but I think we have to tinge it with the sense that it is more like a Bataillean meditation, where instead of the subjects losing themselves into a greater nothing, they are dragged into low formlessness.[2] And in so doing, we can also raise the issue of sadomasochism, which is of vital importance in contemporary Japanese aesthetics. As well as inspiration in the form of eroticism, practiced and/or for viewing, it ties us into the physicality of Japanese noise, where, as in the masochist contract, we agree to submit, but not to what we submit (or at least not fully knowing the content of it). Japanese rope bondage stands as a figure for a certain listening: bound for aesthetics, the tied person feels more embodied than ever, in a Bataillean erotics that denies completion, control, orgasm (as the endpoint, purpose, and so on). If Japanese noise is zen, it is also rope bondage.[3]

This chapter will not so much deal with the specificity of noise music from Japan, but with how it is something that goes against specificity. Many of the musicians make a claim for the strong presence of a messy and complex hybridity in Japanese music, and I will examine how this differs from a knowing hybridization resulting from a conscious choice to mix genres or cultures into a new, and newly assimilable identity. That 'Japanese noise' exists peculiarly, and through external and negative descriptions (i.e. it is not x, or, it is y but more so), is what makes it constelled noise rather than a unity. This is different to being a set number of different recognizable musics making a fusion designed to appeal to the audiences of the music so weakly hybridized (for western audiences, southern African 'township jive' was a breakthrough example of this in the mid-1980s, combining the authenticity of African music and of European rock 'n' roll). For these reasons, I begin with a consideration of McLuhan on globalization, to raise the question of what kind of 'world' is in or behind world music. From there, the specifics of Japanese noise music's refusal of tidy indigeneousness or neat combinations of genres will emerge. Japanese noise music separates from a cosy genealogy with 'noise in music'—instead of noise as music or vice-versa, it is close to a genuine noise music, existing *as if it were noise, as if it were music*. It does this not only for the above-mentioned reasons, but because in many cases, it is noise 'all the way down'—form resisted as pieces develop, noises unresolved into composition (except as listened to, if on repeated listening), music continually thwarted. This does not sound like much of an appealing prospect, even when compared with the potentially cathartic variants of industrial music, but if there is not pleasure as such, there is something in its place. For some, this could be a sense of triumph at their 'extreme' listening capacity, a sense of mastery—but this runs counter to noise, as it is a return to centredness (this time of the listener, if not the player) and dominance. Such mastering is something that Japanese noise tries to undermine as much as possible. That the listener acquires an experience of listening to harsh noise music such that he or she can understand it, or be tired by it, is as much the listener's problem as that of the musician. Noise music is the living-on in this loss, and as they are to some extent in a Cagean world where listening is as creative an act as producing, noise musicians play out this loss, to extremes. Instead of recognition and relief, we are drawn into uncertainty and, very often, sensual assault. Something like pleasure can emerge, but the question of pleasure is kept alive, kept away from completion (the *jouissance* referred to by Barthes, Kristeva and their generation of literary criticism).

So Japanese noise is unspecific, either in genre or culturally, and yet, it has acquired the status of genre. It has done this not only in the context of its reception and/or locatability in avant-garde trajectories, but because it occurs in the context of a technologized and late-capitalist globalization. The Internet has increased access to marginal musics, whether in terms of information, contacts for touring, or commercially. The globalized backdrop, though, is commercial and dominated by American, or at least English-language culture. Noise music (and others that the market would identify as 'niche') offers an alternative globalization, its other. As opposed to resisting it, through nationalist, traditionalist, or authenticist claims about cultural production, Japanese noise music's messiness and particular type of hybridization make it a carrier of, if not a virus in, globalization, then an unwanted symbiote.

World

Marshall McLuhan has claimed that our world 'is a brand-new world of allatonce-ness. "Time" has ceased, "space" has vanished. We are now living in a *global village* . . . a simultaneous happening. We are back in acoustic space' (*Medium Is the Massage*, 63).[4] His theorization of the contemporary world (as seen from the 1960s) is based on the primacy of human media—whether communications, travel or war media. Few can dispute that the world is a 'global village' today, but as well as globalization, we have to consider the village aspect. We are not in a global city, but a dwelling of proximity, of community and shared dominant values, with close monitoring of both those and deviant values, or critiques of value. All of this being, as Baudrillard has long noted, a simulation, a hyperreality. The global village is a hyperlocality, where we are to feel connected, where to be online, or communicat-ing in general, is increasingly a social obligation, and interaction is a necessary good. For Baudrillard, this means we are becoming terminals, and the problem is not our passivity, but that we are exhorted to participate.[5]

It is not immediately clear why we are back in acoustic space, when what seems to characterize the contemporary is the proliferation of images. The reason is that we are leaving a rationalized seeing—leaving writing behind. Before and after writing is the acoustic ('until writing was invented, man lived in acoustic space: boundless, directionless, horizonless' [*Medium Is the Massage*, 48]). The total visualization of culture frees the image from its grounding in representational meaning. Or, conceived slightly differently, total textualization leads to the disap-pearance of text (this is what Baudrillard had to say about Foucault's notion of power in *Forget Foucault*).[6] Our eye actually becomes ear (McLuhan, *Medium Is the Massage*, 121) as we can no longer close it—images surround us acoustically. The organs of sight lose their identity, and vision loses its privileged link to reason (uprightness, controlled, focusing viewing, the dialectic between sight and thought): 'where a visual space is an organized continuum of a uniformed, con-nected kind, the ear world is a world of simultaneous relationships' (*Medium Is the Massage*, 111). At a very literal level, visual media have developed to the point of emphasizing sound quality and ultra-realistic ambience (surround sound). Where stereo mimics our sensory apparatus, surround sound mimics the unstoppable, directionless, sound world. At another equally literal level, music is a medium of globalization and vice-versa. The image is only effective to a certain point, and its perfection needs extraneous enhancement. At the same time, 'perfected' music disappears—the CD does not visually reveal the texture of a recording the same way vinyl does, and with digital forms, music is a pure medium of itself. We have gone from instruments and performers to transcriptions, and then to dispersal into binary code with, ultimately, no visual element.[7]

Jean-Luc Nancy writes of a 'becoming-music of sensibility, and a becoming-global of musicality' (*À l'écoute*, 29).[8] Globalization has been uncannily echoed in the growth of world music, understandably, if Bruno Nettl is at all right in claiming 'music is one of the few universal phenomena' (*Theory and Method of Ethnomusicology*, 3). Even more obvious, though, might be the spread of a globalized, homogenized music, which is generally English-language rock or pop. World music, and the study of it, seeks to resist this homogenization, to the point of contesting itself as a term, as being potentially reductive. World music is the attempt to spread 'indigenous' musics, musics that would authentically represent particular cultures. Although it is utterly compromised in market thinking, it also supports the specific musics it reifies, bringing them to new audiences and perhaps enhancing their status 'at home'. These audiences can, in turn, come to question their cultural presumptions about what music necessarily entails. World music, and its academic relative, ethnomusicology, look to the other both to know the other, and to re-assess music as universal, while rethinking the place of western art music. There are clear orientalist problems here, but ethnomusicology, like postcolonial theory after it, is there in some measure to address that problem. But ethnomusicology still performs a subtle form of reductionism the same as that of the world music labels.

In the case of world music, the culture-specific sounds spread and infiltrate each other, and usually combine with western elements, so world music comes to exist, confirming that the simulation is not a bad copy, but an extravagant reality with no real grounding. Ethnomusicology is more self-aware than this. Philip Bohlman is able to write that 'world music (and by implication, ethnomusicology) is very much a construct of modernity, which is to say the encounter with and interpretation of the world that was unleashed by the Age of Discovery, the Enlightenment, colonial expansion and the rise of the nation-state' (*World Music*, vi).[9] It is nonetheless caught up in a sanitized exoticism that still praises 'diversity' in itself, and of course sees diversity both everywhere and everywhere *else*: from the same book, we hear that the 'abundance of world music today offers the opportunity to experience the diversity of human societies like never before' (ii)—thereby enhancing 'our' capacity to assimilate and learn from the other (sometimes this other is internal, in the form of folk music). We can learn not only about music and cultures, but understand the notion of experience itself (Bohlman wants his reader 'to engage more directly with world music as *experience*' [vii]), presumably enhancing 'our' identity through the other.

This cosy humanism insists on diversity as a value in no need of further exploration, and modifies Derrida's notion of *différance* into a homespun, patronizing judgement, refusing alterity in favour of a recognizable, proximate form (to praise difference is to control it as a judged otherness). To think the difference between difference and alterity is to pit Lévi-Strauss' positive view of culture being an accumulation of beneficial encounters against Baudrillard's insistence on alterity and turning the domesticated and/or familiar into the threatening.[10] In the case of Japanese noise music, these alternate and undermine each other and the ferocity of 'unlistenable' music infiltrates the assimilation and more amenable domestication of foreign musics.

Japan has a history of hybrid forms of music, and despite rigid distinctions between high art styles and performers, reinforced by the education system, it was only when western music was encouraged in the late nineteenth century that a term evolved to describe properly Japanese music (*nihon ongaku*).[11] Terence Lancashire argues that "'world music" in Japan cannot be seen as a contemporary phenomenon', but dates from that time' ('World Music or Japanese', 23).[12] The usual issues in listening to world music are altered in the case of Japan, even if, like most 'world music', the presence of its music in the world is always pre-emptive of the western economical term of world music. Its music cannot be reduced to a clear national style, representing a traditional, hitherto culturally or politically oppressed society, and authenticity is not a resistant virtue.

Even so, ethnomusicology ascribes an identity, however hybridized, and a contextual determinism that insists on 'Japan's opening up to the West'.[13] Hugh de Ferranti praises the culturally specific hybridity of recent(ish) Japanese pop music, which '[does] not conform to the essentializing expectation that popular music of a given culture must sound ethnically grounded in some clearly recognizable way' ('"Japanese" music can be popular', 205). In such an outlook, a new authentic quality or capacity replaces the presumptions of an earlier liberalism. But de Ferranti is not wrong—the music does nothing more, formally, than what he wants it to—it can often be an easily identifiable collaboration of components from different cultures. For Lévi-Strauss, each culture is inevitably such a collaboration, but following McLuhan, these cultures are not identifiable discrete hybrids (i.e. this culture is a hybrid of a and b, this other one of c and d), as there is nowhere to either be a 'pure' culture of a voluntary hybrid (except perhaps with musicians as consumers, buying into 'local colour', 'ethnic feels' etc.). Hybridity has globalized, and is not enough by itself to demonstrate radicality, whether formal or political. Hybridity in noise music is a dimming of differences, making a new alterity, a new strangeness, rather than matching familiar items in an 'unfamiliar' way. Its hybridity is incidental, if inevitable. Does a popularizer of strange new Japanese music such as John Zorn fall into the same trap as the ethnomusicologist? After all, he has a dedicated set of releases entitled 'New Japan', as if we were to learn something about the country from what we hear. Zorn is a key figure in the reception of Japanese noise, but is an odd kind of participant-observer, in that he has joined in, encouraged and been influenced by music that is only messily Japanese in a cultural sense. His own music, which has included collaborations with, for example, Yamatsuka Eye, most known for the Boredoms, is always veering between genres, often in the space of a few seconds (as in Painkiller, or Naked City, *Torture Garden*). If he and others are some sort of neo-anthropologists, or exoticists, they are ethnographers of a future culture, and in the meantime, engage in neither the ethno- nor the -graphy.

Noise music does not oppose hybridities, but offers a weak or minor hybridity (as in Deleuze's idea of 'minor literature') with no control, no imposition of will (as these would create a new identity from 'successful' hybridization), while also being a self-conscious operation. It is consciously hybridizing, but does not take its sources as discrete, secure identities in the first place, and the process continues rather than closing once negotiated. Noise is a hypergenre (one that is an active simulation), and, as I have asserted elsewhere, the 'development of a cross-genre, cross-category, ultra-amplified and often ultra-processed music is something specific (in its breadth and range at least) to Japan' (Hegarty, 'Noise Threshold', 194).[14] Emerging as a bastard genre of free jazz, progressive rock, contemporary classical, Japanese traditional musics (sometimes), and later on, hardcores of both punk and digital forms, it coalesces through musical objects that are formally noisy, as a crucial part of noise is that it keeps altering (white noise is not noise, in this sense).

The 'noise' musicians undermine the ethnomusicologist—Kawabata Makoto: 'we experienced rock, jazz, blues, contemporary composition, ethnic music—in fact, every variety of interesting music—as pure information, and so we felt no need to learn about the history or social background behind these styles of music' (*Japanese Independent Music*, 48).[15] Yuko Nexus 6 adds that 'Japanese music has its own peculiar characteristics because of a misunderstanding of foreign messages' (52–3). Uchihashi Kazuhisa emphasizes Japan's lack of tradition: 'it is because we have no traditional, strong music roots. That's why we can go anywhere' (58).

Noise loses itself in its transmission, just as music disappears as noise accumulates over time (it being an organization of sound in time). Unlike music, though, it resists narrative. It is not a pure object, though: in listening, in being produced, noise asks for meaning, and, as Attali says, 'despite the death it contains, noise carries order within itself; it carries new information' (*Noise*, 33). Attali's point is that the avant-garde or the marginal is initially noise, but can become the new norm. At the same time, it operates outside of power relations, as it brings the world as other, and other to itself. It does this in itself, but also how it relates to a globalized muzak regime.

Ethnomusicology and world music tend to seek to preserve musics as distinct cultural expressions (what Alan P. Merriam termed the 'White Knight Concept', quoted in Joseph Kerman, *Musicology*, 159),[16] just as ecologists seek to preserve endangered species. Here is Bohlman, for example, writing of UNESCO's world music collection: 'classical and traditional musics are emphasized and many endangered examples are preserved' (*World Music*, 34). Noise music follows Baudrillard's dictum that 'we must not reconcile ourselves with nature' (*Illusion of the End*, 82).[17] Japanese noise rejects its environment and eludes the musical naturalists, eager to learn, to save, preserve, and position *outside* the globalized world. Noise works across globalization, neither in nor out, and exists in a marginal form of the world economy.

Noise moves Japanese music beyond a hybridity of discrete forms becoming new discrete forms to an absence of form, or more accurately, what Bataille termed formless/informe, where the absence of form plays across form (so a Merzbow track is still a track, with title and duration). Noise is, as if it were music, and as if it were noise. It offers a model of unpredictable interculturality, one that challenges the notion of intercultural exchange between two readily identified participants with agency, or the enforced relation of colonizer and colonized, in order to not be, not be itself, not be other, let alone the 'same' of a tradition.

Material

It is not just its cultural or historical position that makes Japanese noise music other to world music, or to other globalizing forms like pop. What we encounter is a relation to the world that is played out formally (*not* represented). Japanese noise relates the world both as world and undoing of world, and it does this through its materiality. At the most basic level, this is in the choice of materials: metals, objects, electronics, samples, playback devices used for sound making (or in the case of Nobukazu Takemura, absence of playback devices, with the 'no-input' system of making a mixing desk set up noise circuits), distortions, feedbacks, effects used not for effect but as action (i.e. not as ornament). These materials have of course featured in many of the styles of music or categories of noise mentioned in earlier chapters, but it is the combination of so many of these that sets Japanese noise usage apart, at least at its peak in the mid-1990s, since when the techniques and approach have spread. Even more important is that these sound sources are specifically maintained as residual. Where mid-century *musique concrète* brought the residual into organization, or where Cage sought to signal the potential musicality in everything, in music made by Merzbow, MSBR, K2, CCCC, for example, the residual is continually returned to its uselessness, to its place beyond pleasurable desirability in appropriation. In industrial music of the late 1970s and early 1980s, the noises, the residues, the purposeful incompetence *signify*. In 1990s Japanese noise music (one part of it at least), the residual is brought into form (a performance or recording of a certain duration, made up of components which however unusual or unpleasant have to a large extent been patterned by the performer and/or listener). However, this is a form that undoes itself, that acts as form, while in fact offering something else where form is supposed to be. Arguably, it attains something of the essence of music, as, like repetition, it reveals that music is a structuring of time, and that this appears in or through the perception of the listener. The disruptiveness of this 'form' or formless, as Bataille would have it, through volume, unpredictability and relentless change, makes a settling or dwelling difficult. This ecstatic non-music continually structures and destructures both the listening subject and music, or, in another theoretical register, it deterritorializes and reterritorializes them. It is the movement and alternation between that makes it noise. Pure deterritorialization is an end to noise, a new locatedness, but as de- and re-territorialization play out as listener and performer alike find and lose structures, find and lose repetitions and recurrence, *this* is the noise of the territory undoing.

Music offers a world, and inhabitability. Noise offers something more like dark matter which may be what allows a structure for everything else to exist (i.e. music, meaning, language, and so on, emerge from and against noise), but also the living on of that other material that is excluded as, or, for being, noise, and, beyond that, the continual limit of expansion of matter (or meaning/music). Noise is not a turning away from the world into an imagined pre-linguistic self, but it does recall, like Derrida's *Of Grammatology*, that language/music/meaning dwell in the sense of both always having existed and having been brought into being. They therefore own an origin, while at the same time, the absence of that original coming-to-mean must always be hidden, excluded. Instead of being primordial sound, noise is that which comes to have been primordial. This is why it is important that the musicians that veer toward 'pure noise' mobilize the residual, rather than primary sounds (to remind us, the Big Bang is not the first sound, the beginning of all sound, but only ever the residue of a sound never to be found, and this only to be heard in hindsight as something that has always already been, and gone).

Adorno questioned whether untreated material could count as music. While little Japanese noise is untreated, it aims to be material that is unmusicalized. Adorno argues that 'the work of art without content, the epitome of a mere sensuous presence, would be nothing more than a slice of empirical reality. [. . .] The unmediated identity of content and appearance would annul the idea of art' (*Sound Figures*, 197). Maybe it is not music, but it is what occurs in its place in the case of many Japanese noise musicians, for whom material is to be restored to material (not just left as material). Noise music does treat sound, even if only in the framing, but it returns it to noise. Koji Asano's *Quoted Landscape* seems to be only the sound of a microphone dragged over land, but even this is structured by choice of area, conditions there, the length of a CD, and the properties of a microphone. But these very properties are what create the piece, as the microphone is 'too close' to its source and loses a proper signal, as the microphone becomes not only a bad recorder but a percussive intervention in its own right. So at one level, we could just ignore Adorno's comment, but Japanese noise certainly presents itself as a letting play of material, often through relinquishing control of machinery or recording situations. It wants to be the kind of empiricism that *musique concrète* tries to remove. Unlike a large amount of sound art which considers a peculiar sound source to connote interestingness—the empirical 'in its own terms'—noise music does not buy into this fallacy of the object world, observed sympathetically by the sound artist. Noise music is intervention to keep material material (or make it back into this, now, again, for the first time) rather than idealized, organized musicality. It is interested in material being stuff, not a source.

Against idealist materialism, that talks of 'the real world', or conceptualizes it in any way, Bataille's concept of 'low materialism' is about the matter that still gets left out: 'base matter is external and foreign to ideal human aspirations, and it refuses to allow itself to be reduced to the great ontological machines resulting from these aspirations' ('Base Materialism and Gnosticism', 51).[18] According to Bataille, modern art (or some of it) is capable of being 'the expression of an intransigent materialism' (51), so importantly, 'material' is not idealized as outside, but that which can come to be as matter when presented as that which cannot be represented. Bois and Krauss suggest that part of this shift occurs in the rejection of verticality, of the primacy of looking at images on walls, which insists on humanity's upright, logical, ostensibly visually-dominated reason (*Formless*, 93–103). But I think we can go further than that, and ask whether sound offers something lower than vision. At the physical level, we have less option when hearing than when seeing—but this goes beyond the point about not having a natural cover for the ears. We 'hear' through the body as well—hence the possibility of torturing and killing people through low frequency sounds. Sound can disturb more directly than things seen, and hence noise featuring as a problem—noise brings *us* into the realm of the animal, of the material—we are things that hear.[19]

K2 (Kimihide Kusafuka) produces a residue-based noise that differs subtly from MSBR and Merzbow. These latter produce layers, masses, strata of noise which have sounds piled on top of each other, but merge so the verticality of layers becomes a horizontality of noise. K2's noise compromises linearity differently. The 'instrumentation' is metals, electronics, processed voice on occasion, and bursts of coloured noise, and he keeps this potentially unlimited range of sounds from the ironic fate of seeming limited through cuts. The album *Molekular Terrorism* cuts relentlessly between bursts of percussion, noises and so on to create a structural percussiveness, hinting at a rhythm that might be there, but the more this is sought the more noisy the tracks become as they resist. The cutting is the narrative, or, more accurately, the refusal of narrative in the place it is supposed to be. A difficult recurrence replaces repetition and/or reference, one that recalls Nietzsche's eternal return, where it is each moment that is returned to, and only ever for the first time. On *Metal Dysplasia*, part 2, both music and noise are replaced by micromusics of noise—broken into tiny elements, while spread over 23.33 minutes. Part 1 suggests discernable shape through regular noise bursts, but in the context of his overall practice, these have to be seen as punctuation, as the moments the pieces are made not to fit. If such pieces are noise, are they actually music in any meaningful way? Have they taken disjointedness to the point where they cannot claim to form or even deform time and listening? This of course is the question that is 'noise music', and I would claim that this playing out of the question is what brings it near enough to music to have something to do with it without being it. Both albums mentioned here might recall the strategies of Pierre Boulez, where music is disassembled into areas, floating zones of notes, or even plateaux of experience, but the difference is the virtuosity required for Boulez, and for listeners, who are also called on to be virtuous, to learn before and during the listening. K2 plays out the limits of music in a low process of unlearning.

Such playing of material, as material, would only be content, even if displaced, if it did not transpose into the actual material production—and this at the most blatant level, which is the use of a variety of formats, releases on small labels, in small runs, and the use of analogue formats such as vinyl. The CD (and downloaded formats even more so) reveals too much of a noise album—the track times in their own right (which is played with as a parody of structure by the musicians) but more importantly in the imposition of temporal location, which helps situate the listener. Vinyl is literally noisier than digital formats (although new noise has been introduced in the shape of low grade formats like mp3 and most current variants, such as music for mobile phones, ringtones, etc.). For a time, in the 1990s, vinyl was commercial noise as music companies tried to dispose of it in favour of the significantly cheaper to produce CD. Many Japanese noise musicians have released many vinyl records (and also brought out home-produced cassettes).

Beyond this, artists such as Merzbow and MSBR have tried to emphasize the objectness of the recording purchased (this even in CD format).[20] Works are made as ludicrously limited editions, often with handmade or at least very detailed packaging (Aube's vinyl releases). There is extensive use of coloured vinyl, and often bits and pieces (pictures, notes, etc.) tumbling out, like the DIY artwork of punk and post-punk, or releases on, say, Constellation Records. All of these emphasize the materiality, the objectness of the item—the exact opposite of a commodity, which tries to ascend to value, to gain a worth that becomes an essential part of the thing-made-commodity. While it is clear that this is a parody of the capitalist music business, there is still the symbolic capital for the 'collector', who possesses rare items which are hard to find and which acquire the status of art objects, and, over time, many of these become financially valuable.[21]

One MSBR object (the single 'Electrovegetarianism') raises many of the above questions about commodification and plays them out. The single comes in a seven-inch pizza box, with title and band name stencilled on. In most people's case, it was probably delivered to their door, like mine was, just like a pizza. This kind of a box is cheap, disposable, maybe recyclable. It not only suggests lazy consumerism, but also is rubbish-to-be—a disposable container. I think that in the case of this object, a continuum is formed with the record, which is a slurry of heavily flanged noise pulses, with searing tones coming in on occasion. The green vinyl record, far from being carefully housed in an anti-static sleeve, is supposed to be placed on a springy spindle, and fixed to it with washers, the whole to be connected to a seven-inch wood block (these all come in the box), immobilizing it as sound producing object. It is now mobile as green circular object, as you can tip an edge and watch it bounce for a while. Is this the fate of the record—i.e. to have a second existence after being played (mirroring the use of records as clocks), or is the purpose to be thwarted from the start? Is there a correct use? Should we follow what is deemed to be correct anyway?[22] The lowly materialized object has its ghostly exchange value taken away in becoming more objectlike, its transcendance of the plastic lost, even if played, as the sound emitted is just one thing about this set of objects. This is not an anti-commodity though; it is an ultra-commodity, an ultra-fetish.

Volume

Away from the power electronics and junk materials (not entirely though), another strand of Japanese noise is essentially rock-oriented, or at least occurs as if it were rock, while dramatically questioning the format. Groups like Zeni Geva, Boredoms and Acid Mothers Temple have even broken in to the 'mainstream' of 'alternative' rock. Fushitsusha, Ruins, High Rise and Musica Transonic have also had a subtle but noticeable impact on both faster types of rock and the doom/stoner side in the first decade of this century. But ironically, many noise musicians beyond these re-developing genres see themselves as carrying on the project of rock, jazz or both (MSBR, Masayoshi Urabe), with many citing King Crimson (Merzbow, MSBR, Acid Mothers Temple) and Black Sabbath as key references (very rarely does punk feed into Japanese noise, even if certain types of hardcore do filter in). Much of what the 'rock' noise bands do can be matched with developments elsewhere in the late 1980s and early 1990s, but rather than match up bands, or spend a chapter insisting that the Japanese equivalent of an American band always went further, I would argue that the key element that works through the Japanese noise take on rock is volume—and this not just in terms of level of sound. As well as this, all of the musicians mentioned here have combined what would normally be many discrete western genres and often played each of those to or beyond its limit. Rock has long had time for excess, but a different kind of excess can be heard at work in Japanese noise, much of which would seem to recall Spinal Tap's boast about their amps going to 11. It goes without saying that all the above Japanese groups play at extreme volume. What counts is that it occurs in small spaces, and that it is too much for the space. Two major strategies evolve at this high volume: first, repetition, and the sense of an ending being impossible; second, disruption, so that ears cannot settle at a new norm (however loud that might be). Unlike the volume of a rock or metal gig (although like new variants such as Sunn O)))), this is not volume as signifier (of power) or carrier of the music (as privileged passenger, like many imagine Descartes' mind to be in relation to his body). The volume is integral—the sound continually overdriven, to the point where the rock element thwarts and, better still, exhausts itself. Feedback is not mastered, and neither are overtones from electronics. There is often skill at work, but it at least seems to defeat virtuosity (although we might except Keiji Haino here).

The volume structures the listening space, and engages bodily hearing. Paul Collett argues that Japanese noise musicians 'share a common concern with space. This ranges from the extremes of the annulment of space via sonic density to the creation of new aural spaces from a combination of existing sounds' ('Spacious Paradise', 25).[23] The volume collapses back into the music, as more detail/information/meaning is lost due to levels being too high (although sometimes, as in the mid 1990s Merzbow, the mastering is higher than nearly all other CDs, providing an excess of detail as noise of the noises therein), so this playing with volume as space occurs within the sound as well. Fushitsusha present an exemplary version of these combinations on *Pathétique*. Like Acid Mothers Temple, rock is first (or last?) undermined by the expected time boundaries being ignored. Track 4 on *Pathétique* is in the 'rock idiom', but is 44.12 long. The volume is such that the individual instruments mulch together—not completely, but making it hard to pick out the variations. The first twelve minutes or so take on repetition, turning it into a suspension of time that is more violent than that typical of 'krautrock'. One riff is circled around, and the drums are almost static in their punctuation. As it moves on, we hear continual, unresolved finales (see also Boredoms, *Vision Creation Newsun*, and especially track 1, for more of this, and any one of many Acid Mothers Temple tracks). The second half is more expansive, and between 34 and 39 minutes, there is a more or less tuneful roll around some doleful powerchords, but, even then, payback is withheld. The track closes with a minute and a half of clatters, highlighting the fact that the listener has been stuck in a parodic rock finale for an excessive stretch of time up to now, and the piece ends with a few seconds of speaker hum. The track drags rock out, pulling it in many of its already implied directions. Its excess is in length, in what it does with rock moves (and there are no solos that emerge from the 'failing' recording, where the mass of band sound melds a further communality to that already there from group improvisation), and the volume is too much of itself, along the way worrying at the 'perfection' of the CD.[24] A similar effect occurs in Boredoms' music, abetted by electronics and cut-editing. Their audio 'space' is configured within the multiple drummers on *Vision Creation Newsun* (and some of their subsequent recordings), such that stereo expectation and/or naturalism are prevented. The spatial imagining that would save this (they're all literally between drummers, and recorded from the centre, or, alternatively, from behind drums sets, etc.) is disrupted by the editing, and the alterations in speed within the track.

Noise performance is not a self-contained style, but has to be consumed in relation to other approaches—so some groups may well build on the energetic rock performance where individuals are playing instruments—but even with groups as straightforward as Acid Mothers Temple, eventually as the pieces unwind over 20 or more minutes, the identifiable source of individual sounds dries up. The performance of noise is always collective, shunning the individual, who would be a carrier of meaning and of subjectivity. Incapacitants, CCCC and Hijokaidan play within rock settings (as opposed to art galleries and events, although increasingly, noise music finds a potential outlet in that sphere), and the volume becomes an extension of punk, rock, or industrial musics. But the performance of Incapacitants is minimal—two people with electronics on tables—a style familiar to any who attend 'experimental' music events, often accompanied by rummaging, fiddling and adjusting objects, devices, etc., all of which non-spectacle has been heightened by the advent of the laptop.[25] Incapacitants set up an immense quantity of noise as foreground, and then other sounds emerge, but overall, the noise music is left to come out—it does not have to be further signified by accepted sign-posts of the performed (i.e. identifying provenance of sounds, indicating narrative and skill). Instead of subject controlling object (instrument) through their own motive power, it is as if noise musicians are assembling something that has already started to make itself.

Ultimately, what characterizes even the rock end of Japanese noise is that it cannot be held separate from 'pure noise' power electronics or where sound is fedback to the point where a rock aesthetic cannot even briefly emerge. While Keiji Haino's guitar is usually more or less recognizable as such, KK Null and the later Masayuki Takayanagi often lose the guitar sound entirely. KK Null's *Ultimate Material II* processes the guitar through effects, and like Robert Fripp, the consummate skill is denied through a removal of it as identifiable evidence. To disguise the guitar is to de-phallicize it, and the playing of it (which may not always be a good thing, as it hints at an idealized sound, away from physical production). The guitar in this situation is no longer an expression of virility (discrete power riffs, sequences of quickly played notes in a solo as the individual male stands in front of the pack, moving the guitar as if an extension of the body). Masayuki Takaya-nagi, on *Action Direct*, for example, sits the guitar on a table, instantly detumescing the machine, and according it other possibilities: now it can be a conduit for sounds other than played through human (often male) fingers, part of an electrical circuit (which of course restores the material object to what it is, just as flatness in paint-ing brings us back to painting).[26]

Somewhere beyond even these is Hijokaidan's *Romance* album, which lures us in with its Cluster/ECM style cover. If Ground Zero and Fushitsusha stretch the rock format to breaking, and then keep going (feasibly reinvigorating rock rather than dismantling it), then this album is the red shift of the universe expanding. All hope is removed, all possibility of resolution gone, as narrative is slowly and stonily buried in wailing guitar, over its 77-minute duration. This does raise the prospect of a masculine listening, of phallic consumption, once the performing rock phallus has been denied (but it is consumption, not control). This would take the form of the toughness of what you listen to magically giving you some sort of reflected strength. I don't doubt that quite a bit of noise listening is done like this, but I would claim it still involves a degree of subjection, of handing over control, and, possibly, assertions of 'that was the harshest album I've ever heard'—which I apply to this one—are a defence mechanism, a way of reasserting ownership precisely where it is most inaccessible or unavailable.

Body

Noise affects and alters the body's relation to its surrounding, and also how our thinking relates to the environment we are in. However theoretically dismissed 'Cartesianism' is (mind-body dualism), this is not the day-to-day functioning assumption, particularly for those placed in a context where aesthetic experience occurs. Noise disrupts rational mental control—of course this is not to be taken fully literally, especially as most people buy into noise knowing to some extent what they are getting, and presumably extracting some kind of desired experience from it. However, noise does block thought, blocks attempts to structure meaning and coherence. It is a coalescence that never arrives (thereby keeping our interest, suggesting resolution, purpose, etc.). To counter this, we disobey the imagined purpose of noise music (to be as loud as possible), and turn recordings down to a manageable level. As noise music is nearly all noise, 'noise all the way down', it still resists. To think about Hijokaidan's *Romance* entailed turning it down to a level where I could exert some control. Its duration, though, pre-empts escape. Some noise music, even Merzbow, but especially Aube, can be very soothing, the wide frequency coverage offering undemanding stimulation for non-listening. *Romance* is not—the entire piece consists of competing fedback guitar and microphone (the main sounds), but the level of feedback makes the question of source largely irrelevant. These sounds sometimes merge within a vat of gradually accumulated white noise, mostly arguing, but not quite at each other. Howls occur frequently enough to stop immersion, and not regularly enough that you can fix on that. Nothing seems to offer any narrative. This is music about resignation and its impossibility, and is seemingly without any logic, other than to exist. It removes the listener's resources, forcing imagination, but making itself an obstacle to imagining away from the persistence of the sounds. The piece does not really end or begin—just fades in and out, as if a glimpse of another world, immanent, dense, breathless and infinite. Listening is replaced by hearing, for both performers and listeners—unlike the standard concert performance, deafening noise music is not inflicted from above, but from within, in a relation, an aesthetic version of Foucauldian power at work.

All those present at a noise event, or recorded version, to some extent, are embodied by noise—noise is the equivalent of Foucault's power: 'power must be understood in the first instance as the multiplicity of force relations immanent in the sphere in which they operate and which constitute their own organization; as the process which, through ceaseless struggles and confrontations, transforms, strengthens, or reverses them' (*History of Sexuality*, vol. I, 92). As Baudrillard notes, though, if power is everywhere, constructing everything, it is also a containment of reversibility of power itself—i.e. power itself can be undone in exchanges with 'itself':

> Power is *in its form reversible*, because on one side and the other something holds out against the unilateral exercise and the infinite expansion of power, just as elsewhere against the infinite expansion of production. This resistance is not a 'desire'; it is what causes power to come undone in exact proportion to its logical and irreversible extension. (*Forget Foucault*, 42)

Noise, especially in the case of Japanese noise music, is the play of power against itself, within itself, and the subject made in that process is a dissipating one. This music is neither complicit with 'power structures', nor against them. It is a *staging* of power, as a form of symbolic exchange Baudrillard sees as gone, writing 'there was a time when power allowed itself to be sacrificed according to the rules of this symbolic game from which it cannot escape. A time when power possessed the ephemeral and mortal quality of what had to be sacrificed' (54). I think this needs to be fed back into the *staging of power* and the earlier point drawn from Foucault.

As a noise subject is created, it is also undone (subjectivity as a coming undone of subjectivity), and is replaced by something closer to 'bare life', where existing is the sole purpose of existing.[27] However, performers do have to be patient, do have to exercise some control, however much the decision might be to lose control of equipment, and they do control the duration, however long the performance. Furthermore, volume has to be controlled so that people are not actually deafened—anyone in search of that would be finding the easy way out from any more noise. This is just another way in which noise can never be enough, while always seeming to be too much, along with the questions of familiarity and connoisseurship.[28]

While we would be tempted to attribute more noise to a live setting, many noise performers eschew performance, sometimes in the guise of 'letting the sound be', but also as a rejection of performance convention, where the skilled, trained musician is to be the centre of attention, as they control the space they have made. Japanese noise musicians might not avoid intervening in the noise they make, but, outside of the more rockist noise groups, they try to act as if not intervening—hence the lack of movement. Henritzi notes, 'Sachiko M and her near immobility on stage' ('Extreme Contemporary', 36), and also that Japanese noise musicians (especially those concentrating on a more electronic sound) tend to try to disappear behind machines and/or installations (36). One way to think this would be to claim that such stage inactivity implies a belief in the superiority of the sound produced to the material, and to the fleshly. Alternatively, the stasis can be imagined as a recognition of the limits of performers signifying the sound they are playing (through their visible actions), and a wish to establish a shared body, something like a noise body, perhaps, that is jointly structured (and challenged) by noise. It is another part of the discipline noise listening demands—to the point of being guilty of asceticism, of punishment and pain as new goals, new outcomes to be aimed for. Again, disappointment will be inevitable here, as noise will always fail, as noise at least. It can never realize itself, because any success means it has failed. Any outcome signals the end of noise. Also, literally, as noise ends, the noises we have structured into meaningfulness (i.e. all or most sounds encountered outside of noise performance and listening) return. The disruption is only ever temporary, fleeting, lost from the moment it begins.

The more electronic end of noise is home to more static 'performers', as subtle movements and adjustments are the mechanism, particularly where quiet is involved. Use of sine waves and other electronic tones can make just as much audio impact on listeners, as relentless notes and sounds are literally sustained by the listener. Clicks, hums, whirs add to the manipulation of electronic waves, in the work of Ryoji Ikeda, So Takahashi, Sachiko M, among many others. This approach (sometimes referred to as *onkyo*) is noise as brutal reduction—a judgement that would simply appreciate such sounds would miss the fact that much is happening on the fringes of the listening. It is also important that a human head is doing the listening: even fixed tones vary with movement, and Ryoji Ikeda gives one of the more purposeful uses of this on *matrix* (CD 2), which was initially a sound installation. He specifies on the sleeve notes that 'matrix (for rooms) forms an invisible

146 • noise/music

pattern which fills the listening space. The listener's movement transforms the phenomenon into his ± her intrapersonal music'. True, of course, but it is also true of all music. What is going on here is a purification of listening, which is maybe too didactic. Sitting totally still creates a more interesting effect, as further overtones are produced—as the movement of parts of the ear become 'manifest', the listener is hearing the process of listening. We have been given instructions as to how to listen, and the question of discipline comes up again. The listener at an electronic event, or any other where quietness is an essential component not just for reception, but also for production of sound, must stay still, maybe moving their head. While *matrix* lays claim to being an interactive physical experience of sound, the 'live' listener to quiet noise must become disembodied, except for the hearing and seeing parts. But this is still a play of embodiment, as the listener becomes aware of their body—stillness is not absence—and, in terms of hearing, the intensity of sound transforms the processing of listening as processing into the process of hearing.

If there is a noise body, it is between the participants, or how they relate; it is also the body in receipt of noise; also the subject struggling to be subject; but there is also ecstasy. The experience of noise has been thought of as ecstatic (Thacker, Reynolds, most people writing on Merzbow), and this is far from wrong. The listener at a loud noise event is taken out of the subject body to be dumped back into embodiment, lowered into something like ecstatic noise consumption. The mistake would be to imagine any lasting freedom emerging from that ecstasy. It is certainly more ecstatic than pleasant, and closer to the sublime than the beautiful, with which it cannot share anything. Like Kant's sublime, though, it is also in the framing of the moment the self is lost as the rational reflection on the moment the self was lost. Noise strives for a pure expression where it is other in a way that listeners and performers are also made other, taken out of themselves, free from the networks of power that have built them. That said, without the restricted economy of meaning, rationality, and so on, there would be no ecstatic moment, as this has to fall outside of something else, and be temporary to the other's permanence. Once again, noise is going to fail, and noise is this failure, making itself as if it will not fail, and living on in the failure, as residue.

Masonna plays out this interplay between noise and failing to be noise (which goes alongside music and failing to be music), in a way that seeks to merge body with noise. In recordings, voice, guitar and effects (ocassionally percussion) combine, with (often) the loss of identity of those sounds, and the arrival of squalls of noise in feedback, echoes, overtones, etc. Masonna imagines himself as a rock musician, and this is clearest in his performances, which verge on the cathartic body art of Viennese Actionists, or Carolee Schneemann. These are generally very short and can involve his body working as a percussion device. On the DVD *Like a Vagina*, we see a collage of several of Masonna's performances, mostly for 'solo vocal', sometimes harmonica, and at other times, wielded hi-hat and stand. He is continually moving, although always returning to the effects pedals—as if to home—but distortion is not a home suitable for dwelling. While sometimes kneeling at the pedals, he will also throw himself down on them. His voice alternates between screams, panting and murmuring, and also between the effects on the several microphones adding howls, blasts and so on. In terms of movement, there is walking around while shouting, which is about as rock a gesture as we get, but there is also stumbling, falling, awkward jumping, crawling, lying down and rolling around. The sound produced is of a mediated embodied voice (which all voices are, but not generally as exposed as this). The voice is caught within electric and electronic circuits. The voice and body caught in these processes decline into a variant of noise body—i.e. neither is it just Masonna throwing himself around, nor is it just the spectral processed sound Masonna. It is the being caught in between these, and as a result, between self and other (noise, audience, machinery). Listeners are directly involved in the physicality of the performance as they hear it. Moments of weakness alternate with the masculine grappling with the object world to transform it. These alternations and crossings are what make these performances work as noise rather than just outburst (even if 'just outburst' is what it is presented as), and why it is an ecstatic parody of rock and also of singing in general.[29]

Quiet

The fate of Japanese noise might lie in silence—or close to it, in *onkyo*. Electronic musicians have, in Japan and Europe, in particular, moved on to experiment with small sounds, and the use of silence as a compositional component (like the rest in written music, like pauses in music, but with more emphasis as digital recording made it possible to use silence without hiss). I will arbitrarily stay largely with Japanese examples. Sachiko M's music tends toward removal of sound—with machines feeding back on themselves, loops, waves and gaps alternating. In the groups Filament (with Otomo Yoshihide and Günter Müller) and ISO (also Otomo), this adds not only texture, which in turn gets lost in the rest of the sounds produced, but also noise, in that it surges and disappears, often contrary to the rest of what is going on. In solo form, it is about the gaps as much as the sounds. Sachiko M's *Detect* is very quiet, hums and tones drifting in and out of audible sound (for humans, but not totally). Clicks come in, occasionally noticeably louder than the rest. As well as silences, and silences that quite probably still involve very high pitch tones, there are quiet tones, sometimes continuous, other times more staccato. In this music, volume is just as much a tool as in power electronics, or feedback guitars. It is just as much of a noise device, even if instead of accumulating sound, volume and noises, this is noise as dissipation. The separation of units of sound disrupts musicality, prevents the listener getting a distance from which to properly understand and therefore listen. As the piece goes on, the listener inevitably does get a sense of movement, compounded by the solid tone that ends it, lasting over two minutes. Awareness is never stopped by noise, just hindered, cajoled, fooled, offered but withheld, and no more so when silence comes into play.

Silence within noise music is not about awareness of musicality beyond the music, but about anticipation, shock, and testing limits that are not just about hearing endurance in terms of excess volume. Francisco Lopez exploits this in his *Untitled #123*, which takes over 10 minutes to gradually emerge from silence—the slowness is almost noise in its own right. The turbine-like sound is halted by buzzes of digital noise, and crisp static. This expands, again, very slowly, into a combination of chimes and hiss, and then it cuts out. From 19 minutes to roughly 33, there is almost nothing—an even quieter emergence of what eventually comes out as something like the sound of air (or the sound of a recording being made) and then becoming a humid throbbing, which lasts 24 minutes. From 57.10 to near the end, a quiet hum starts up and descends to impossibly quiet levels. The recording cuts out at 72.52, leaving a few seconds of silence, except that to hear any of the previous few minutes required turning up to very high volume, so when it ends, it does not. This is because as the recorded sound gets quieter, it merges with the analogue residual sounds of the music system, and at the cut-off point, those sounds have already gone past the other sounds from the CD. The use of silence and quietness is evocative, atmospheric, and so on, but more than that, this piece is a severe test of listening, such that listening, as with Ryoji Ikeda, is forced back on itself—mere listening, which is not just concentration, but concentration without product—there is nothing to figure out here.

Silence as pause to heighten effect is of course a resource for many of the more overtly harsh noise musics—Masonna often features gaps, but the example I want to give here is a single by Kazumoto Endo, which not only uses silence as a kind of punctuation, but as material. 'Most of my problems are solved by an afternoon snooze' builds as a piece through blocks of clear, I think digital, blocks of noise, and among these are patches of silence. The section from 0.32 to 1.15 is mostly silent, broken by short bursts of noise. The individual gaps vary in length from 4 to 10 seconds, and as well as the suspension of noise creating an effect of waiting for an inevitable blast, the returns to silence are their own noise—as the record offers only the sound of vinyl playing.[30] Another brief silence comes in around 2.50, emphasizing the arbitrariness of noise cutting out. These silences do not seem like pauses but like the record or the track failing. Is 0.32 to 1.15 the snooze of the title? If so, it is disrupted. Maybe the snooze is the rest as it is more constant. Either way, relaxation is a decoy.

Henritzi claims that Japanese experimental music has moved away from the harsh, ever more extreme forms of the mid 1990s, and is heading toward a different exploration of sound ('Extreme Contemporary', 36–7). If we are to look at what constitutes a new avant-garde approach, imagining that noise has become a style, then this might be so, but investigation of any of the major performers of noise music will show that they are all aware of this problem, and vary their approaches accordingly, whether in different bands, totally different types of noise, or combinations thereof, or, in Merzbow's case, by the sheer volume (numbers) of releases.

NOTES

1. See Toop, *Ocean of Sound: Aether Talk, Ambient Sound and Imaginary Worlds* (London and New York: Serpent's Tail, 1995), where he writes that 'moral judgements and oppositional categorizations imposed on noise and silence, or human and machine, are less clear cut in Japan' (150). See *Japanese Independent Music* (Bordeaux: Sonore, 2001), for continual reiteration of this idea.

2. Jibiki Yuichi claims that 'European noise is conceptual and logical, meanwhile Japanese noise is meaningless, coming from emotions within the soul' (*Japanese Independent Music*, 49). There are many problems with this statement, but I think it accurately reflects the thoughts of many noise musicians in Japan. Keiji Haino's album titles would back up the belief in what, rather than absence of thinking, we would have to imagine as a nihilism that incorporates emotionality: *So, Black Is Myself*; *Abandon all words at a stroke, so that prayer*

can come spilling out, or, inside the slightly more black than usual cover, *I said, This is the Son of Nihilism*.

3. Famously, there is also noise within Japanese visual pornography, in the shape of the taboo on pubic hair. Hair is noise.

4. Marshall McLuhan and Quentin Fiore, *The Medium Is the Massage: An Inventory of Effects* (Harmondsworth: Penguin, 1967).

5. Baudrillard, *Télémorphose* (Paris: Sens et Tonka, 2001).

6. Baudrillard, *Forget Foucault* (New York: Semiotext[e], 1987)

7. At this point, sound is hyper-visualized in wave forms, or via the progress of tracks in software-simulated machine frames.

8. Nancy, *À l'écoute* (Paris: Galilée, 2002)

9. Bohlman, *World Music: A Very Short Introduction* (Oxford: Oxford University Press, 2002).

10. See Lévi-Strauss, *Race et histoire* (Paris: UNESCO, 1952), and Baudrillard, *The Transparency of Evil* (London: Verso, 1993), especially 124–38. He writes that 'one might even say that difference is what destroys otherness [altérité]' (127).

11. On this, see Hugh de Ferranti, ' "Japanese music" can be popular', *Popular Music* 21 (2) (2002), 195–208, particularly 197.

12. Lancashire, ' "World Music" or Japanese—the gagaku of Tôgi Hideki', *Popular Music* 22 (1) (2003), 21–9.

13. Michael Henritzi writes of 'a double exoticism: [Japanese music] is music that is both distant (geographically but also temporally as representative of a techno-future), and extremely contemporary (the noise)' ('Extreme Contemporary: Japanese Music as Radical Exoticism', in *Japanese Independent Music*, 31–7).

14. Hegarty, 'Noise Threshold: Merzbow and the End of Natural Sound', *Organized Sound* 6 (3) (2001), 193–200.

15. This is not the knowing hybridity of Japanese pop (J-pop), but a collision of styles, making a morass of near-undifferentiatedness, which forms an unformed alterity. For a knowing hybridity that ironizes itself, the Yellow Magic Orchestra's rendering of exoticist composer Martin Denny's take on Japanese music, in their track 'Firecracker'. A self-conscious pastiche and homage is redone as self-conscious pastiche and homage to Denny.

16. Kerman, *Musicology* (London: Fontana, 1985).

17. Baudrillard, *The Illusion of the End* (Cambridge: Polity, 1994).

18. Bataille, 'Base Materialism and Gnosticism', in *Visions of Excess*, 45–52.

19. As Bataille notes, in Gnosticism, matter is 'an active principle' ('Base Materialism and Gnosticism', 47).

20. Labels like PSF also established their own aesthetic. Many releases of Japanese noise are produced outside Japan, mainly in the US—a further example of noise as internationalism that runs with and counter to commercially driven globalization.

21. Nick Smith develops this into a vigorous criticism, that this playing with the commodity is a very profitable game (writing on Merzbow's 50-CD box *Merzbox*) ('The Splinter in Your Ear: Noise as the Semblance of Critique', *Culture Theory Critique: Noise* 46 [1], April 2005, 43–59).

22. The record comes with instructions as to what to do with it, concluding with 'display proudly in your home'.

23. Collett, 'Spacious Paradise: Psychedelism in Japanese Music', in *Japanese Independent Music*, 25–30.

24. This is not an incapacity on the part of certain manufacturers, or CDs from a particular period, but a specific strategy which is a crucial part of crossing rock into noise, as can be heard on Boris' 2006 album *Pink*. Once this is a widespread strategy, and features in music from places other than Japan, the Japanese noise use of this in the late 1980s and up to the mid-1990s is the reference point for it. Also, even if recognizable, it does not alter volume as the thwarting of rock volume still unfolds in the duration of tracks as they play (and clearly in excessive sound levels in performance, where the volume not only has a physical effect, but prevents detail recognition and diminishes capacity to hear the full frequency range being presented, even though this range should be a key bearer of a noise 'message').

25. The laptop, particularly if in 'solo' performance, offers the spectacle of a person looking at a machine. While it refutes the need to see performance/production of music, it is not enough of an anti-spectacle: remove the laptop performer from view altogether.

26. Keith Rowe of AMM has long been using this technique, and clearly it does not pre-clude noisiness. It is a loss of the expected manipulation of the instrument, an improper use, and it encourages loss of control, allowing in chance influences (in his case, for example, fans, radios).

27. For Agamben, we are witnessing a strange unravelling of bodily subjects, where we are perpetually, potentially, returnable to the fundamental conditions of biopolitical power: 'just as the biopolitical body of the west cannot simply be given back to its natural life in the oikos, so it cannot be overcome in a passage to a new body—a technical body or a wholly political or glorious body—in which a different economy of pleasures and vital functions would once and for all resolve the interlacement of zoe and bios that seems to define the political destiny of the west. This biopolitical body that is bare life must instead be trans-formed into the site for the constitution and installation of a form of life that is wholly exhausted in bare life' (*Homo Sacer: Sovereign Power and Bare Life* [Stanford, CA: Stanford University Press, 1998], 188). No way out, only other ways in.

28. Smith reads this properly tragic condition of noise as a sort of competitive listening, where mastery is always sought. This mastery can only be served by increasingly harsh or 'extreme' sound ('Splinter in Your Ear', 55–6). There is of course some truth to this, but also a certain moralizing tone in the criticism, whereby young people (mostly male) are drawn into a downward spiral, starting out with 'soft' noise in metal, and 'graduating' to the hard stuff, of which there is never enough.

29. Masonna also does some dismantling of the record industry and its consumption, as he performs in a record shop, with loudhailer and effects. Among the carefully ordered racks which will be processed into similar racks in collectors' homes, Masonna rolls around, screaming. Proper singing can be subverted in many ways, as seen in preceding chapters, but also with Diamanda Galas, whose extreme singing range and operatic use of the voice is bludgeoned by herself into a tool for vocal subjectivity that goes beyond the person, most notably in 'Wild Women with Steak Knives (The Homicidal Love Song for Solo Scream)' on *The Litanies of Satan*.

30. One pressing of Coil's *How to Destroy Angels* has 'blank grooves' on side 2, as does Merzbow's *Live at 2000V*.

10
MERZBOW

Masami Akita, aka Merzbow (there were others on some of his earlier recordings), is the paragon of noise, its 'godfather', its master. Having outlined the theoretical issues in Japanese noise in the previous chapter, this chapter seeks to look at the concentration of noise strategies in his work. Merzbow's position is as the ultimate example, the reference point, for Japanese noise music, and for the consumption of and writing on noise. It is impossible to avoid a vocabulary based on excessiveness, extremity and harshness. These are characteristic of many individual works, and of his oeuvre as a whole. Merzbow's music is all noise, almost always presenting (and ultimately, therefore, absenting) itself as the culmination of the messy genre of Japanese noise. Duration, volume, harshness, interference, luring a listener into attributing meaning, and anti-virtuosity are all tools that work through the layers of harsh noises, pulses, oscillations, crashes and explosive bursts in Merzbow recordings. The quantity of his releases, even within the prolific production of Japanese noise musicians, is immense, to the point where Masami Akita could constitute a genre in his own right. The excess, though, like that of all noise, must be thought of in Bataillean terms, where excess is not just more, but an attempt to be more that sacrifices itself as it goes along (i.e. loses itself in excess, but also as excess, as we get used to it)—and this excess does not reach a high point in Merzbow—Merzbow is the *lowering* of sound, noise as lowering—i.e. there is no endpoint to aim at, no 'ultimate' moment, despite the temptation to see his music as the 'ultimate noise'.

Excess is a constant negotiation of the normal, the taboo, the structured. It does not get rid of those, but acts as if does. Eugene Thacker, referring to Merzbow's *Music for Bondage Performance*, puts it like this: 'the body of music filled with excess and volume, presented as the tension-filled inability of excess to fulfil itself' ('Bataille/Body/Noise', 58).[1] Noise is excess to the normal economy of music, that which is to be excluded as threat. Merzbow's recordings are about occupying this space of threat, and not just reincorporating the threat into music. His releases make something out of noise that approximates music, while refusing most ideas of musicality. The excess is also what Bataille thinks of as eroticism—where individuals lose themselves in death, non-reproductive sexuality, sacrifice, drunkenness, and, with Merzbow (and in Thacker's article), noise.

The temptation is to read this extreme noise as a form of ecstasy, and in terms of taking individuals out of themselves by forcibly rooting them in bodily experience, this is the case, but it is not an ecstasy of harmoniousness: we do not come together; we just keep nearly doing so. The energy of this catharsis depends on it being burned up. Music, even at its freest, aspires to some sort of development, and things do occur in sequence in Merzbow, but seem to undo what preceded. Thacker locates the catharsis beyond us, at least when stating that 'the music of Merzbow is of course not music at all, but rather the intensive expenditure of sound and silence in a whirlpool of electronic catharsis' ('Bataille/Body/Noise', 63). In other words, it is always expiring even as it grows. This is a music of waste, expenditure and sacrifice, and whatever there is, however momentary, comes from waste. Merzbow music is all residue, all noise. The name comes from dadaist

Schwitters' *Merzbau*—his house, gradually reconfigured on the interior by the incorporation of found material, i.e. largely rubbish. The building gradually got fuller with this more or less random stuff, unified by paint, and, as shown in the few remaining photographs, the building of the stuff into crystalline forms. Merzbow's music does some of the same work as Schwitters, making a form that is so complex it becomes formless, out of junk (sound instead of physical material). Excess fills volume with infinite possibilities, and there is the sense of an alternative world being built, but within this one. Schwitters' stuff becomes *merz*, Merzbow's sounds noise, but the latter does not stop working the components—they can never settle. I suppose this is not a great difference—both artists accumulate, but accumulate to distort (and vice-versa).

From early work with percussion, tapes and samples, Masami Akita moved on to 'music' characterized by overdriven, fedback and effect-laden noises from analogue equipment, notably analogue synths and electronics. It is often seemingly nothing but feedback and explosive residue, with metallic scrapes, howls, myriad types of pulse, or of coloured noise. Many layers counteract each other, sometimes creating a dense mass, at other times, offering more a sense of strata or depths. The recordings, from the mid-1990s on, especially, are all of extreme volume, some of the CDs even mastered at levels far beyond standard (e.g. *Noisembryo*, *Pulse Demon*). More recent releases relentlessly circle around particular tones, or a limited number of sound sources, but in the main, his different 'styles' all feature disruption (noise to the noises within the tracks themselves). Tracks finish abruptly, and the semblance of an orderly album, with titles and track times is made ridiculous. On titles, Masami Akita says that 'when I use words, say, album titles, they are not chosen to convey any meanings. They are merely selected to mean nothing' (in Woodward, *Merzbook*, 40). This is not quite true, and some recent albums do tell us something about the sound source, particularly the albums based on nature samples. What the titles signal is the arbitrariness of the noise that results from those sources. Titles and apparent themes mean it is not 'just noise', but noise in the place of music. Feedback and distortion are not incidental, but drivers of arbitrariness. '"I was able to control feedback", Akita claims proudly, "The feedback sounds of equipment is a central concept for Merzbow. Feedback automatically makes a storm of noise"' (in Edwin Pouncey, 'Consumed by Noise', 30).[2] This control is more a sense of being able to use it, I think, than actually mastering it (in the same way Derek Bailey uses a volume pedal to play with attack and decay, as well as effects).

Merzbow noise is going to be difficult to put into words, but this has if anything encouraged writing, theoretical speculation, not-quite-analysis and theory riffing. As one of the guilty in this respect, it seems to me that the openness of the work encourages thought, its extremity suggesting the limits of all music, and all that defines music, while at the same time standing as a negation of thought. Unless played very quietly, analytical thought is thwarted while Merzbow noise occurs, and even at quiet volume, there is still a jaggedness in the cutting, the bursts of sound, the alterations, that hinders the development of analysis. This is the case in much Japanese noise, but there is always more, more to come, more to unravel, more as the unravelling of the not-more of the simply-there. With Merzbow, in other words, there probably is more of noise, but above all, there is a continuous thought that not only is this already more, but that more is to come. Also, some might imagine that if all music or art is somehow misrepresented through being thought about and written on, then noise is fundamentally betrayed by trying to understand it. Maybe that is so, if you imagine that art emerges out of nowhere in the head of a genius, that it can be pure or authentic. I do think, however, that to think about Merzbow is about missing the mark, speculating, imposing, and distorting—all of which are in tune with what Masami Akita is interested in. He himself has a keen sense of European theory, citing Derrida, Deleuze and Guattari, Foucault, Baudrillard, and of course Bataille as reference points for what his noise does.

These assertions do nothing to answer the problem of how to process Merzbow—the listener can veer between thinking it is all just noise, and that it's all basically the same, or be awed by the sheer infinity of possibilities unleashed. Is the first encounter the most important? For any one album it probably is, and Merzbow *uses* this idea, in the form, for example, of albums beginning at high volume with no attack, with no lead-in. Alternatively, the listening can be read as a case of getting there, being able to consume it and being consumed by it only gradually—'the fact is that to understand, enjoy and eventually reach noise nirvana through Masami Akita's work, you have to listen to a hell of a lot of it' (Pouncey, 'Consumed by Noise', 27). Beyond these problematic possible listenings is one more profound: how can music, or even something approximating it, carry on, once the gesture of total noise has been played? Is it not just a playing out of the last moment? Is music still possible after Merzbow? In which case, why does he carry on? Of course, we could also ask whether noise is possible, if its ultimate expression has somehow been reached. These arguments rely on a profound misunderstanding of noise as being a fixed, definable object, with clearly measurable noisiness, but noise, especially in a near-musical context, is precisely the non-measurable, the fluctuating, the interruption, the interference, so it can never end. One answer to this problem returns us to Adorno's question in *Negative Dialectics*—once meaning, truth, fairness and life are questioned, what can aesthetics do? Its duty might be to disappear, but this disappearance is to be staged, thinks Adorno. Beckett, for example, quite literally plays out 'art after Auschwitz', and this without having to write about the Shoah. So we can think of Merzbow arriving at noise, and deciding whether to continue. At this imaginary moment, it turns out noise cannot be arrived at—it is always withheld (just as it holds off music and meaning). In this case, it makes sense to continue in the light of the impossibility of ever attaining 'ultimate noise'. If music is brought to a terminal condition by noise music at its fullest (made only of residue, full with noise, both oppressively total and unmanageable, always moving), then this can be a site of living-on in the decline of music. But it would be more accurate to say that Merzbow's noise music brings a terminal condition that turns out to have always been the case—music, language, meaning, culture always haunted by that which it is not, that which surrounds it, threatens it, and structures it by providing a frame that dissolves itself. Over and over. Merzbow is the playing out of the fundamentals of music, to the point where there is little left.

The answer to 'why go on' all of these lies in the volume, in the other sense, of Merzbow's production. You may get used to one album, even start thinking of it as music, but the next one will do something else. It is also more or less impossible to keep up, and properly collect Merzbow. Smith has complained that Merzbow offers a paradigm of collectability and cultural capital, aided by a rhetoric of extremity (see references in previous chapter). I would argue that Merzbow gets around this by limited editions, releasing on many different labels, in different formats, thus making collecting farcical, extremely effortful and unlikely to succeed—thereby presenting a deconstruction of all collecting. Merzbow must have produced over 200 releases by now, including the monumental 50 CD *Merzbox* (released 1999) and several smaller multi-CD sets (these being individual albums—returning us to the original definition of album, which was a collection of 78 rpm records adding up to one release). Among these are the mythical CD in BMW or Mercedes, a one-off with the CD playing every time the car was activated, or the 2006 release *Metamorphism* in a marble box with what looks like a fossil in the lid.

The *Merzbox* presents itself as the extreme album release, comprising rare releases and over thirty CDs of unreleased material, packaged in fetish-style bag, with book and other paraphernalia. What does such an amount of stuff mean? How is it supposed to be listened to? It is about listening, about consumption, about pushing listening to the point of consumption (in many senses of the word). But is it really so odd now? Box sets abound—U2 put all their music on a dedicated iPod, Depeche Mode have offered their entire oeuvre as a single download, and anyone else can make an immense collection of one artist in digital form. Jazz collections with alternate takes, vast numbers of concerts and so on are not exactly rare. But none of these demands a suspension of music—Merzbow's box should not exist, as it implies a work that builds into a whole, but while it does cover the length of his career, the material is not additive—it is not about learning. More interesting, in any case, are the albums consisting of many CDs, which is still rare (e.g. *Houjoue*, *Day of Seals*, *Timehunter*, *Turmeric*). In an era where the album is apparently under threat from isolation into individual tracks, here are albums that can be five hours long.

Analogue

Merzbow persists with anachronistic machinery, its unpredictability and noisiness (i.e. chances for residual sound) key elements in his work up until the end of the 1990s. Analogue equipment can be overdriven, brought to noise, and layers of their sound recombined without suggesting tonal relations between separate parts. The limitations of the machinery are precisely what allow the possibility of a going-beyond (like transgression's relation to taboo). Merzbow's early releases were on cassette tape, wrapped up in apparently discarded porn images. Like many avant-garde musicians, this cheapness was as much out of necessity as design, but he has persisted with vinyl releases (as with 2006's *Minazo* vol. 2). We might think, especially if we like vinyl as a medium, that recording on vinyl would best represent the analogue work, but Masami Akita was, it seems, just waiting for CD to come along to expand the range and potential for loudness that he felt records lacked (quoted in Pouncey, 'Consumed by Noise', 41), while still suspicious of digital sound making. It is good, and faithful, in one way, to hear vinyl struggle, as it does even more with releases by CCCC and Incapacitants, where the range is compromised into a bulbous headache-inducing frequency lump. CDs do *contain* sound (and mp3s even more so), compressing it in ways we are not supposed to be able to hear, and Merzbow's records do not seem to suffer by comparison to the CDs, even if quite a bit quieter, which does limit the effect even if turned up in compensation.

The duration of a vinyl record is important, too—a piece longer than 25 minutes has to be split up, or drastically reduced in quality and volume—and Merzbow does not want these limits (even though it is rare to have one track occupying a full-length CD). The visual element means we know where we are as well—how long is left (this is at its worst in music consumed on computers, so not restricted to analogue technology), and maybe even work out from the texture of the record where the loud bits or changes are going to fall. On the other hand, the materiality of vinyl allows play with the format—and Masami Akita and Russell Haswell's digital fight *Satanstornade* is one such, with each track ending in a locked groove.[3]

Many of what are considered Merzbow's harshest works come from his 'analogue period'—albums such as *Noisembryo*, described by Keenan as 'the quintessential Merzbow album' ('picks the best of Merzbow', 33).[4] This is indeed a fierce album, but the question of listening to Merzbow is raised even as the album is praised. If this is 'the one', surely it can stand in for all the others? This is to misunderstand the scale of Merzbow's project, and even if we think of the plethora of releases as arbitrary, variable in quality, sometimes not really adding much to previous releases, we have to think in terms beyond individual releases. Like a single, one CD or record, however focused, is a tiny part of Merzbow. *Noisembryo* can remain quintessential because any album can be—the whole is in each part, even if the whole cannot be summoned comfortably into the part. Released at pretty much the same time, it is *Venereology* that catches the attention of Thacker, whose take is this:

[Venereology: The conjunction of sex, disease, and death; the diseased body in an intense, often anguish-filled zone of hyper-sensitivity; coitus, expiation, and decay—the measured curve of the body of a sound—attack, body, decay; technology and electronic abnormalities, illnesses; sound and the microbial transference of bodies.] ('Bataille/Body/Noise', 60)

The opening track 'Ananga-Ranga' starts with lumpy pulses and shrieking flanged sounds. Layers cut in and out; piercing notes drown out the rest for brief moments. As it goes on, coloured noise vies with busy electronic sounds, as slices of high pitched blocs of sound interfere. The middle section sees several layers taking over and falling back, or seeming to, because there is no background from which specifics emerge, however much the listener might conceive it that way. Different layers grind against each other, and continue to be blasted with short bursts of high oscillating tones and wide frequency white-ish noise. After 22 minutes, the sense of convoluted layering densifies, so that sounds now do seem to come to the surface, but like algal blooms or dirt particles, their rising does not end up in either exit or getting above the rest. Throughout, microphases of sound acquire consistency only to be caught within as the layered whole moves on, closing over whatever looked to emerge. There is emergence at play here, of the simplest kind, where some order is formed chaotically, but this forming is no sooner established than it unforms. After 29 minutes, it just cuts straight into the next track. The patterning and seaming of layers of *Venereology* are the 'style' of 1994–5, perhaps the period where Merzbow is most focused on a world-defining aesthetic (i.e. noise music that can supplant the world, like Roy Lichtenstein's gradual colouring in of art history in his style, or a virtual world where the laws of this one do not hold. *Pinkream* (1995) furrows the same groove, the three-sided vinyl album full of squawls, bursts, throbbing, accumulations of feedback toppling under their own weight. 'Tuku Tuku' leads in with a faltering alarm-style drone, presaging its inevitable incorporation into an array of noise after nearly 2 minutes. At moments, rhythm is injected into noise, neither anchoring it, nor free; just arriving, to not really work as rhythm (except as lure or parody). Electronic whizzing gradually goes out of control, and around the 10-minute mark, a relentless pounding, speeding and slowing, comes in, to give way to staccato tones, a final clattering and a rising pitch to the cut point. There are opening and concluding gestures on this album, but they only work retrospectively—they occur too rapidly to be signalled as an impending end, so the conclusion is heard only after the end—and this in fact reminds us that even apparently closing gestures like a rise in noise, a quick change, a cut from high volume, are all arbitrary as 'closures', as these kind of sounds occur throughout the tracks.

Analogue Merzbow is mostly richer in both sound and noise than the digital versions. For one thing, the liquefying stratification of the mid-1990s goes away, as the digital stuff is more linear, and ironically, more revealing of the processes that made it (listening to 'Looping Jane' on 2002's *Amlux* is dominated by awareness that the whole track has been slowed down on the computer). In digital, Merzbow is happier for layers to stay longer, set up rhythms, even beats. The early computer experiment single 'Happenings 1000 years time ago' (1999) sets up a sample as rhythm, which stays throughout both sides, and he cuts, disrupts, and intersperses it with more obvious metallic noise. This release could well be seen as trying to replicate what he was up to with analogue equipment, thus making the digital an analogue of analogue. 'Takemitsu' on *Amlux* has many pulsing beats, which are, at any one time, reasonably straightforward, and, with this, crackles, rumbles and steel sheet-like interjections more or less above the beat. This is a consistent pattern on recordings which are made exclusively on laptop. *Merzbuddha* (2005) is almost techno, so much is it oriented by beats. Each of the three long tracks has a dub style bass riff/rhythm that goes on throughout, and it not far from, say, Richie Hawtin or Drexciya. This album is effective, and relentless in its own way, but for me, it raises the question of how much we are waiting for Merzbow to do what we are anticipating. Each of these tracks does have electronics, squelching, hissing, howling bits of noise. The beats themselves all have a glitch as an integral part. In the last couple of minutes, everything is ratcheted up, but unconvincingly—the intensification not so much withheld as telegraphed. But turn the CD up, and a curdling bass throb between industrial and techno does something 'noisy'. Many Merzbow listeners will be disappointed with this CD (and many others), as an annoying tension exists between valorizing variation and unpredictability on the one hand, and the likelihood that you didn't buy a Merzbow album to hear ambient industrial techno. This frustration is of course a crucial part of noise listening: i.e. that interference, unexpectedness and divergence are inevitable. This is all heightened by the amount of releases meaning that anyone who listens to anything other than Merzbow, will only buy some, and usually more or less randomly, and that would be the case even if you could notionally afford and track all new releases.

Why would analogue Merzbow be better? Would such a belief entail the sense that analogue is to digital as speech is to writing, i.e. the false presumption that one form is superior to its opponent? Is analogue 'more human'? Certainly, whether it's Russolo and Cage, or John Peel, or many that insist on the quality of vinyl, the claim is that vinyl more closely approximates the authentic human listening experience (the same goes for stereo, which helps illustrate that these are only imagined realities that belong to a specific moment in history, however long that might be). Digital sound carries the posthuman, a way of experiencing that moves beyond what we have accepted as fundamentals of the human condition. Why should listening be determined by biological chance? So Merzbow's digital moments might be much noisier than they sound, as they resolutely stick to the post-machinic, sounds with no origin, or with origin lost (Merzbow has, after a brief bout of digital purism, recombined digital and analogue, as on *Metamorphism*, and gone on to work more with samples, referred to below). Computer-based noise can be as harsh as any, as Kazumoto Endo, post-2000 Whitehouse, or the collaboration of Masami Akita with Russell Haswell show.

Ecologies of 2006

The periodization of Merzbow into analogue and digital is not straightforward, as analogue releases kept coming, and the way in which samples come to be used in the 'nature-based' albums at least brings back non-programmed sound as source. A few years ago, it could be said that Merzbow rarely used field recordings as a basis for noise pieces (although there are certainly source materials to be cut, such as percussion). Music has been sampled and then exploded, broken into fragments that recombine in Merzbow's soundworld, and notably in 2005 and 2006, nature recordings have featured strongly, carrying on from *Frog* (2001) which even has a recognizable frog sound at the beginning. Chickens (his own), whales, seals have all been part of how Merzbow's noise ecology feeds back into the other one. Have these sources become content? Prior to 2000, samples were mostly lost in the midst of layers of noise and noising of the samples. But the 4-CD set *24 Hours—A Day of Seals* (2002) changes that, as not only are some of the source sounds clearly signalled, they are also suggested in turn by the final piece. Once this has occurred on one release, it is tempting to listen for similar reference points, on albums 'about' other animal life. Given Merzbow's view of the arbitrariness of his titles, we might be advised to not read too much into sound content as musical content (i.e. meaning). Like Jackson Pollock, we should, I think, take it that what is content is shifted—in Pollock's case to the expression of his subjectivity in chaotic paint patterning. This would be hard to do in Merzbow's case, but in both examples, we can take the 'formless' forms as their own content, form and content caught in recursive relation, and continually crossing one another. And yet, you cannot ignore that a Pollock picture is entitled *Galaxy*, or that a Merzbow album is named after a specific elephant seal (*Minazo*).

Recent albums from 2004–6 surmount the divide between digital and analogue that listeners and critics perhaps accept too readily. The incorporation of audio samples from nature is one level at which this occurs, but more important is the merging of organic and machine, and in many cases the unclear collision and drift between the two. Where exactly is the chicken? At some point is it subsumed

Tetsuo-like into Merzworld? In the general cacophony of Merzbow, it is slightly fool-ish to look for where the sound source is noticeable, and, more important than the individual specific sound source is the crossing of machine/animal, culture/nature, as played out in analogue and digital. Merzbow's music is a general ecology of noise, and opposed to the organization of sound into species, types, forms. Noise is the material of the ecology and what continually emerges (like lava). These are not just metaphors—once noise music presents itself as ecological, we are justi-fied in thinking of it as a chaotic system where order does occur, as islands within a wider formlessness. Like the pre-Darwinian theorists Hutton, Cuvier and Lyell, it is geology that is the key to animal and plant life—fossils are raised, displaced, trapped, loosened—if we make the timescale long enough, there is constant movement, even of mountains, tectonic plates, etc. (this is also a commonly used set of images for noise and dirge musics). Contemporary evolutionary theory can see evolution occurring at incredible speed, especially at a viral level—another possible language for noise. But what Merzbow most resembles is the negativity of Darwin and the interactions of an ecosystem—i.e. evolution occurs because of death, and is not an upward, triumphal narrative, but a clustering that is endlessly branching, failing, sometimes succeeding—but only provisionally.

At the heart of 2006's output is the 4-CD *Turmeric* (with 'bonus' CD 5, an EP-length blast that accompanies it). At any one moment, the listener is caught within a mass of pulses, whirs and so on, sometimes with an absolutely unchanging beat (the second half of CD 1, CD 2 and 'Black Blood pt.4' on CD 4), and at other times, in an expansive flowering of crashes, roars, howls, and so on. At some point on this album, all Merzbow styles appear—as if Merzbow, like Gerhard Richter, is working out the fullness of a piece, and this by making a total piece that is not unitary. CD1 features bird sound, and most likely a good deal of heavily processed versions of it too. 'Black Flesh pt.1' howls, pt. 2 smashes and clatters, pt. 3 pulses unstoppably, while pt.4 is a play of bashing and strangulated howls. 'Black Flesh pt. 3' is the most interesting part of this CD, a digital pulse building into a genuine techno-industrial backdrop (which is never fully submerged). The contrast is between the fixed form of the beat and the formless expanse of it (the track is 19.34 long). Noise clatters and blasts supply an illusory variety, as if relieving the listener from the noise effect of the rolling stasis of the beat. In this track, the per-cussion is not the beat, and grainy percussions interfere with the relentless pro-cessed beat; CD 2 ('Black Bone') presses and presses, through over 70 minutes of repetition within, and sometimes above, the interruptions of noise bursts, twisted so it is never 'just' white noise (this is at its peak toward the end of pt. 1). Individual layers cut out, but there is no let up as other layers settle in (as much as something like a piercing whistling can settle). CD 3 ('Deaf Composition') is two lengthy tracks, the first 34 minutes covering the whole range of Merzbow styles, volume levels irregularly changing, and CD 4 ('Black Blood') pursues this further, with incredibly loud moments (in pts. 1 and 3), and, as if in an ironic reversal of Spinal Tap, it transpires that all the noise so far has been kept down, held in.

Why this description, why put forward a list of key moments or moves? It could be because Merzbow removes most of our other resources—it strips down musi-cality, and also suggests it is beyond discourse. All music, and a considerable amount of music criticism, wishes music (or noise) to possess a certain ineffability, wishes it to be beyond the powers of language. At one level, Merzbow is the extreme of this, but like Kant's sublime, or indeed Bataille's excess, it is surrounded by attempts to understand it, to process it, to listen to it rather than just hear it. Human ears cannot just hear, they are part of a system of perception. This perception involves judgement, framing, even of what eludes understanding. This latter becomes the sublime, *understood* as that which eludes understanding. In Merzbow's case human listening is drawn into an ecology that is unfamiliar, or even if recognizable after a while, is still not under control. Despite this, our listening, no matter how theorized, seems unable to let listening go, let judgement fail. Beyond how this occurs when listening to individual CDs, the mass of Merzbow's quantitative sublime is always brought into qualitative terms, leaving us, however mundanely, with the question of what is 'good' Merzbow? Is it all good? This would be to make the error implicit in a lot of sound art, which is that the existence of an unusual sound piece is enough. 'Good Merzbow' should presumably fail to meet the expectations of the listener, exceeding them, but maybe the listener prefers the busier analogue squawls of *Pulse Demon* and wants that same thrill repeated, or perhaps the relentlessness that parts of *Turmeric* offer. The key is arbitrariness—there does not seem to be a *reason* to judge from. Even if you have heard it all, what would it mean to be the master of all that—surely that would be against the spirit of this noise?

Bariken, from 2005, uses repetitive pulsing at a different level of structure—much more of an anchor, as clatters and reverbed chickeny sounds (suggested by the bird on the cover) come in over low throbs ('Minka pt.1'). Huge squawls sustain themselves over an unchanging beat: 'Bariken (reprise)—Mother of Mirrors'. This last track suggests an interaction of an unchanging Nature, with continual variation of natural processes—each framing the other. Of course, much music has variation over repetition, but this is arbitrary variation with no specific endpoint to aim at, played out over an absolute value, but one that will disappear just as finally (as both individual and species will). We are further authorized to think in these terms by the ecological suggestiveness at levels of content, form, packaging (as with *Metamorphism*), and of materiality that is both organic and not, alive and not (reminding us of Russolo's thought that life is noise, as well as human culture being noise).[5] Merzbow's ecology is not part of the panic that seeks to keep humans at the top of the food chain by 'saving the environment'. While he has a genuine commitment to preserving animal life, and indicates links to animal welfare agency PETA on his albums, his is a posthuman ecology—one where humanity is not the peak of anything, whether 'Creation', or evolution. Humanity submerges into the crossing of animal and technology. To kill is to control, and to maintain that whales, as a notable example, are fit for killing is an attempt by humanity (although less of it today) to keep the line firmly drawn between 'intelligent life' (i.e. humans) and the rest (food, living objects to be tested). As Japan is a keen advocate of whaling (for 'science') this is a significant position to take for a Japanese artist, part of that rejection of conformity and superiority *in* conformity that some societies have.[6]

Bloody Sea is not discreet about its motives—'stop whaling now' is on the front cover of the CD, the tracks are 'Anti-Whaling Song' parts 1, 2 and 3, and the title is clear enough. Sue Arnold writes about the brutality of whale hunting on the cover. However, how can we read this surfeit of content into the music? There is nothing, or very little, to suggest the subject matter, let alone a position on it. Nonetheless, the insistence on materiality means the packaging is not irrelevant but a framing which infiltrates our listening (as any titling of instrumental music would do, arguably). I think the listener is being asked to listen for content—i.e. the position against whale hunting, but the sound resists. There is no signalling of whale music, no presentation of their song culture, even processed, unlike Psychic TV's *Kondole*. New Age recordings have whale music as a staple, and however uninteresting these may be, or have been made, they probably contribute to understanding the complexity of whale culture. Merzbow has no such aim with *Bloody Sea*. Why not? Arguably, because 'whale music' is a human construct, and has always had a use value: either 'whales are ok because they communicate', or, more perniciously and more commonly, the use of whale song as soothing balm for stressed humans, 'as if' it were music. This use value can be laid next to the use of whales for cosmetics, food, experiments, etc.—to record for use is to abuse. Maybe the squalls of noise show humanity's alienation from nature? Perhaps with an other artist, but in Merzbow, noise is not alienation but communication, ecstasy, and, feasibly, a messy encounter with nature, as opposed to its rejection in the form of the strictures of proper musical form (if you wanted to make the case for such alienation, you could nonetheless, refer to the separation of sounds between channels in 'Anti-Whaling Song pt. 1', which fills over half the album). So is the noise of *Bloody Sea* a celebration of whales' cultural complexity, ineffability? Maybe, but there are no markers to suggest whale input, samples, or connections. There is no direct connection whatsoever, nothing to distinguish it from Merzbow's procedures he has followed on many other occasions. Instead it seems more of an evocation, if there is one, of the ecology mentioned before. The vast array of sounds, volumes, shifts in rhythms, moments of abrupt change, interferences, violent encounters of layers of sound, all feed into an ecology, a zone which incidentally hosts a variety of sounds that maintains itself as potential, while also establishing various, provisional stabilities. If pt. 1 covers a range, pt. 2 focuses in, through an unpleasant arpeggio, switching to a slow oscillation after 7 minutes. As it suddenly ends, pt. 3 delivers a horizontal range of noise—i.e. everything at once, over and over, recalling the mid-1990s albums, and shot through with piercing tones, ending oddly, with a measured fade, and about 10 seconds of clattering. Still, there seems no connection to either the evil of whaling or the greatness of whales, and there are elegaic Merzbow tracks elsewhere, such as *Metamorphism*, pt.1, where there is an exhaustion brought through falling noises, dropping tones, volume drops, and also the closing track on *Bariken*, where the harsher noises seem to be fighting the beat and failing, or struggling. The answer is that, unlike on *Day of the Seals*, where low sounds suggest marine ambience, there is no such connection on *Bloody Sea*, but this does not mean it has nothing to do with Masami Akita's position on whaling, or nothing to do with the sea, or nature. The sea is full with noise, fuller than the air, for ears that are prepared for it. The sea is where land life came from, just as sound comes from noise—and both relations can only be attributed retrospectively. The sea is where many mammals, including whales, returned to, and their vocalizations are meaningful, even if noise to us. The sea to them, though, is a carrier of meaningful sound. However we think about this album, it seems not to deal with noise for sea mammals, as opposed to noise for humans, especially as the former is largely created by humans, looking for oil, navigating, searching for enemy movements. In the end, however suggestive the noise of this album might be, what it does is revert to materiality of sound, and refuses activism as a component. This is not engaged art, but engagement as a place art occurs in.[7] The reading of *Bloody Sea* is nothing but arbitrary, nothing but failing, but if anything, it is also the illustration of insufficiency as a consequence of the formless process of Merzbow. Merzbow's noise unfolds, and then, the arbitrariness of which

NOTES

1. Thacker, 'Bataille/Body/Noise: Notes Towards a Techno-Erotics', in Brett Woodward, *Merzbook: The Pleasuredome of Noise* (Cologne: Extreme, 1999), 57–65.
2. Pouncey, 'Consumed by Noise', in *The Wire* 198 (August 2000), 26–32.
3. Other examples are many of Boyd Rice's records, the highly creative Underground Resistance label, Mars Volta's *Frances the Mute*, which deals with the problem of long tracks on the CD by just cutting a locked groove into them, creating a listening that recalls My Bloody Valentine's *Loveless*, and an insistence that you continue with the rest of the album. Beyond these examples, the noise single is an oddity, but there are many of them, and pretty much all Japanese noise musicians have released several. The limited duration of a vinyl single can be read as an admission that slices of noise can be extracted, more or less arbitrarily. The noise single is not a single from an album, so is more self-contained—a shrinking of the album. Aube's 4-single box *Quadrotation* is a good example, with a different sound source informing each record, while the whole suggests a punctuated continuity—elements that maybe should not merge but might.
4. Keenan, 'Picks the Best of Merzbow', *The Wire* 198, 32–3.
5. Russolo took noise to be an indication of life, liveliness, creativity and the unexpected. Life can be thought of as a supreme example of structuring—after all, it is a way of holding entropy at bay, a slowing of decay, but life can also be thought of as noise, an interference.
6. On Japan in general, Masami Akita says that 'sometimes I would like to kill the much too noisy Japanese by my own Noise. The effects of Japanese culture are too much noise everywhere. I want to make silence by my Noise. Maybe, that is a fascist way of using sound' (in 'the Beauty of Noise: An Interview with Masami Akita of Merzbow', in Cox and Warner, *Audio Culture*, 59–61), 61. This apparent intolerance is a knowing one, complicit with what it attacks—presumably the noise of the ultra-commercial because it intrudes so much. The answer is a bigger intrusion. It is also a self-conscious statement because clearly he does not have the power or the strategy to take power to enforce his views.
7. This is a problem with what is generally viewed as cynical involvement in spectacles such as Live Aid or Live 8. Why not here? The principal difference is that neither anti-whaling groups nor Masami Akita is set to make huge commercial windfalls, and the latter is unlikely to perform in front of gigantic TV audiences.

11
SOUND ART

According to Walter Benjamin, western art moves away from art having a sacred value toward having exhibition value. Art's value becomes secular, aesthetic and social. It moves from sacred buildings to private ones, and gradually becomes more public: aristocrats and monarchs build collections of art and curious objects, which are displayed to their peers, the bourgeois class follows suit, and the public museum is created. Eventually, the public, including members of lower classes, are allowed in, to be educated into the great heritage of the culture that sits atop them. Exhibition value constrains works to being portable, of recognizable form (e.g. a framed painting, a statue on a plinth), and exchangeable. From the late seventeenth century onwards, art as an institution develops, including galleries, museums, criticism and a public of connoisseurs. This setting of art excludes noise—audiences must behave correctly, demurely; buildings must clearly show works that are autonomous, and simultaneously part of a narrative. Far from disrupting this, modern art leads to a booming of the art institution, and fuels the idea of art history as a narrative where we move from one picture to the next. But modern art does introduce noise, in the form of avant-gardism, and even if ultimately this adds to the teleogical story of art, at any given stage, from the 1850s onwards, some part of art was regarded as noise: as not carrying meaning, lacking skill, not being appropriate, disturbing of morals, etc.

Music, too, is harnessed in the modern concept of a concert where the audience sits silent, except for regulated participation, and the musicians are separated, elevated in more than one sense. Even as late as the eighteenth century, audiences at musicals are raucous, but gradually they are disciplined,[1] and however we might imagine a Wagnerian *Gesamtkunstwerk* as a sort of noisy crossing of artforms, it completes the subjugation of the audience. Sound is totally banished from the gallery—where art is to remain visual. The framed painting on a wall allows rational contemplation, and so massages the verticality of appreciation and analysis, over the potential messiness of horizontality.[2] Futurist and dada performances occurred elsewhere—with their collisions of theatre, early sound poetry, film, dance, shouting, music and fighting happening in theatres for the most part, but also on many occasions outside of any cultural institution. It is only really with Fluxus in the late 1950s that sound is tentatively staged in galleries. Where dada's radicality was in not being in a gallery, Fluxus, as a second generation of the same impulse, was able to be radical precisely for performing in official art settings (as well as elsewhere). This is the early days of performance art (also in Japan), and Fluxus flows into the outpouring of movements, or approaches of the 1960s: conceptual art, happenings, installations, body art performance. As well as the acceptance of art's radicalization and disrespect for categorical borders between artforms, there is also the question of technology. Sound creeps into galleries in the wake of affordable technologies, notably in tape technology in the 1960s, and the development of video in the late 1960s. This is the first point at which, I would claim, we can begin to talk of sound art, and, just as the (temporally amorphous) advent of Japanese noise music authorizes a retrospective rethinking of 'precursors' in noise, so the sound installations that begin to appear in the late 1960s allow, or suggest ways in which sound was used to construct art, or was made as art rather than as music.

The Pompidou Centre in Paris proposed an intimate connection between sound and modern art in its *Sons et lumières* show (2005), looking at how artists were inspired by music (like Kandinsky), made sound-producing sculptures (Moholy-Nagy), or incorporated sound as content. Duchamp's *With Hidden Noise* plays with the possibility but unlikelihood of the trapped ball of string etc. producing audible sound. Duchamp's actual musical experiments do not produce sounds that are particularly challenging. Kurt Schwitters' sound poetry is there of course.[3] The second part of the show looks at actual sound performances/installations/objects that were designed for the gallery setting, and usually had been located there in the first place. I am not complaining about the hindsightfulness of the show, rather using it to show a problem at the heart of definitions of sound art: namely, that it comes to apply to pretty much anything that has to do with both together. Sound art, like 'noise music', is a noisy genre, something porous and very hard to define, but as I will argue below, following Krauss' take on minimalist sculpture, it is too self-contained, and sets up the listener as self-contained, in order to challenge not sufficiency, but only the way in which that has been constructed (i.e. it's going to 'make you think', and in so doing reveal to the listening subject some part of a hitherto hidden sound reality).

Sons et lumières goes on to gloss over the longstanding incompatibility of sound with the gallery/museum setting. Sound in the gallery is noise—not only inappropriate until recent times, but it spreads beyond its location, or demands more of a sense of location than a painting, say, requires. Sound-based art in a show can be overbearing, and, if there are several pieces, they risk clashing. Contemplation of any given piece is disrupted, and in turn the sound piece becomes an ambience rather than a discrete work. To get round this, space can be allocated away from other works—a sort of quarantine. Alternatively, the piece can be totally isolated and accessed through headphones. So sound art continually raises the question of noise, even if often to be closed off (sometimes by the artists themselves). Once it is safely positioned, it then becomes a highly appreciated commodity of the gallery, as a CD, sound files, or even messier older media are transportable, convenient and probably not unique (however aleatory the actual playing out of the piece might be). This convenience must be part of art's acceptance of sound art in its most restricted form.

Sound art takes many forms: sound installations, performances, recordings, whether for direct public consumption, or as purchasable objects to listen to domestically, interactive pieces, pieces designed for headphone use, transmission of sound (often from other locations). Each one of these has many variants. The sound source could be the most important factor, or the process of listening it establishes. Sound art is not just sound working as art. Brandon LaBelle notes that

> in bridging the visual arts with the sonic arts, creating an interdisciplinary practice, sound art fosters the cultivation of sonic materiality in relation to the conceptualization of auditory potentiality. While at times incorporating, referring to, or drawing upon materials, ideas and concerns outside of sound *per se*, sound art nonetheless seems to position such things in relation to aurality,

the processes and promises of audition, and sonic culture. (*Background Noise*, 151)[4]

The communal element of performance might be what counts, or the enclosedness and peculiar isolation of headphones. It can also basically just be experimental or avant-garde music brought into an art location. This is part of this music's attempt to get away from music and its standard settings, but, again, it is also a way of getting music heard that maybe does not function in concert settings, and that has found a new outlet. Sound art often reflects on its own production, and this can be the effective content of the piece (1960s/1970s art using tape recorders is fond of this). It does this in combination with an exploration of sound—as in Paul Kos' *Sound of Ice Melting* (1970), which has blocks of ice in the gallery, surrounded by microphones. Here sound becomes spectacle of its own production. Sound art extends this into a questioning of listening, and the position of the listener.

Labelle insists that the importance accorded listening and sound production means sound art is process at least as much as product (sound consumption requiring the time of its playing feeds into this): 'sound art as a practice harnesses, describes, analyses, performs, and interrogates the condition of sound and the process by which it operates' (*Background Noise*, ix). That this often supplants the 'what' of what is being listened to might be a problem on occasion, but it is essential to the process. Sound art is also about space, he argues, writing that it is 'the activation of the existing relation between sound and space' (ix). Sound and space are inherently linked, as sound for us is what disturbs air, and that is not going to happen in the absence of space, but sound also structures space, and sound art aims to both illustrate that and do it. Space is not fixed, but permanently forming and reforming, with sound as one of its constituent parts, and this occurs through human intervention and perception (as far as we can hear: humans cannot functionally have any other perspective). Following on from that, 'the acoustical event is also a social one' (x)—it is not just the interaction of human subjects with an object world; it is also interactivity as society. Hence, from these three points, the centrality of Cage's *4' 33"*, which opens these perspectives. Once we have these ideas as ways of thinking and listening, then our whole body is involved, as it is not just a matter of deciphering an encrypted block of sound—i.e. a musical piece. The performances of Fluxus accorded sound a significant part (on Cage, see chapters 1 and 2; on Fluxus, see chapter 2 of this volume), as did the later happenings, and performance art. These approaches sought to break open the rigidness of artwork and viewer, and sound's mobility offered a heightened connectivity.[5]

If sound art is to do all these things, then it either has to be an installation where the sound occupies a certain space (or exceeds it) or a performance. Transportable works can be sound art (particularly if we take self-description as a useful marker), if they are headphone pieces that 'guide' you around a town aurally (Hildegard Westerkamp, Janet Cardiff) or maybe set up an environment, through site-specific sound recordings, other than the one you are in (Richard Long, Chris Watson), even if only listening on headphones in the gallery. A CD of sound art that gets played at home seems less fully part of sound art—despite the growth of field recordings, ambiences, and recordings of installations. The key in any case, is the installation, of which Labelle has the following to say: 'the developments of sound installation provide a heightened articulation of sound to perform as an artistic medium, making explicit 'sound art' as a unique and identifiable practice' (*Background Noise*, 151). Some of those 'ideas and concerns outside of sound' are to do with disjunction, for LaBelle, and I will return to that below. The installation does not have to do any explicit bridging itself, as it can be sound in a place where the visual is supposed usually to be. The visual is supplanted through a display of the machinery of production or reproduction of the sound, and the visitor to the gallery is now made primarily an auditor.

As sound art expands its remit (colonizing other forms?), and the innovations brought by Cage, Fluxus, conceptual and video art are now taken for granted, the performance of sound art can often be very straight—i.e. basically a concert. So to define itself as sound art, it reverts to the 'what' is being played—supposedly non-musical objects, homemade instruments, odd noises, field recordings . . . at what point this stops being a concert is hard to tell. Conversely, sound art performance that looks uncannily like a concert generates its own audience—i.e. sound art expectations are different from events described as concerts—the quality or type of sounds takes on an autonomous importance, and the listening is thought to be more creative, as the work establishes an ambience (however aleatory or loud or monotonous or dynamic) that encourages reflection or its loss (as opposed to engaging with the content/form of music). Artists like Scanner play to these expectations, with different approaches according to context (in a sound art setting, he would use a radio scanner to sample the city's speech; in a club, he would play electronic dance music). Of course, defeating those expectations works too—it's win-win. An audience in a major gallery might also not recognize sound moves familiar to those who listen to avant-garde music, so are more easily 'disturbed' in their expectations.

On this question of the audience, it is worth going back to Cage. He was highly didactic in his advocacy of listening, and this has been inherited ever since by sound art followers, who have become incredibly deferential to sound in the guise of liberating their listening. A sweeping statement, but in my experience, the only exceptions are the sanctioned 'play' of a 'subversive' disco style party in a gallery setting, or of an art event in a club (like Paul O'Neill's *Mingle-Mangled* [2005]), where the deference is to the curated setting. Cage's *4' 33"* is a time and space for sounds to occur in, a space, as Labelle rightly notes, for bodies to make noises, for ears to hear beyond the confines of the pianist in front of them (one of the less-commented on elements of the silent pieces is that there to be a performer, even if it is you deciding on a duration on which to hear in). By all accounts on its first performance people got restless, some left, and it was not met with rapturous applause afterward, but there can be no failure, because whatever happens, listening has occurred.[6] The most likely unwitting purpose seems to be to discipline those bodies into correctly listening bodies, static, tensed, if excited in anticipation, about someone or something else intruding. This is no dismantling of music but a heightening of its conventions' hierarchies. Only now the musician is included too in the enforced silence.[7] Today's attendance at sound art performance is docile—and this can be interesting too, with quietness of the sounds produced an even better strategy than silence for heightening listening. But if we are thinking about noise, it seems to me it is being swept away even as it is being listened for. At some point, noise has to be allowed to to come into hearing, not be caught and musicalized before coming into fleeting being.

Acoustic ecology (or sound ecology) has tried to capture the soundworld in a concerted way. Started and inspired by R. Murray Shafer, and his notion of the soundscape, it pursues the soundworld that we now conceive as opened up for listening by Cage. As with Cage, the principal idea is that there is a soundworld 'out there' and we should appreciate and be part of it. It is more interventionist, though, more of a purposeful bringing of the soundworld to the newly sensitized ears of the listener, in the form of examples of that soundworld. Drawing attention to sounds from around the world becomes important, as does the preservation of 'soundmarks', whether natural or well-established social sound. Acoustic ecology also seeks to limit noise, especially human noise that interferes with the sound-scape of 'the world'. It does not quite see human culture as noise, but identifies numerous points at which humanity overpowers its own good sounds and those of nature—basically refusing Russolo's love of industry and advanced technology as noise creator. It is absolutely against noise, and for familiar sounds, and familiariz-ing people with sounds that elsewhere are a more or less natural part of the sound-scape. LaBelle sums it up well in writing that

> what acoustic ecology lends to a history of sound art is a social, musical and ontological register, for in proposing sound as a category for bureaucratic consideration, sociological study, and environmental concerns and design, acoustic ecology raises the bar on auditory understanding and its relational nature. (*Background Noise*, 203)

Sound becomes part of what we inhabit, our inhabiting has consequences, and we should alter our thoughtless noise production and consumption to properly dwell in the soundworld. The production of field recordings or works that draw our atten-tion to our surroundings in terms of sound and noise is a means of doing this, not a fully separate mission, so in that sense acoustic ecology has a different kind of open listening to that of Cage, and it is one that *judges*. Noise is always a judge-ment that certain sounds (or actions, practices, attitudes) are noise, but many would agree that this judgement does not only dismiss things as noise, it discerns good and bad noise. This might be theoretically untenable, but it is what is being done by the Merzbow listener as much as by noise abatement, or 'authentic' sound recordings. In terms of sound art, as well as bringing in elements to the gallery, or onto recordings, acoustic ecology emphasizes that listening should not be restricted to those occasions, and sound artists, at least as much as any other type of artist, have looked beyond the institutions for its works, and situated them or identified listening places in many different types of location.

Sound art is an essential part of both conceptualism and minimalism, writes LaBelle (*Background Noise*, 143), and ultimately separates off from them, while still pursuing their objectives—in the case of the former, in drawing attention to listening, to sound as object, to sound as questioning of perception, and as for the latter, this is the environmental or spatial element, particularly in the case of sound installations. The minimalist Robert Morris made a corridor of wood, entitled *Pas-sageway* (1961), Bruce Nauman making a very similar piece, *Sound Corridor* (1969). Both establish an oddly differentiated space in the gallery, on the inside resonating from the body that visits it, and the sounds from the rest of the gallery partially excluded from it. This intrusion in the gallery restructures the space around it, as minimalist sculpture aims to, introduces listening, and alters the movement of the visitor, setting up a disjunctive space. For Krauss,

> Minimalism was indeed committed to this notion of the 'lived *bodily* perspective', the idea of a perception that would break with what it saw as the decorporealized and therefore bloodless, algebraicized condition of abstract painting in which a visuality [was] cut loose from the rest of the bodily sensorium [. . .] its insistence on the immediacy of the experience, understood as a bodily immediacy, was intended as a kind of release from the forward march of modernist painting towards an increasingly positivist abstraction. ('The Cultural Logic of the Late Capitalist Museum', 433)[8]

Sound is initially part of this project, then sound art reverses its priorities, so that creating an environment is *part* of what sound art does. But all the while, it offers a regenerated perception of situatedness. There are limits to the realization of such an aim, as it is based on a simplistic view of the body, of how experience relates to it, and how a controlling mentality then processes the experience:

> Minimalism's reformulation of the subject as radically contingent [i.e. transformed through experience of the artwork] is, even though it attacks older idealist notions of the subject, a kind of Utopian gesture. This is because the Minimalist subject is in this very displacement returned to its body, regrounded in a kind of richer, denser subsoil of experience. (*Ibid.*)

Sound art tries to affect the individual that encounters it, drawing a sense of disjunction from incongruous sound (its presence in the gallery in the first place, then the way in which it makes the visitor think about listening, the oddness, in some occasions, of the sounds themselves), but in so doing, requires belief in an otherwise fixed subject. Put differently, sound installations relocate the individual as a centred subject encountering an object situation, with neither troubled in its respective unities. Nonetheless, despite Krauss' warning, sound art's attempts to fix the listening subject could, despite itself, actually signal the continual de-centredness of individuals.

Sound art also ties in with the development of video art. Sound is a long underplayed elements of video art, being a crucial part of Nam June Paik's work, and now a commonplace in video art that tends toward narrative film or music video (i.e. where either sound or vision purposely *accompanies* the other). 'New Wave' filmmakers like Jean-Luc Godard had a keen sense of disruptive use of sound, and 1960s art as a whole exploits all the potentialities of sound and visual media, including where sound is absent, because now it has been made absent, rather than being a result of technical insufficiency. Video art (or experimental film) introduces the moving image to the gallery, thus already questioning the position of 'the' image (as Duchamp's did to a certain extent with his 'rotorelief' machines). It subtly brings an added disturbance in the form of sound, notably exploited by Nauman in numerous videos, where sounds are repeated, voices distorted, and other sounds (like feet jumping) occur. Video artist Bill Viola, known for his grandiose reworking of 'the great themes of the human condition' is part of this noisy interference. In a 1999 show at San Francisco Museum of Modern Art, some of his works are described as video/sound installations. The silent ones take part of their supposed emotional power from the contrasting silence (as well as the silences and gaps in the 'video/sound' pieces). This is a more disjunctive use of silence than that of Cage, at least in the museum context, as your attention is drawn to sound and its absence, across something else, as opposed to setting up a purist space of listening creativity. With an early work, *Hallway Nodes*, consisting of two bass speakers positioned opposite each other, Viola configures space as heavy air. The piece is cordoned off by plastic curtains, with a warning about disorientation. This is sound made physical (resonating the air almost visibly) and has a deep effect on the visiting body, which has to readjust to the unbassed air outside. This installation, then, not only structures space, but it also makes the structuring itself physically perceptible.

Nauman revisited his video oeuvre for *Raw Materials*, in London's Tate Modern. The long turbine hall was lined with speakers, from which Nauman had constructed a sound piece. It is a radical move to not only place sound in this vast setting, but to remove all other elements. Unfortunately, it illustrates the limitations sound art often encounters. Nauman took the audio tracks from his video pieces, and channelled them through individual speakers. The polite sound levels (or perhaps the presence of bodies) prevented cacophony, or any interference, and isolated what were now sound tracks, such that no interesting recombination was possible. The problem with this work is that the idea of it has taken over, and the idea is very small: here's the sound from video artworks, put together. This is an emptied conceptual art that might be interesting as a critique of conceptual art, but offers an unwitting critique of how sound art's move to the materiality and/or reproduction of sound displaces not only content, the interestingness or noisiness of content, but also any purpose beyond self-sufficient existing.[9] This problem crosses into the audience, who are too often called upon to marvel at the fact of the work existing rather than anything else. This is not exclusive to sound art of course, and applies to swathes of large scale and/or public art, but sound art is not incidentally or cynically doing this; it is a fundamental condition of its working.

Sound art can do more than this, and it deals in perception, both structuring it and positing it as a question, but too often this is not enough; it is kept at a level of sufficiency, the presentation of sound in its own right, in a rejection of formal experimentation and judgement alike. Maybe like other noise 'forms', it does not bear repetition too well, but more than most types of noise music, it seems caught within its remit to explore perception, to the exclusion of all else. Ryoji Ikeda's *matrix* CD recalls the installation where a visitor would move within the sound, and interactively structure the sound, becoming aware of the processes of physical as well as mental listening. The long tones are also difficult for the listener, highlighting a problem for sound art as it requires a durational participation (i.e. you're not supposed to identify the sound or type of sound, then move on), so noise is going to be thwarted by itself. Sound art has to self-censor to begin to be noisy, rather than be simply rejected as *mere* noise.

Alternatively, sound art can take a musical turn. The Pompidou Centre's *Sonic Process* show of 2002 (first presented in Barcelona) purposely blurred the lines between music and sound art,[10] exploring sound production in a primarily digital form, or as created in the context of an era of digital reproduction. Janet Cardiff achieved a popular success with her *Forty Part Motet* (2001). As presented at Tate Liverpool in 2003, it consisted of the forty speakers placed in eight groups, forming a circle, occupying one room. The sound is of a piece of sixteenth-century music, as performed by the Salisbury Cathedral Choir, with each speaker allocated to a voice. The piece includes peripheral sound in the form of the moments before the music begins. Cardiff states that with this piece she 'want[s] to be able to "climb inside" the music, connecting with the separate voices. [She is] also interested in how the audience may choose a path through this physical and virtual space'.[11] This piece investigates sound as produced in a musical context: audiences are kept from the performers, and the performers are perceived as a bunch, rather than as individuals, thus undermining the voice in favour of the effect. Cardiff's point seems to be that music has lost something, and that this can be restored through restructuring, or, feasibly, deconstruction, but it falls into the problem that Krauss identifies in minimalism, where a hitherto buried authentic experience is restored by the new artwork. Doesn't *Forty Part Motet* deny the sociality of choral sound production, in favour of individualism? A riposte to that would be that they are not ultimately separated off, but that the interaction between individual and group is brought out.

The speakers do more than stand in for the individuals of the choir; they represent them, and do so as specifically absent—one of the recurring themes of sound art being the uncanniness of the playing of sounds both present and signalling a presence now gone, whether of people, of place, or of the sound artist as recorder of another place, then present, there, at least, and now not. The visitor's involvement is to do with them rethinking music as spatializing, as positioning (of the listener). At one level, this not much different than the aural positioning of stereo, except with 40 channels, or perhaps the questioning of this by Brian Eno, who aimed for a more total sound with his ambient music (see sleeve notes on his *Discreet Music*). In other words, it is part of a quest for aural perfection and authenticity. However, *Forty Part Motet* is messier than that, as the number of channels questions notions of 'surround sound'—the unity of the listening is not achieved by the number of channels, as these are so rigorously discrete.

To return to the gallery's staging of sound art, it seems as if sound art can successfully be allocated a space, and it can also be given control of a space (I mean this literally, not in terms of sound's spatialization and critique of same). The *Sons et Lumières* exhibition not only took an entire gallery space, but it also configured it as separate sound cells, allowing, for example, the reconstruction of Lamonte Young's *Dreamhouse*, whose 'total environment' principally located it forcefully in its historical moment, with its 1960s futurological décor, rather than it highlighting Young's quest for infinite and eternal sound. Once sound art makes up a whole show, the noisiness of sound is reduced, becoming expectation on the part of the listener, while, conversely, certain areas are permitted to be more disruptive, loud, unpleasant. Headphones are never far away, though, especially in new media shows such as the Whitney's *Bitstreams* (2001) in New York. Here visitors were presented with the rather sad spectacle of the sound art component being a row of headphones with accompanying seats. Maybe this illustrates the refusal of the visual or spectacular, in favour of a pure listening, but if this is sound art, it is too little: no spatial structuring, a poor substitute for personal stereos, and a rigid separating off from the real art. The presentation of video art was closer to the aims of sound art. Indeed, as video art increasingly pays more conscious attention to sound, headphones are provided for the viewer/listener.[12]

Headphones can work, though, in sound art, providing another means for reconfiguring the individual as a listening subject, interacting with space.[13] Place as well as phenomenological space can be invoked, evoked or disturbed. Cardiff, often with George Bures Miller, specializes in recorded walks.[14] The listener takes a personal stereo out of the gallery and retraces a walk done by Cardiff and making up the recording you are now listening to. This system parodies the audio guide available in museums, offering so much detail it disturbs the walker. Things observed by Cardiff become uncanny—if they are there, there is a hallucinatory doubling of what is in front of you and an odd sense of being followed (even though preceded); or, if not there, the place of the recording separates off from the present location. The walk takes sound into a wider sensorium—and heightens awareness of even a familiar place. The boundary between recorded sounds and those occurring now becomes fuzzy. The whole adds up to a respatialization of the self, actually enhanced through submission to instructions or recorded events. The anarchistic Situationist movement had proposed a similar strategy with the *dérive*, where a walker could reconfigure a place, generally a city, as something they intervened in, rather than passively reacted to, or got moved around in ('parcours'/'parkour' tries this through playful physicalization of the city). It also recalls Fredric Jameson's idea of 'cultural mapping', where the individual in postmodern, globalized society could position themselves, so as to not ignore the connectivity of that society, which is often oppressive.[15]

If such strategies mobilize sound, and use sound as mobilization, then we also have to note sound art that occupies a location, framing it for aural observation, instead of providing a contrast. Akio Suzuki tries to get people to listen to the city, usually the city they inhabit. His 'Oto-date Cork 2005' consisted of twenty locations marked with ears, a map helping you find these locations. Once in place, the person takes in the soundscape as present at that spot, at that time. This draws attention to sound as such, to sounds as usually neglected, and to the listener's relation to the cityspace. Such work recalls the holistic outlook of acoustic ecology, but is hard to conceive of as functioning as sound art, except insofar as sounds other than music are worth listening to. Other artists are not just recording a place, but their intervention in it, interaction with it (Scanner's early performances and recordings using a radio scanner, or, more generally, a recording from a specific time and place, i.e. 'when I, the recorder, was here'). In this case, the subjectivity that sound installations want to deal with is represented rather than brought into direct confrontation with the individual who has now become listener. Whether such work is sound art is a matter for another study, or for record shop genredefining, but like much of sound art, it is not noise, nor is it engaging with it. Where it does, it tends to be where the line between it and noise music is at its finest. This line is not even noisy, as so many artists do both, or do the same thing but get defined in two different ways according to institutional location. The disjunctions are mostly in the relational aspect of sound art (how it makes us aware of relatedness, and our position as related to environments), in its other relation to the visual arts and its homes, in the relation set up between a here and a there in the representing of sound from somewhere else or another time.

sound art • **177**

NOTES

1. See Leppert, 'Desire, Power and the Sonoric Landscape: Early Modernism and the Politics of Musical Privacy' in Layshon, Matless and Revil (eds), *The Place of Music*, 291–321 and 301–2 in particular.

2. On this opposition, and how certain art, mostly since the 1950s, undermines it, see Yve-Alain Bois and Rosalind Krauss, *Formless: A User's Guide* (New York: Zone, 1997).

3. The exhibition does not consider the sound poetry field to any more than a minimal level, peculiarly given the central role of Henri Chopin and Bernard Heidsieck in the spread of the style. Bob Cobbing and Sten Hanson offer more playful versions of sound poetry. Sound poetry makes noise of language, but seeks a return to a primal human communication through voice, and a deconstruction of language that would reveal its true arbitrariness (as in Schwitters' *Ursonate*). For more on sound poetry, see www.ubu.com/sound.

4. LaBelle, *Background Noise: Perspectives on Sound Art* (New York and London: Continuum, 2006).

5. On this point, I think LaBelle is hasty in dismissing Marina Abramovic and extreme body art of the 1970s, on the basis that it is trying to be cathartic (103–4), unlike Vito Acconci in *Seedbed*, who is dealing with questions of interaction. LaBelle is right to dwell on this piece, where Acconci masturbates from under a raised floor in the gallery, as the speaker conveying his declamations is a central part, and is generally ignored. LaBelle refers to Abramovic's piece *Freeing the Voice*, a lengthy endurance piece, where she vocalizes for the full duration, recalling Artaud, but how is this not a piece that demands listening, or does something to and with listening, and complicity? Other works, such as *Rhythm 10*, where she stabs between her fingers, and then tries to repeat the exact pattern, would surely be worth attention in terms of sound, music and noise. I think the same could be said of much of her 1970s work, even if the point about ecstatic catharsis is probably right.

6. Sound artist Danny McCarthy curated an event (Cageday 4' 33") at the Crawford Gallery, Cork, in 2002 to commemorate fifty years since the first performance of *4' 33"*. One of the two performances of the piece featured considerable intervention from people working in the venue, just outside the door, while the other was incredibly silent.

7. Kahn has a similar outlook to this, in his *Noise Water Meat*, which Labelle dismisses (*Background Noise*, 14–16). I think LaBelle's view works, but I'm with Kahn, and his critical take on Cage is not an attack, but an examination of the philosophical limits in Cage's conceptualizations.

8. Krauss, 'The Cultural Logic of the Late Capitalist Museum', in Krauss et al. (eds), *October: The Second Decade, 1986–1996* (Cambridge, MA: MIT Press, 1997), 427–41.

9. Colin Harrison has suggested to me that the failure of Nauman's piece is a rejection of the drama usually required or expected for the large space, and that this makes it a refusal rather than a failure, or more accurately, failure as refusal.

10. The same can be said of *Sonic Boom: The Art of Sound*, staged at London's Hayward gallery in 2000, and curated by David Toop.

11. www.tate.org.uk/liverpool/exhibitions/janetcardiff/default.htm

12. Video art, and many other art forms, carries its own noise, or potential for noise. This can involve critique of art institutions, questions about and to publics and so on, as well as involving the formal properties of specific artworks. Site-specificity in or for any medium would be one rich source of noise, or of noise prevention or domestication. Only sound art connects directly with the issue of noise and its relation to music within the boundaries here, though.

13. Early concerts of the band Cornelius featured them dispensing headphones to the audience, which is how they would hear the music. Recent years have also seen the spread of the 'silent disco' or silent club, where clubgoers listen through headphones, if they want.

14. Hildegard Westerkamp also works in this area (see LaBelle, *Background Noise*, 205–15).

15. Jameson, *Postmodernism: Or, the Cultural Logic of Late Capitalism* (London: Verso, 1991).

12
CUT

Many noise strategies involve misuse, reisue or abuse of instruments, machinery, contexts and practices. Such improper use is part of the failure that constitutes noise (recalling that this failure is only 'failure'—it is not a judgement about badness, but one of a refusal of heroic success in the form of musical mastery or mastery of musical forms). Recording media contain a continual potential for failure exactly where their functionality lies, in what Baudrillard identified as reversibility. There are, then, a sequence of practices that use this 'potential' of recorded media, or already reproduced sound. These media contain completed music, and act as a type of storage that fixes performances, making the recording a reference point. In this chapter, I will look at how use of the turntable, sampling and glitching all try to break through this reification. In so doing, they use pre-existing material and work on that material through the materiality of its storage. More curiously, they end up revealing disruptions, cuts and interferences that are always already present in the 'proper' functioning of those media.

Rut

The vinyl record's capacity to receive sound, then convey the resulting electrical impulses as sound, relies on the permeability of vinyl—the sound material structures a surface and can be disrupted as that it is from there that it must always emerge. The pliability of vinyl, in other words, is a necessity and a risk. Tape's storage of an untextured whole, especially when guarded by the plastic of the compact cassette, is lost as the tape recovers its texture and tactility in unravelling. Even short disruptions of tape have effects elsewhere. The endless looping of eight tracks allowed the sound storage but means the entire recording is at risk if one tiny section fails. CDs can seem to skip when the disc's surface is marked, dirty, etc.—when the encoded surface is broken through (Hainge has pointed out that CDs do not really skip; instead what we encounter is an alteration, or a different reading of the information received as sound ['Of Glitch and Men', 33–4]).[1]

Vinyl's particular susceptibility to manipulation encouraged Cage and, to an even greater extent, Pierre Schaeffer, to begin to use vinyl as an instrument. This takes two forms, both of which persist through to digital media: first, the acceptance that pre-recorded sound, including music, was a legitimate sound source for musical creation; second, that the vinyl record itself could be made to work instrumentally. In the 1970s, this gradually began to inform emerging hip-hop, going via DJ Kool Herc's isolating of rhythmical elements on records (extending dub practice), Grandmaster Flash, Grandmaster DST, and eventually becoming a given, in the form of scratching (actually moving the record manually, or as Peter Shapiro puts it, 'the sound of a record being rubbed across a stylus', which I think conveys the materiality of the practice that is maybe less consciously used once away from sound artists and 'experimental' DJs, but still there ['Deck Wreckers', 165]).[2] Scratching alters the forward narrative of a record, singling out a phrase, a beat, or a section to work as a new loop, or pattern of sound, in the case of more noise-oriented turntablists like Otomo Yoshihide. Cuts in sound recall the original cutting to embed the sound signal.

Form is sought through destruction of the previously inscribed form, but other than that most irritating of scratching staples, the back and forth palpating of a record, it matters what the sound source is, so destruction is not complete. Christian Marclay, who hovers between being sound artist, DJ and experimental noise collager, made what has come to be seen as a marker in the history of music made through a 'failing' medium, with his *Record without a Cover* (1985), part of his overall project where

> Accentuating the natural erosion of vinyl through use, Marclay constructed collages out of the skips and pops and hiss of discarded thriftstore records. By foregrounding surface noise, Marclay attempted to jolt the listener out of the reification created by the medium of recording. (Shapiro, 'Deck Wreckers', 170)

For Marclay, the record is not just being deviated from its original use; it comes from disuse (being discarded) and inutility (damage), and it will continue to descend into something formless. If such works are then put onto CD, the process might be over at a literal level, but the sounds will be a constant parody of the perfection attributed to CDs, a reminder of the hopelessness of attaining perfection.

All these interventions are clearly ways of disrupting the finality of the music commodity in purchasable recorded form. They are also ways of impinging on the teleologies of music: beginning, middle and end, no matter how strange the sounds that fill that time. Beyond this, the stability of a musical object (whether the music itself, the record, or the way music is *contained* by the record) is nullified. A scratch does not even faithfully repeat itself, so as to become an unobtrusive part (unlike where lumps have formed in grooves, either through a pressing fault, or later, then there is a stability, as long as they are low enough for the needle to continue; for then, as it is an excrescence rather than an incursion, it can almost be adjusted to). As such practice continued, the 1990s saw representation of vinyl limitations introduced on CDs as a sort of nostalgia. DJ Shadow, Massive Attack and Portishead popularized this use of represented vinyl, featuring not only samples from vinyl, but samples of warmly static vinyl. While the increase in quantity of such practice, or 'analogues' of it, shows a nostalgia at the level of musical content, it also carries a melancholy for vinyl itself. Soft crackles and a fuzzy static gradually creep across a much played vinyl record, and its decay mirrors that of the listener, who now has their own version of a piece. But the record is becoming *more* complex, less entropic; it is the integrity of the music only that decays, revealing itself as mere sound. The CD that features this is not simply melancholic for the passing of linear information, but it also celebrates this passing, in offering tainted memorials to the supposedly defunct.

In a different context, Hainge warns us not to attribute agency to a CD (*a propos* of CDs themselves affecting CD players, 'Of Glitch and Men', 36), but what I am suggesting is more abstract but also more entwined in an entire complex of sound production, listening, consumption and music-making: where a CD is like Foucauldian power, omnipresent but non-directional, i.e. a vector, with no one in charge of the effect produced. The celebration of vinyl's warmth is, in this context, also part of the 1990s attempt to consign vinyl to the past. Ultimately, sampling fixes the vinyl record as a category, as well as in its individual avatars, just as remasterings fix the original in ever greater detail and perfection. That is to say, this perfection always nearly happens, but never gets completed. At a commercial level, remastering is profitable and panders to a desire that is far from thwarted by endlessly 'having to buy' the new formatting of a 'perfected' classic. However, record companies and stores eventually noticed that another listening was occurring, and from being noise as a format (to be excluded as unwieldy, unreliable, space-consuming, relatively difficult to make, and against the standard mass form of the CD), vinyl has been restored as a newly valued prestige commodity.[3]

Vinyl has great noise potential, and, as Cage, Otomo Yoshihide or DJ/Rupture show, the machinery that goes with it can also be used and misused. It can disrupt, be disrupted, or both at the same time. Manipulating records, though, takes us back to the malfunction of a scratch or of blockage on a record, and then, onto the 'proper' functioning, now intimately connected to its improper use. There are noises other than the sounds 'in the grooves' of a record, even with a proper playing—the placing of the stylus (to be smoothed away by dance DJs, to be used as percussion or sound source in its own right by e.g. Otomo, DJ/Rupture), the hiss of the 'silences' in or between tracks, and the run out grooves ending in stylus removal, all contribute extraneous sounds. A damaged record will add to this, and the primary thing it adds is rhythm: the stuck record has made an incursion into the music, but re-established a rhythm, either from a loop of the recorded sounds, or just the stylus playing the record itself. This phenomenon led Pierre Schaeffer to make samples in the form of locked grooves, which would set up a loop. Scratching does a similar trick (adding in the mixer controls as potential contributors to rhythm), and the locked groove has now become a recognized tool in its own right for DJ-ing. There is a great range available to the locked groove—it can try to represent itself as caught, as a damaged part of a record; it could attempt to hide its repetition through concentrated complexity and/or slight variation between fast repetitions, or it can simply be a beat.[4] The listener to a record with a locked groove (or made entirely of them, as Non's *Pagan Muzak* is, or samplers like *lock-ERS* (162 locked grooves by that number of artists) and *RRR500* with 500) has a great deal of freedom—choosing entirely how long each piece will be. There is also a lot of work for a listener or player, and, in the case of the sampler type, there is a choice between really learning the record or letting a more random playing dominate. Vinyl has other tricks available to it—playing from inside to out; etching records oddly (Non again, Crawling with Tarts, Alva Noto) so that what gets played is uncertain; alternate holes; or double tracking, so that two tracks alternate. At one level, these pre-empt the listener becoming performer; for all their 'interactivity', this is still an imposed interactive process, as opposed to the more ostensibly resistent linear record. At another, they immediately highlight the materiality of the object and the process of sound transcription.

Such work on the vinyl is a literalization of the work of the DJ, or, feasibly, a spread of DJ-ing to encompass the listening demanded by the non-standard record. As DJs developed physical strategies beyond the proper use of vinyl, the DJ was accepted as a genuine musical contributor, or, in the standard DJ setting of playing records to people in clubs, was increasingly accepted as much more than a transmitter of other people's work. That older type of DJ represents an ana-logue of radio, and that started to fade with dancehall and dub. In a way, those innovators were almost too obviously adding artistic intervention, whereas the DJ since the 1980s offers a site of creation that comes through pre-existing sounds. It is important not to lose sight of that, as DJ culture claims a different kind of origi-nality, one that is not just sonic or manual manipulation. For Paul D. Miller (DJ Spooky), 'the records, samples, and various other sonic material the DJ uses to construct their mix act as a sort of externalized memory that breaks down previous notions of intellectual property and copyright law that Western Society has used in the past' ('Algorithms: Erasures and the Art of Memory', 353).[5] The breaking up of sound, of self-sufficient pieces of music and of authorial control alter the under-standing of sound production before digital technology intervenes, making such technology a constituent part of playing technologies, rather than a driver or deter-minant of musical perception.

Bit

Sampling and scratching are allied operations. While sampling is now a common-place digital practice, it has been done with other music technologies.[6] In fact, sampling and scratching should more properly be thought of as technologies in their own right, phenomenological interactions rather than human operator $+$ machine and/or digital technology $+$ 'abuse' of that technology. The sample in contemporary mainstream music is generally a small section of another piece of music, looped into a riff or beat, or sometimes used as a recurring ambient texture (one version of this being the incorporation of extra-musical sounds). The sample is a fragmentation of the unity of 'the' musical work as a whole, and, as Élie During argues, constitutes the destruction of 'the author' ('Appropriations', 94). Sampling would then be the epitome of a key concept in French theory of the 1960s (Roland Barthes and Foucault in particular explicitly stated the idea, then also Kristeva). The argument is that at a certain point, we have come to recognize that a novel, say, has not sprung from nowhere, nor from the soul of the author. We should mis-trust authorial intention, because he or she will often be unaware of unconscious and socialized sources. Furthermore, no text is independent—instead what we have is intertextuality, where texts move, change shape, reappear, disappear con-tinually. While this has always been the case, the argument goes, a certain kind of late modernist writing makes this evident, and exploits it. So, similarly, music is intertextual, and sampling is the explicit recognition of this. Alternatively, we could think of it as representing a change in music, which perhaps works retrospectively.

The original work is also broken up in sampling—and while it questions the first originality of the piece sampled, many others would question any claim to orig-inality of work containing, featuring heavily or exclusively, readymade fragments of existing works. Before coming to the implications for this in a capitalist and individ-ualist society (i.e. in this case, the belief the artist is somehow separate or above society and dispenses works of autonomous genius), I want to consider other aspects of sampling. Sampling ties in with scratching because the integrity of an existing work is modified in both, and the newness of the now sampled is in what the second artist does with that material. Even if absolutely unmodified, that will have been a choice made about the 'original' material, and the same applies to hit songs that take a track in its entirety and substitute a new lyric for the old one, or to 'mash-ups' which might take whole tracks in order to play with them (as in plunderphonics). In that instance, the track as unity is still lost, as it has become only fragment, a set of organs without a body.

Sampling is not restricted to pre-existing music, as it can come from any-where. Field recordings, speech, sounds from other instruments, sounds from musical works played through a keyboard, and even sounds not generally audible (e.g. storms on another planet) can all be thought of as part of sampling—a means of realizing the dreams of Cage and R. Murray Shafer. Pierre Schaeffer took frag-ments of extra-musical sound, and set them up as loops. William Burroughs applied his cut-up to tapes, as did Cage, Pauline Oliveros and a host of composers in the 1950s and 1960s. For Burroughs, a hidden truth would emerge from the reconstituted material, once the ostensible meanings had been scrambled. Some of that idea persisted in industrial music, and would become too meaning-laden with the incorporation of often extremist speeches by political or religious leaders. Generally, though, even when mobilized as part of a musical piece, the sample is always a fragment, displaced, adrift from context.

Like scratching, sampling, from the outset, involved interference with record-ing and reproductive media—tapes literally being cut and spliced. Digital media merely make this process more accessible, and facilitate mainstream popular use. This ease of access (and use) is what has led to a noise within commodified music (even as it too becomes commodity), in that ownership of music has come under threat. If the view of the sampler, or cut-and-paste combiner of scratching and sampling technologies, is that there is no such thing as definitive ownership, then formed music is just as usable as a field recording. Listeners are now able to con-tinue this trend through downloading, but it is only the music industry that sees these activities as the same. The downloader of 'pirate' material is a consumer that pays less, or pays nothing, rather than presenting a challenge to ideas of musical ownership. In fact, they could be seen as replicating the actions of the music indus-try in exploiting producers of music. Sampling does not fully dispose of traditional ideas of artistic creation, as the defence that has to be made is that the sampler is adding something, and only making audible their inspiration or sources (and in general the sampler artist still takes their share of royalties). Not only that, but in so doing, sampling is clearly not copying or imitating. Early hip-hop use of sam-pling for melodic fragments or beats to be looped explicitly set out to make audible the connections between forms of black American music, now becoming inter-locked layers, and a history always available for reuse.

Beyond the use of short elements of pre-existing tracks and extended use of a track as backing for a new one, there is a usage where the presence of the first material is both more and less: more in the sense that the entirety of a piece is developed within a new one, or that a section is fragmented at length; less in that this fragmentation eventually undoes the original track and the notion it could claim originality—if you break a track down into microscopic sections (which is much more feasible with digital and software technologies than before), how could any-one claim ownership of such a section they probably were not aware of? At that point, though, the sampler might have to emphasize the source, making it an uncanny cover version, where it is unrecognizable as such because you had never heard the bit you are now hearing. Fennesz' 'Paint It Black' is a good example of this approach, and pleasingly, as well as being a CD single, it has also appeared on vinyl, a medium on which, prior to software that can break sound down to infinitesimal levels, it could not exist, thus adding to the anachronism of or in sampling.[7]

For sampling not to settle into being an equivalent of lining up a sequence of notes, it has to keep the referentiality (as opposed to becoming referent). Although the idea of ultra-smooth sampling, which uses tiny sections of sound adrift from their original reference, offers a critique of recognition (of sounds, of music, of specific tracks, of sources), smoothness and full incorporation remove a layer of noise. To stay somewhere near the realm of noise in or with sampling is not necessarily about making something totally discordant, or relentlessly changing so there is no pattern at all, and nor is it achieved by posing as critique. For noise to occur across sampling, it would have to engage all those strategies, recombine them so that 'noise' in its most literal sense was itself disrupted by recognizable elements or moments of musicality, and perhaps to show awareness of its fate of losing its noisiness as it went on, or was listened to on repeated occasions, or the style became familiar. Ground Zero's *Revolutionary Pekinese Opera (ver. 1.28)* (1996) works in this way, while also working as an almost beautiful formal narration, even if fragmentary and multi-layered (its noise continually compromised and continually coming near to being, and then dissipating). The album takes an already sampled version of the actual *Revolutionary Pekinese Opera*, from Heiner Goebbels and Alfred 23 Harth. The band, comprising 'real' instruments and samples from Otomo's turntables and Sachiko M's sampler, plays with, against, under and over the pre-existing layers. This alteration of positioning between layers is important in not letting the album work as a kind of sound track to an already existing album, or having the first recording work as ambience for the new playing. Other works are sampled, including works by Marclay and Steve Beresford, weaving in traditions of avant-garde play and referencing, so the Ground Zero piece avoids being a patronizing reworking of now kitsch material. There are humorous moments, usually near the lounge music elements, but there are also epic sections, elegiac transformations of sections of the pre-existing material, and parallel cover versions as the band plays along with the 'original'. The position of the samples within layers shifts, and meanwhile the band's style goes from lounge to rock to jazz-ish thrash via soundscapes and what at least sounds like (non-jazz) improvisation. These pile up as the album goes along, rather than either simply colliding or forming a clear sequence. The intense layering (even when the sound is coming from a reduced number of sources, layering is still the dominant process) summons an effect noted by Burroughs and Bryon Gysin, in juxtaposing two pieces of writing—there seems to be at least one more thing going on than there should be, or can be identified. This effect is 'achieved', perceived or structured through dissonant layering, where the concern is not matching up, but something approximating musical overtones. There are more obvious noise moments, with the playing of short samples and actual bursts of noise ('The Glory of Hong Kong: Kabukicho Conference'), and also many occasions where sounds of vinyl being played come in, sometimes very loudly or lengthily (there are more of these as we approach the end, a formal melancholy echoed by the use of 'When You Wish Upon a Star' at the very end of the last track 'Paraiso 2', after four and a half minutes of [mostly] the sound of vinyl crunching and crackling, interspersed with long gaps). So if we are reading for content, we can take the audible dispersal of sound into information that is no longer coherent enough to form meaning to signal the Maoist experiment disintegrating, but it is still a utopia that is falling away as opposed to being thought of as a mistake. The return of music at the end is not simple, in noise terms, as it comes in the shape of samples, separate from sounds from the first Opera, so does not resolve the 'question' of the material (i.e. take a view on its purpose and context), but it does work in and around that context. The resolution that is suggestive of such a position is not one—it returns us to citation, to music as material such that its content does not matter (while suggesting it does)—this because of the return of musical sounds (messily) after the emphasis on vinyl/stylus sounds.

Overlay and pile-up can take place with the use of samples alone, as in plunderphonics, with John Oswald's *Plunderphonics* a standard-bearer, in huge part for negative reasons, due to copyright pursuits. This is due to Oswald's principal method being the 'plundering' of well-known rock and pop songs, and manipulating and/or drastically re-arranging them. Oswald positively and purposely values recognizability, and this to the point of threatening it:

> a major ingredient in perceiving any plunderphonic piece is the recognizability of the source in the transformation. In *Plexure* we were experimenting with the threshold of that recognition [due to shortness of samples]. (*Plunderphonics 69/96* sleeve notes, in interview with Norman Igma, 14)

> A plunderphone is a recognizable sonic quote, using the actual sound of something familiar which has already been recorded. Whistling a bar of 'Density 21.5' is a traditional musical quote. Taking Madonna singing 'Like a Virgin' and re-recording it backwards or slower is plunderphonics, as long as you reasonably recognize the source. But the plundering has to be blatant. (17)

Clearly, ownership of music is going to be an issue here, as the rights of the perfomer, writer, record company are ignored. The taking, or removing of these ownership rights is as important as the sounds themselves, hence Oswald's extensive use of the most successful pop and rock musicians, including the Beatles, the Doors and Michael Jackson. Eventually someone was going to notice, and Sony, Michael Jackson's label, did, when they found Oswald's 'dab', a dramatic retooling of 'Bad' on his original *Plunderphonics*. Oswald insisted that as he was giving the new material away he was not pirating, and not profiting, so therefore, he claimed (slightly disingenuously), his plundering had nothing to do with questions of ownership. In more general terms, he imagines plunderphonics as empowered listening, saying, 'it all comes from being a listener who actively changes things' (*Plunderphonics 69/96*, 9). But this type of listening threatens the saleability of passive listening, of the more cynically commodifed music that emerges from major record companies. The irreverent attitude, visualized on the cover, in the form of Jackson being morphed into a nude white woman, might have exacerbated the problem, but according to Oswald, Jackson himself never complained, as the Canadian Copyright Agency (CRIA) took it upon themselves to make a claim for breach of rights (*Plunderphonics 69/96*, 25–6), and ordered the destruction of all remaining copies.

Oswald takes tracks and cuts them into fragments, some of which can be so brief their provenance becomes strange. Often, the Oswald track will combine numerous songs by the artists 'under consideration', or different versions of the same song as in 'vane' "by" Sonic Mylar/Erastus Spyfact. In that track Carly Simon and Faster Pussycat alternate between combining, colliding and taking over from each other in ways that throw the forward movement of the track—such as when Simon's voice is 'time-stretched' while saying 'you'. While this sound acts as a kind of chorus, it also implodes, opening up echoes within the 'original' recorded sound, setting up a rhythm within what we imagine to be discrete sounds. All sounds in Oswald can end up like this, and despite his avowed impatience with repetition, there are moments in all time alteration where rhythm appears (to dissipate at higher or lower speed). With the tracks on?of? James Brown, those who have used sampling as a technique are included along with the much-sampled Brown. The Beatles feature regularly, with *Plunderphonics* launched with 'Day in the Life's closing piano chord. Listening to 'way' and 'sfield', and reading Oswald talk of his 'abandoned early eighties project to make a more-or-less backwards Beatles album' (*Plunderphonics 69/96*, 11), the parody that is the Martins' Beatles album *Love* is apparent. Instead of worrying about whether it is a real Beatles album, the question is whether it is anything other than a bad copy of a plunderphonic album.

Oswald's plunderphonics involves incessant movement and cutting—the sound of CDs 'catching' features as a further display of the process. In 'dab' the catching, or repetition through digital error, occurs both directly 'represented' as the clicking sound of a glitching CD and in the massed repetition (of, e.g. 'bad'). The fixity of the digital recording (its 'perfection') is shown to be infinitely malleable, as many fragments, in layers and in line crash in 'dab', and then other sections are stretched to an equal if opposite dissipation.

Interrupt

Many have taken a utopian view of the deterritorialization of music production, as it is reterritorialized in 'home studios'. As well as the evidence of Aphex Twin, Squarepusher and a good proportion of those involved in the nebulous genre 'electronica', we have Attali in 1977, thinking of that kind of activity as 'composing' (*Noise*, 133–48) (even if, in 2001, he has little in the way of analysis to offer now that it exists, although not quite how he predicted). In *Sonic Process*, Bruno Heuzé praises the creative potential of this unheard-of autonomy.[8] Kim Cascone sees computer technology as a liberating force, both creatively and in terms of eluding the dominant commercial industry, writing that 'computers have become the primary tools for creating and performing electronic music, while the Internet has become a logical new distribution medium. For the first time in history, creative output and the means of its distribution have been inextricably linked' ('The Aesthetics of Failure', 396).[9] Along with a rhetoric of freedom comes a puritanical praise for self-teaching, as techno-autodidacts master new machinery, software, concepts and sometimes programming. Cascone writes that 'composers of glitch music have gained their technical knowledge through self-study, countless hours deciphering software manuals, and probing Internet newsgroups for needed information' ('Aesthetics of Failure' 397). Access to and increasing control of digitally produced or processed music move computer music beyond strictures of existing musical convention, and almost inevitably, it seems, to the digital dismantling of music, and ultimately, to the dismantling of digital music (music as presented digitally, or digitalized). Familiarity with the working of digital encoding simulates a questioning of the claims made for it by the music industry, particularly with regard to perfection (material) and fidelity (to the sound content), and this is what leads to glitch music (or microsound)—music constructed from digital debris, errors, processing of normally extraneous sounds (microphone sounds, electrical connections, cuts, evidence of editing).[10] This can be re-organized using some of that material as beats, as is often the case, or left as isolated sound moments (these two can occur together—in Pan sonic, Oval, and much on the Raster-Noton, Mille Plateaux or Mego labels). What it adds up to is what Cascone identifies as an 'aesthetics of failure'. This occurs in the context of a digitalized environment, and

> more specifically, it is from the 'failure' of digital technology that this new work has emerged: glitches, bugs, application errors, system crashes, clipping, aliasing, distortion, quantization noise, and even the noise floor of computer sound cards are the raw materials composers seek to incorporate into their music.

> While technological failure is often controlled and suppressed—its effects buried beneath the threshold of perception—most audio tools can zoom in on the errors, allowing composers to make them the focus of their work. ('Aesthetics of Failure', 393)

Unlike some of the sounds I mention above, Cascone is keen to keep the sound source itself digital, to emphasize the attack on spurious perfection of digital media. I am not sure such a divide is necessary, as the processing of error sounds still works essentially through digital encodings and alterations of material sourced from outside the computer. Glitches, in the sense of unwanted interruptions, can occur in any media, and do not even need recording to occur; however, the glitch aims to carry an additional critical, as well as creative, charge, by virtue of undermining the CD, for example.

Eliot Bates argues that glitch exposes the medium as such, and is most significant in digital media, where 'glitch is the *betrayal of the simulation*'.[11] Hainge argues that while this is not wrong, it only goes so far in assessing what the glitch is and how it works. Failure is not so straightforward an exposure it initially seems, as failure is always already integrated into the CD, in order for it to claim perfection ('Of Glitch and Men', 35), as the CD does not skip, and neither does the laser scouring it for information, no matter how much the CD has been tampered with, or 'prepared'. While jumps can be made to occur through jarring the playback machine, Hainge's is a valuable precision, and leads to an important rethinking of glitch as noise, as exposure, as disruption. It still is those things, but this occurs within a different economy, an economy of *différance*. The CD and its successors are always moving to greater perfection, revealing that perfection is not present in the CD, and the belief that it is is completely reliant on incorporation of software to control the limitations of CD ('Of Glitch and Men', 34–5). To praise glitch as the undoing of digital reproduction media is to reify their perfection in order to dismantle an otherwise flawed medium. The CD is a permanent playing out of success and failure, argues Hainge: the glitch turns failure into successful artistic creation, solving the 'problem', and in so doing, moves on from the failure, such that 'glitch not only stages an avowal of this failure by contracting its plane of immanence into a perceptible realm but also succeeds this failure' ('Of Glitch and Men', 40).

Advocates of glitch as a material critique suppose that the glitch is noise to the CD signal. This is true for the listener (see below) but not for the machinery. In any case, even if it is noise to some other signal, I think, following Hainge, that we have to conceive of the noise being the relation between the ostensible good signal (music on a CD) and the sound of skipping, jumping, hiss, etc. Like all noise, glitch presents a noise, or set of noises, and the interplay of these with the structured sound is noise to where the specific noises occur. This is more than moving the location of noise in glitch; it is to show that glitch is itself a differential, like noise, and crosses between success and failure, in the context of a perpetual failing.

Beat

Hainge warns of a tendency to identify the potential for glitch to be mobilized against the system that spawns it, where one analyzes the '*modus operandi* (of insert name of preferred glitchmeister), [how] his or her music averts the catastrophe that is foretold by the tarnishing of the apparently infallible sheen of digital technology through a positivistic aesthetic act' ('Of Glitch and Men', 32). A benefit of such positivistic theorizing about a given glitching is that the music is left to theorize itself—not as a moment of autonomy or purity, but as a location where theorizing is already occurring. Against is the temptation to find final answers through assertions of triumph—in glitch this triumph being a navigation of failure, but still an interventionist triumph. Glitch extends its attempts to dwell in the interstices of digital functioning by using computer code, using programming language conventions for odd album titles usually featuring a surplus of misplaced punctuation. Farmers Manual's Web site is a paradigm of this (http://web.fm/twiki/Fmext/Web-Home)—language and meaning are breaking down, into strange encoding, is what is says, too loudly, but, as Hainge argues with glitch sounds, the glitch aesthetic makes failure work, and comes along after failure that is already contained (perhaps this explains the derisory Markus Popp [Oval] presence on the Web).

The same problem could be said to apply in attempts to find noise working, even if construed as always provisional, as yet-to-come, as gone, as dissipating, mounting, but never there. Chosen glitchmeisters would be selected to demonstrate this, but as with all examples in this book, there is a purposeful arbitrariness that raises exemplarity as a question. Examples of noise locate it too precisely, claim a moment, however absent, that can be equated to an Idealism via ineffability (noise is out there, but we can never quite get to it). Noise occurs though, often negatively, and the same occurs with glitch. The negotiation of failure occurs in the listening, the playing out of the sounds in time: noise is phenomenological as well as base material. The lowering of all noise is there in glitch, and in its transitions between different failures.

Cascone proposes Panasonic's *Vakio* as a key moment in glitch.[12] This album was, in 1993, a 'sonic shockwave' and 'conjured stark, fluorescent, industrial landscapes' ('Aesthetics of Failure', 395). The album combines tones, clicks, hums, hisses and beats made from signal generator tones. The equipment is either taken away from its original lab use or demonstrated in its peripheral sound making capacities, for example in disconnection hums. The vinyl edition, comprising four clear vinyl 10-inch singles, is a magnet for noise. Playing these short sides disrupts the flow of an album, and if these are soundscapes, they are slices of them, placed under a microscope lens and then whipped away. Even on later albums, Pan sonic feature many short tracks of single wavering tones, or some sort of electrical or electronic residue, by itself, but for so short a time it cannot take on significance as commentary or representation.[13] *Vakio* requires a lot of handling, and as many of the tracks already feature hiss, static, and quiet hums, the mind-body sound-medium Cartesianism of most recordings slips away. The transparency of the vinyl enhances this, as sound, material and location almost merge. Instead of this forming a holistic unity, the endless ending of sides keeps these mergings from completion. This noisiness is residual, rather than central, as in Marclay's *Record without a Cover*, and as a result *Vakio* is less of a conceptual mastering of the failing medium. Panasonic/ Pan sonic are never far from setting up beats, which brings the residues into musicality, and layers that almost mirror a band, where the beat is steady and other sounds veer in and out of it. Except that the distinction is far from clear, as percussive elements occur in all parts, all layers.[14] The beat in glitch is not simply a recuperation, as it continues the looping of a locked or damaged groove on record, and in this sense, the beat mediates technological change, such that for all its belonging largely in the digital realm, it cannot loosen itself fully from the undead format.

Beats are often there to be thwarted, either through complexity, or purposeful variation, often as an odd take on microsound, where dissected sound (or information) is stacked up, as in, for example, Autechre. Their 'Flutter' on the *Anti-ep* (1994) seems to have a beat, seems to be rhythmical, but is perpetually changing so that 'no bar is the same', as the cover claims. This ep was made in the context of the UK's Criminal Justice Bill which sought to ban raves through direct control of beat-oriented 'repetitive' music. Side one declares itself illegal under the new law, while side two is designed as a lure which will prove to not be repetitive. The disciplining of raves led also to their commercialization where the utopianism of music gatherings away from 'proper' venues went overground, into clubs.

Alva Noto's *transspray* (2004) does not look to be a political intervention, but its beats are not only messy, they are overridden by hums, blasts, failings and direct glitch sounds, or hums signalling spaces between instrument and functionality. Short tracks prevent a unity forming, and glitch has become a component, in a realization it is now part of musicality rather than a gesture that takes the medium from music to being medium, and failing at that. The glitch 'effect' transfers into the relation between sound and listener, and, while losing the specificity of glitch, lets it play across tracks where glitch features (in the same way that noise in any 'noise music' plays across tracks featuring or consisting entirely of what are generally though of as noises). Once away from the unwitting reification of glitch left to its own devices, we have something like hyperglitch, where it is an effect, not an essence of material and materialist commentary.

A more literal version of this can be heard in Disc's 'cover' of Joy Division's 'Love Will Tear us Apart', essentially consisting of (or purporting to be) a glitched CD of the original (on *Gaijin CD4*, 1997). This is also an extended playing out of plunderphonics, where as the original comes apart, it also reveals what makes it. As a commentary, the track could be taken as a formalization of separatedness, failure, alienation, as tiny sections circle in their own orbits, more stuck the more they try to emerge (i.e. the track continues to play rather than stopping entirely), and the voice seems entirely absent. The track reimagines failure as a creative resource, except there is still no resolution. While elegiac tones build, there is still the jarring of back and forward movement, as even stasis cannot settle, and the whole clicks (is read as containing those clicks). The noise of this track (as with many Oswald tracks) is not so much in the documenting of a failing medium but the loss of control over that failing that machine and listener are supposed to exert. The track inexorably blunders on, and, as with Merzbow, there is no reason for the many end moments (the sound is always ending, as it cuts) to ever really be the end. Toward what turns out to be the end, the track cuts out and 'skips' more often and it closes with what could be extraneous beeping sounds. But do we really need to hear this track to know enough, or even too much, about it? Unpleasant though it is, and allowing for the duration being a key part of its noise, we get the message soon enough, so the noise itself fails (even if it continues on, in its failure). Jimmy Edgar's 'I Hate When People Make Tracks Like This' works glitch through a plundernoising of Will Smith's 'Miami', and signals the frustration of listening to tracks that are just interruptions of the first version, while using that as a playful device.[15] The track follows 'Miami', but cuts it, layers it on itself, time compresses parts and stretches other sections. Parts are made staccato, broken into fragments, with some of these forming perfect new microrhythms that disappear in a second. Beeps, clatters and momentary granular synthesis bursts scatter through the piece. DJ/Rupture does similar stuff while Dj-ing, and, just like Edgar, toys with the seriousness of noise or 'experimental' music listeners' expectations. Only small sections of Edgar's track could actually be thought of as glitch, but it takes us away from the austerity and didactic oppressiveness of microsound and glitch aesthetics at the purest. Glitch is not there to be worshipped as the means and end, but is to always already have occurred and be *re-played*, or be itself disturbed, for glitching to have anything to do with noise.

NOTES

1. Hainge, 'Of Glitch and Men: The Place of the Human in the Successful Integration of Failure and Noise in the Digital Realm', *Communication Theory* 17 (2007), 26–42. This argument builds on one developed by Caleb Stuart. Yasunao Tone, who tapes over sections of discs to alter the sound, has said as much: 'It's not really skipping. It's distorting information' (Christian Marclay and Yasunao Tone, 'Record, CD, Analog, Digital', in Cox and Warner [eds], *Audio Culture* [341–7], 341). For more on Yasunao Tone, see LaBelle, *Background Noise*, 218–29.

2. Shapiro, 'Deck Wreckers: The Turntable as Instrument', in Young (ed), *Undercurrents*, 163–76. He goes on to say that this practice came to resemble the rock guitar solo, in that virtuosity came to take precedence.

3. Vinyl as noisy format does contain a hint of its fragility and capacity to be manipulated away from its mission to transmit its proper signals, but a noisy format can be of high quality but be rejected or marginalized, and therefore hinder the all-pervasiveness of a mono-medium.

4. Rose notes the complexities involved in repetitions that emerge from prerecorded sound sources in *Black Noise*, 67–72.

5. Miller, 'Algorithms: Erasures and the Art of Memory', in Cox and Warner (eds), *Audio Culture*, 348–54.

6. Mixmaster Morris says that all media involved in recording are open to sampling (cited by Élie During, 'Appropriations: Morts de l'auteur dans les musiques électroniques', in *Sonic Process*, 93–105 [97n24]).

7. The single declares itself as 'Fennesz Plays: Paint It Black/Don't Talk (Put Your Head on My Shoulder)', giving the further implication that the tracks are only being played—not only only, but less so.

8. Heuzé, 'Home Studio', *Sonic Process*, 61–7. This is part of a continuum that begins with pirate radio and home taping, and on through techno, into the 'home studio' and Web transmission.

9. Cascone, 'The Aesthetics of Failure: "Post-Digital" Tendencies in Contemporary Computer Music', in Cox and Warner (eds), *Audio Culture*, 392–8.

10. For more on this, see Phil Thomson, 'Atoms and Errors: Towards a History and Aesthetics of Microsound', *Organized Sound* 9 (2) (2004), 207–18.

11. Bates, 'Glitches, Bugs and Hisses: The Degeneration of Musical Recordings and the Contemporary Musical Work', in C. J. Washburne and M. Derno (eds), *Bad Music: The Music We Love to Hate* (London: Routledge, 2004), 275–93 (288), cited in Hainge, 'Of Glitch and Men' (31).

12. The electronics corporation of the same name soon decided to pursue the group for ownership of the name, partly, I imagine, due to Panasonic the band using exactly the same font as the company. They then became Pan sonic, keeping the font, keeping a space for the excluded 'a'. The space continues the noise the band introduced through their exact copying of a logo, as the company more or less fails, even though Panasonic also failed in a minor way. The net result is that it looks like the company name misspelled: for the company as questioning as well as the band as questioners of ownership. For another moment of an 'a' on the move, this time inward, see Genosko, *Baudrillard and McLuhan: Masters of Implosion* (London and New York: Routledge, 1999).

13. Panasonic and much glitch music is a post-laboratory sound, not so much following on from the experiments of mid-twentieth-century avant-gardists as rethinking the stereo test record in vogue in the 1970s, to verify the fidelity of your hi-fi, and the correctness of its physical set-up, through bursts of noise, single tones, panned sound and so on. The label Underground Resistance label has also 'made reference' to these in short sine wave tracks between more musical pieces.

14. Recalling Stockhausen's truism about rhythm and musical notes being the same things at different oscillations, and demonstrating it at its most obvious, and in all its obviousness.

15. On *Detroit Underground 06* (2004) also includes, between tracks on each side of the record, a set of locked grooves by Richard Devine, which work as powerful noise moments, both in the disruption of listening and playing and in the loops that do not quite settle (i.e. altering enough to not be obviously loops for the first few rotations) and are largely blasting beats (the second set in particular).

13
LISTENING

There is no sound, no noise, no silence, even, without listening. The range of audible sound is just that: 'of audible sound'. Certain wavelengths register as sound to those who have evolved a capacity for it. But listening is more than physical, and is something often striven for by humans, but with difficulty. Cage wonders 'if I did or somebody else did find a way to let a sound be itself, would everybody within earshot be able to listen to it? Why is it so difficult for so many people to listen? Why do they start talking when there *is* something to hear?' ('Composition as Process: Communication', 48).[1] Ever alert to listening as an inherent part of music and musicality, Cage raises several issues here, centring on the competence of those who would be listeners. People are easily distracted, have been socialized into this distraction, and prefer their assertions of presence over a more communal sound production and consumption. While we might question the didactic element here, once we take these queries further, they reveal a more philosophical question. Like Heidegger, Cage is presuming individuals to be lost in worldliness, the mundane, the living where existence is unreflective. Heidegger puts it like this: 'Losing itself [Dasein] in the publicness and the idle talk of the "they", *fails to hear* [*überhört*] its own Self in the listening to the they-self' (*Being and Time*, 315). For both, listening is what authentic being-in-the-world should be, because listening is not under your control, is largely undirected, and is capable of working over long distances, but this is made inauthentic in industrialized society, which, they would, I'm sure, both agree, imposes a blanket of noise that prevents listening. While Toop is not at all against this environment, he suggests that sound art establishes an other acoustic space, so that 'when sound artists and improvisers focus on details that would once have seemed just a tiny part of a bigger whole, I believe they are entering the microscopic in order to counter a wider sense of fragmentation: too many signals making too much noise' (*Haunted Weather*, 3). Crowded, industrial societies have added a further hum of piped music, muzak, so that an unwanted ambience seeps through listening. Many would say that this is noise, but bad noise, and if it is bad noise, it is because it controls, limits and ultimately pacifies and smoothes listening, no matter how aggressive or annoying it initially is. It is a tiresome and vacuous cliché to say that you cannot block sound like you can vision, as there are no earlids. For all its literal truth, it is too literal, as hearing does not occur in the ear alone, but throughout the body and in particular, the brain. The problem is in the division of human perception of sound into hearing and listening. Hearing is the simple perception of sound, listening the reflective conscious hearing. Even though on occasion the words can be used interchangeably, or the other way around ('I *hear* you' . . .), there is division into attentive perception and inattentive or unwilled perception, with the latter the lesser. Nancy offers a further distinction, with 'écouter' what happens before meaning is attributed, and 'entendre' (which is also 'understand') what comes after (*À l'écoute*, 19).[2]

Nancy asks what it means to listen properly' (17), to engage listening without full understanding. Cage wanted the mind to be 'free to enter into the act of listening, hearing each sound just as it is' ('Composition as Process: Changes', 23).[3] Both aspire to something between hearing and listening, which, oddly, is only available when listening is at its most intensive and conscious. This type of listening subject is in the process of creating a community with all that is around and whoever is around. For both Cage and Nancy, this listener is open to the world, the world filtering through him or her, such that an awareness of a connectivity that was always already there comes to the attention of that listener. For Cage, this is a revelation about an individual's and humanity's relation to the world, and for Nancy it is that too, but in deconstructed form, as openness goes all the way down, so that there is only ever openness constructing subjects in and around it (see *À l'écoute*, 44). This awareness, in Nancy, is not the end of a process but the beginning of a heightened sociality, as the subject recognizes shared openness (74–5, 82). Cage implies such sociality, as sounds are freed through new listening, 'an attention to the activity of sounds' ('Experimental Music', 10), and this implies an 'ethics of listening', writes LaBelle (*Background Noise*, 20). This listening may start with a challenge to music and hearing of same, but spreads and 'initiates a conversation in which the musical and found sounds merge, making music a cultural paradigm beholden to sound and its situatedness' (*Background Noise*, 21).

This new listening is not content to let music or other sound just unfold over or in time. The attention that loosens listening from a search for meaning restores extra capacity for situatedness, of listener and sound, such that space is formed, audibly. Nancy argues that the reconception of listening as ontological openness is about a spatiality that crosses in and out of listening body or subject (*À l'écoute*, 33). Cage is persistent in drawing attention to the act of listening itself, and its locatedness in both time and space. For Toop, we can intervene in as well as 'observe' our soundworld, and sound art offers this for any listener, in the form of a 'walking through sound', as for example, in Akio Suzuki's directed walks (*Haunted Weather*, 112–13), or any hearing-oriented walk or movement. The locating reduces noise and turns it into a good experience (attentive listening can go the other way, as in *Haunted Weather*, 260). The individual is more in tune with their surroundings, and the society that makes and is made from them. Instead of 'thrownness' into the morass of urban living, in particular, we have imbued the soundworld with either meaning, or at least character that furthers our subjectivity against (but not antagonistically) that of the 'other' (the external soundworld, or what *was* the external soundworld).

While to a certain extent Cage finds more meaning resulting from listening (just not specific meanings) than Toop or Nancy, Oliveros takes listening as a life mission that is a sort of self-improvement, and ethical as a result: 'everyone with healthy ears can hear, listening takes cultivation and evolves through one's lifetime. Listening is noticing and directing attention and interpreting what is heard. Deep listening is exploring the relationship among any and all sound' (www.deeplistening.org-dldef). Instead of meditating on sound, sound becomes the meditation itself (as it is with LaMonte Young), and at that point it can induce a listening which is not directed anymore, but stretched beyond the sound, giving a 'resonance with being and inform[ing] the artist, art and audience in effortless harmony' (*ibid*.). A similar claim could be made for sound art when it engages the listener with the process of sound production and listening itself (especially when in the form of a spatialized installation), but I think that as opposed to Oliveros' single process, the tendency in sound installation would be that one sort of attention (to the sound) creates another (to the way it was made, or the way you are listening to it) and then another (attention stimulated, it moves to think about contexts).

There seems no doubt that listening is good, at least when we renew it as something that is not subjected to unwanted everyday noise. Listening can fix you, as in psychoanalysis or in more behavioural psychologizing—or more accurately, someone's listening can fix someone else, but you too come to listen to yourself. Listening is an expression of concern, of care, and a society made transparent also wants to be transphonic. Where all claims to be on display, and in terms of simulation, it is, then too will everyone's 'voice be heard'. In among the search for a good listening lies the too-soft touch, the too-quiet voice of the 'caring listener', and Heidegger himself is no exception as through listening, any 'I' learns about 'my' own subjectivity and in so doing recognizes it in relation, as always related to everything and everyone else:

> Listening to . . . is Dasein's existential way of Being-open as Being-with for Others. Indeed, hearing constitutes the primary and authentic way in which Dasein is open for its ownmost potentiality-for-Being—as in hearing the voice of the friend whom every Dasein carries with it. Dasein hears, because it understands. [. . .] Being-with develops in listening to one another [Aufeinander-hören]. (*Being and Time*, 206)

This understanding occurs at a deep level of being which is both most authentic and furthest from overt consciousness, and ultimately is a separation from literal hearing, but Heidegger is keen to hold on to the actuality of a listening process, arguing that it 'is constitutive for discourse' (206)—and *not* just receipt of discourse. Listening then is to be revalued, resituated within what is now not a hierarchy, but a process and exchange between sound production and perception. But all this listening has only made things worse—as now hearing has an object, whether that is the world, listening, the subject, the community or the impossibility of not listening. 'Letting sounds be themselves' is still about the listener framing, locating, territorializing sounds, noise into sound, immanence into experience, absence of self into self-awarely absent self. What noise needs, and where noise is, however briefly, is a listening that is brought back to hearing through processes of rejection (as noise), confusion (through noise as change), excess (including of volume), wrongness or inappropriateness, failure (of noise, to be noise, to not be noise, to be music, not be sound, not be). Noise is where all this listening goes when it has had enough.

Curiously, Heidegger does not stop at his subject being the kind of open listener Nancy hopes for. Heidegger's listening is more nuanced, and not restricted to a newly positive passivity of receptiveness (even though this passivity imagines itself as heroic action): The listening of the 'Being-with' mentioned above 'can be done in several possible ways: following, going along with, and the privative modes of not-hearing, resisting, defying, and turning away' (*Being and Time*, 206–7). We could imagine these latter four types as being resistance to noisy urban industrial life, but they seem to apply beyond that, and are themselves part of the constitutive listening of 'authentic' Being. There is as much listening, then, in refusal, as in unlistening. It is important to notice that these are not about fully autonomous individuals choosing how to listen, but situations where subject and other (the world, or others, or something like music, something like noise) are within listening. This is where another hearing takes place, a hearing of loss, of the loss of hearing, even, as loss, and where some sort of subject comes fleetingly into being outside of subjectivity through a sort of subjection, a subjection with no mission. Noise is listening as Foucaldian power—between rather than belonging to subjects, and the listening to something like noise music is the movement of the difference between noise and music as either constitutive power or Derridean *différance*, now a difference between listening and hearing, the noise and the noised listener. All of these keep crossing over into one another, opposites that rely on each other, mutual undoings, oscillating failures. Is this good? No, it is not proper, linear, meaningful. But not bad either, as noise transvalues listener and object, noise and music, hearing and listening, perception and its failure, perform-ance and its failure, noise and its failure to be music, noise and its failure to be noise. And the transvaluation itself, only as if it could ever be. As if it really were noise, after or before, all.

NOTES

1. Cage, 'Composition as Process: Communication' in *Silence*, 41–52.
2. A further complication is that 'écouter' usually translates as 'to listen' and 'entendre' as 'to hear'. The archaic 'ouïr' is closest to simple hearing, making a three-part system. The title of the book could be translated as 'to listening', or 'listening to'/ 'tuned in'.
3. Cage, 'Composition as Process: Changes', in *Silence*, 18–34.

Discography

This list is indicative only, concentrating on albums referred to in the text.

Acid Mothers Temple and the Melting Paraiso UFO, *Absolutely Freak Out* (Resonant, 2000)
Alternative TV, *Vibing Up the Senile Man* (part one) (Get Back, 2002)
Alva Noto, *transspray* (Raster-Noton, 2004)
AMM, *AMMUSIC* (ReR, 1989)
Aube, *Quadrotation* (Self Abuse, 1996)
Aube, *Sensorial Inducement* (Alien8, 1999)
Albert Ayler, *Bells* (ESP-Disk, 1965)
Derek Bailey, *Improvisation* (Cramps, 1975)
François Bayle, *Erosphere* (INA-GRM, 1982)
The Beatles, *Sgt. Pepper's Lonely Hearts Club Band* (EMI, 1987)
Jacques Berrocal, *Parallèles* (Alga Marghen, 2001)
MB, *Archives* (Vinyl on Demand, 2006)
Bonzo Dog Band, *Cornology* (EMI, 1992)
Boredoms, *Super Ae* (Birdman, 1998)
Boredoms, *Vision Creation Newsun* (Birdman, 2000)
Boris, *Pink* (Southern Lord, 2005)
Burzum, *Filosofem* (Misanthropy, 1996)
Cabaret Voltaire, *Methodology, 74/78* (Mute, 2002)
Cabaret Voltaire, *Red Mecca* (Rough Trade, 1981)
Cabaret Voltaire, *The Voice of America* (Mute, 1990)
John Cage, *Cartridge Music* (Wandelweiser, 2004)
John Cage, *Imaginary Landscapes* (Hat Hut, 1995)
John Cage, *Works for Percussion* (Wergo, 1991)
Can, *Monster Movie* (Spoon, 2004)
Captain Beefheart, *Trout Mask Replica* (Reprise, 1970)
CCCC, *Live Sounds Dopa: Live in USA* (Endorphine, 1993)
Henri Chopin, *Les Mirifiques Tundras et Compagnie* (Algha Marghen, 1997)
Cock. E.S.P., *We Mean It This Time* (Sunship, 1999)
Coil, *Horse Rotorvator* (Force and Form, 1986)
Coil, *How to Destroy Angels* (LAYLAH, 1984)
Ornette Coleman, *Free Jazz: A Collective Improvisation* (Atlantic, 1961)
John Coltrane, *Ascension* (Impulse, 2000)
John Coltrane, *Interstellar Space* (Impulse, 1991)
Crass, *Christ—The Album* (Crass, 1982)
Cream, *Wheels of Fire* (Polygram, 1990)

Current 93, *Dawn* (Durtro, 1992)
Current 93, *I Have a Special Plan for This World* (Durtro, 2000)
Derek and the Ruins, *Tohjinbo* (Paratactile, 1997)
Disc, *GaijinCD4* (Tigerbeat, 1997)
DJ/Rupture, *Low Income Tomorrowland* (Applecore, 2006)
DJ Shadow, *Endtroducing* (Mowax, 1998)
DNA, *DNA on DNA* (No More Records, 2004)
Einstürzende Neubauten, *Strategies against Architecture* (Mute, 1983)
Einstürzende Neubauten, *Zeichnungen des Patienten O.T.* (*Drawings of Patient O.T.*) (Some Bizarre, 1983)
Faust, *Faust/So Far* (Collector's Choice, 2000)
Faust, *Faust Tapes* (Virgin, 1973)
Fennesz, *Plays* (Moikai, 1999)
Fennesz, *plus forty seven degrees 56'37", minus sixteen degrees 51'08"* (Touch, 1999)
Filament 2, *Secret* (4 Ears, 1999)
Foetus Inc., *Sink* (Self Immolation, 1990)
Fushitsusha, *The Caution Appears* (Les disques du soleil et d'acier, 1995)
Fushitsusha, *Pathétique* (PSF, 1994)
Serge Gainsbourg, *Rock around the Bunker* (Mercury France, 1975)
Diamanda Galas, *Litanies of Satan* (Mute, 1988)
Genesis, *Selling England by the Pound* (Virgin, 1973)
Germs (MIA), *The Complete Anthology* (Slash, 1993)
Grateful Dead, *The Anthem of the Sun* (Warner, 1971)
Grateful Dead, *Live/Dead* (Warner, 1969)
Ground Zero, *Consume Red* (ReR, 1997)
Ground Zero, *Last Concert* (Amoebic, 1999)
Ground Zero, *Revolutionary Pekinese Opera, ver 1.28* (ReR, 1996)
Jimi Hendrix, *Live at Woodstock* (Warner, 2005)
Matthew Herbert, *Plat du Jour* (Accidental, 2005)
High Rise, *Speed Free Sonic* (Paratactile, 1999)
Incapacitants, *Asset without Liability* (Bulb, 1996)
ISO, *ISO* (Amoebic, 1998)
Jefferson Airplane, *After Bathing at Baxter's* (BMG, 2003)
John the Postman's Puerile, *John the Postman's Puerile* (Overground, 1998)
K2, *Metal Dysplasia* (Cheeses International, 1996)
K2, *Molekular Terrorism* (Pure, 1995)
Kazumoto Endo/Incapacitants, 'Most of my problems are solved by an afternoon snooze'/'Selling Mutual Fund by the Pound' (Gentle Giant, 1997)
Keiji Haino, *Abandon all words at a stroke, so that prayer can come spilling out* (Alien8, 2001)
Keiji Haino, *I Said, This Is the Son of Nihilism* (Table of the Elements, 1995)
Keiji Haino, *So, Black Is Myself* (Alien8, 1997)
King Crimson, *Larks' Tongues in Aspic* (Island, 1973)
KK Null, *Ultimate Material II* (Fourth Dimension, 1995)
Koji Asano, *Quoted Landscape* (Solstice, 2001)
Kraftwerk, *Autobahn* (EMI, 1974)
Kraftwerk, *Tour de France* (EMI, 2003)

Hijokaidan, *Romance* (Alchemy, 2001)
Joan La Barbara, *Voice Is the Original Instrument* (Lovely Music, 2003)
Alan Lamb, *Primal Image: Archival Recordings, 1981–1988* (Dorobo, 1995)
Francisco Lopez, *Untiled #123* (Alien8, 2001)
Love, *da capo* (Warner, 2002)
Masami Akita and Russell Haswell, *Satanstornade* (Warp, 2002)
Masayuki Takayanagi and Kaore Abe, *Mass Projection* (DIW, 2001)
Masayuki Takayanagi, *Action Direct* (Tiliqua, 2005)
Masonna, *Inner Mind Mystique* (Release, 1995)
Masonna, *Like a Vagina* (Vanilla, 1994)
Matching Mole, *Matching Mole* (Sony, 2001)
Matmos, *A Chance to Cut Is a Chance to Cure* (Matador, 2001)
Merzbow, *24 Hours—A Day of Seals* (Dirter, 2002)
Merzbow, *Amlux* (Important, 2002)
Merzbow, *Bariken* (Blossoming Noise, 2005)
Merzbow, *Blackbone pt.5* (Blossoming Noise, 2006)
Merzbow, *Bloody Sea* (Vivo, 2006)
Merzbow, *Hybrid Noisebloom* (Vinyl Communications, 1997)
Merzbow, *Merzbox* (Extreme, 1999)
Merzbow, *Merzbuddha* (Important, 2005)
Merzbow, *Metamorphism* (Very Friendly, 2006)
Merzbow, *Noisembryo* (Releasing Eskimo, 1994)
Merzbow, *Pinkream* (Dirter, 1995)
Merzbow, *Pulse Demon* (Release, 1996)
Merzbow, *Turmeric* (Blossoming Noise, 2006)
Merzbow, *Venereology* (Release, 1994)
Ministry, *Psalm 69* (Sire, 1992)
Mokira, *Cliphop* (Raster-Noton, 2000)
MSBR, 'Electrovegetarianism' (Pinchaloaf, 1996)
MSBR, *2,000 Thousands Contaminate Electronic Acid* (Old Europa Café, 1994)
National Health, *Complete* (East Side Digital, 1990)
Neu!, *Neu!* (Astalwerks, 2001)
Neu!, *Neu! 2* (Astralwerks, 2001)
The New Blockaders, *First Live Performance* (Vinyl on Demand, 2004)
Nihilist Spasm Band, *Record* (Cortical Foundation, 2000)
Non, *Pagan Muzak* (Mute, 1999)
Nurse With Wound, *Chance Meeting on a Dissecting Table of a Sewing Machine and an Umbrella* (United Dairies, 1979)
Nurse With Wound, *Homotopy to Marie* (United Dairies, 1982)
Nurse With Wound, *Drunk With the Old Man of the Mountains* (United Dairies, 1987)
Pauline Oliveros and Reynols, *The Minexico Connection: Live! At the Rosendale Café* (Roaratorio, 2003)
OOIOO, *Featherfloat* (Birdman, 2001)
The Oppressed, *Oi! Oi! Music!* (Captain Oi!, 1993)
John Oswald, *Plunderphonics 69/96* (Seeland, 2001)
Panasonic, *Vakio* (Blast First, 1995)
Prurient, *Pleasure Ground* (Load, 2006)

Psychic TV, *Force the Hand of Chance* (Some Bizarre, 1982)

Public Enemy, *Fear of a Black Planet* (CBS, 1990)

Public Enemy, *It Takes a Nation of Millions to Hold Us Back* (Def Jam, 1988)

Public Image Limited, *Public Image Limited* (Virgin, 1978)

Red Krayola, *The Parable of Arable Land/God Bless the Red Krayola and All Who Sail in Her* (Charly, 2006)

Boyd Rice, *Boyd Rice* (Mute, 2006)

Ryoji Ikeda, *matrix* (Touch, 2001)

Sachiko M, *Detect* (Antifrost, 2000)

Samla Mammas Manna, *Samla Mammas Manna* (Silence, 1971)

Pharaoh Sanders, *Karma* (Impulse, 1995)

Erik Satie, *Relâche/Vexations/Musique d'ameublement* (Warner, 2004)

Pierre Schaeffer, *L'œuvre musicale* (EMF, 2005)

Severed Heads, *Since the Accident* (Ink, 1983)

Sex Pistols, *The Great Rock 'n' roll Swindle* (Virgin, 1993)

Archie Shepp, *Fire Music* (Impulse, 1965)

The Slits, *Cut* (Runt LLC, 2005)

Soft Machine, *Third* (CBS, 1970)

Soft Machine, *Volumes One and Two* (MCA, 1989)

SPK, *Information Overload Unit* (Normal, 1985)

Sun Ra, *The Complete ESP-Disk Recordings* (ESP-Disk, 2005)

Swans, *Cop/Young God. Greed/Holy Money* (Thirsty Ear, 1999)

Swans, *Filth/Body to Body, Job to Job* (Young God, 2000)

23 Skidoo, *The Culling Is Coming* (LAYLAH, 1988)

Cecil Taylor, *Air above Mountains (Buildings Within)* (ENJA, 1973)

Test Department, *Beating the Retreat* (Some Bizarre, 1982)

This Heat, *Out of Cold Storage* (ReR, 2006)

Throbbing Gristle, *20 Jazz Funk Greats* (Mute, 1991)

Throbbing Gristle, *D.O.A. The Third and Final Report* (Mute, 1990)

Throbbing Gristle, *The Second Annual Report* (Mute, 1991)

David Tudor, *Microphone* (Cramps, 1973)

Various, *Anthology of Dutch Electronic Tape Music*, vol. 2 (1966–1977) (Composer's Voice, 1979)

Various, *Detroit Underground 06* (Detroit Underground, 2004)

Various, *Extreme Music from Japan* (Susan Lawly, 1994)

Various, *Futurism and Dada Reviewed* (LTM, 2000)

Various, *Improvised Music from Japan* (Improvised Music from Japan, 2001)

Various, *lockERS* (ERS, 2000)

Various, *Necropolis, Amphibians and Reptiles: The Music of Adolf Wölffli* (Musique Brut, 1986)

Various, *No New York* (Antilles, 1978)

Various, *Oi! The Album* (EMI, 1980)

Various, *RRR500* (RRR, 1998)

Various, *Tokyo Flashback* (PSF, 1991)

Violent Onsen Geisha, *Excrete Music* (Vanilla, 1991)

Chris Watson, *Weather Report* (Touch, 2003)

Whitehouse, *Asceticists 2006* (Susan Lawly, 2006)

Whitehouse, *Buchenwald* (Come Organisation, 1981)

Whitehouse, *Cruise* (Susan Lawly, 2001)
Whitehouse, *Quality Time* (Susan Lawly, 1996)
Yasunao Tone, *Musica Iconologos* (Lovely Music, 1993)
Yes, *Relayer* (Atlantic, 1975)
Yes, *Tales from Topographic Oceans* (Atlantic, 1973)
Frank Zappa, *Threesome No.1* (Rykodisc, 2002)
John Zorn, *Cobra* (Hat Hut, 2002)

Bibliography

Adorno, Theodor, *Aesthetic Theory* (Minneapolis: University of Minnesota Press, 1997)
———, *Beethoven: The Philosophy of Music* (Cambridge: Polity, 1998)
———, *The Culture Industry: Selected Essays on Mass Culture* (London: Routledge, 1991)
———, *Essays on Music* (ed. and intr. Richard Leppert) (Berkeley, CA: University of California Press, 2002)
———, *Quasi una fantasia: Essays on Modern Music* (London and New York: Verso, 1994)
———, *Sound Figures* (Stanford, CA: Stanford University Press, 1999)
Agamben, Giorgio, *Homo Sacer: Sovereign Power and Bare Life* (Stanford, CA: Stanford University Press, 1998)
Altschuler, Glenn C., *All Shook Up: How Rock 'n' Roll Changed America* (New York: Oxford University Press, 2003)
Apollonio, Umbro (ed), *Futurist Manifestos* (London: Thames & Hudson, 1973)
Argosfestival 2003 (Brussels: Argos, 2003)
Artaud, Antonin, *The Theatre and Its Double* (London: John Calder, 1970)
Attali, Jacques, *Bruits: essai sur l'économie politique de la musique* (second edition) (Paris: PUF/Fayard, 2001)
———, *Noise: The Political Economy of Music* (Minneapolis: University of Minnesota Press, 1985)
Bailey, Derek, *Improvisation: Its Nature and Practice in Music* (New York: Da Capo, 1993)
Barr, Tim, *Kraftwerk: From Düsseldorf to the Future (with Love)* (London: Ebury, 1998)
Barthes, Roland, *Image Music Text* (London: Fontana, 1977)
———, *L'Obvie et l'obtus* (Paris: Le Seuil, 1982)
Bataille, Georges, *The Accursed Share*, vols II and III (New York: Zone, 1991)
———, *Eroticism* (London: Marion Boyars, 1987)
———, *Visions of Excess, Selected Writings, 1927–1939* (ed Allan Stoekl) (Minneapolis: University of Minnesota Press, 1985)
Bataille, Georges, et al., *Encyclopaedia Acephalica* (London: Atlas, 1995)
Bates, Eliot, 'Glitches, Bugs and Hisses: The Degeneration of Musical Recordings and the Contemporary Musical Work', in Washburne and Derno (eds), *Bad Music: The Music We Love to Hate*, 275–93
Baudrillard, Jean, *Forget Foucault* (New York: Semiotext[e]), 1987)
———, *The Illusion of the End* (Cambridge: Polity, 1994)
———, *Télémorphose* (Paris: Sens et Tonka, 2001)

————, *The Transparency of Evil* (London: Verso, 1993)

Bayton, Mavis, 'Women and the Electric Guitar', in Whiteley (ed), *Sexing the Groove*, 37–49

Benjamin, Walter, *Illuminations* (London: Fontana, 1973)

Berendt, Joachim, E., *The Jazz Book: From Ragtime to Fusion and Beyond* (revised by Günther Huesmann, sixth edition) (New York: Lawrence Hill, 1992)

Bohlman, Philip V., *World Music: A Very Short Introduction* (Oxford: Oxford University Press, 2002)

Bois, Yve-Alain, and Krauss, Rosalind, *Formless: A User's Guide* (New York: Zone, 1997)

Boldt-Irons, Leslie, 'Sacrifice and Violence in Bataille's Erotic Fiction', in Gill (ed), *Bataille: Writing the Sacred*, 91–104

Boon, Marcus, 'The Eternal Drone: Good Vibrations Ancient to Future' in Young (ed), *Undercurrents*, 59–69

Buchanan, Ian, and Swiboda, Marcel (eds), *Deleuze and Music* (Edinburgh: Edinburgh University Press, 2004)

Bull, Michael, and Back, Les (eds), *The Auditory Culture Reader* (Oxford and New York: Berg, 2003)

Cage, John, *Silence: Lectures and Writings* (London: Marion Boyars, 1968)

Cascone, Kim, 'The Aesthetics of Failure: "Post-Digital" Tendencies in Contemporary Computer Music', in Cox and Warner (eds), *Audio Culture*, 392–8

Chion, Michel, *Le Promeneur écoutant* (Paris: Plume, 1993)

Cole, Bill, *John Coltrane* (New York: Da Capo, 1993)

Collett, Paul, 'Spacious Paradise: Psychedelism in Japanese Music', in *Japanese Independent Music*, 25–30

Cowell, Henry and Sidney, *Charles Ives and His Music* (New York: Oxford University Press, 1955)

Cox, Christoph, and Warner, Daniel (eds), *Audio Culture: Readings in Modern Music* (New York and London: Continuum, 2004)

Culture Theory Critique: Noise 46 (1), April 2005

Debussy, Claude, *Writings on Music* (London: Secker & Warburg, 1977)

De Ferranti, Hugh, ' "Japanese Music" can be popular', in *Popular Music* 21 (2) (2002), 195–208

De Lauretis, Monia, 'About Myths, Common Places and Other (Japanese) Oddities', in *Japanese Independent Music*, 46–64

Deleuze, Gilles, and Guattari, Félix, *A Thousand Plateaus* (London: Athlone, 1988)

Deleuze, Gilles, *Difference and Repetition* (London: Athlone, 1994)

Delville, Michel, and Norris, Andrew, *Frank Zappa, Captain Beefheart and the Secret History of Maximalism* (Cambridge: Salt Press, 2005)

DeRogatis, Jim. *Turn on Your Mind: Four Decades of Great Psychedelic Rock* (Milwaukee, WI: Hal Leonard, 2003)

Derrida, Jacques, *Artaud le Moma* (Paris: Galilée, 2002)

Derrida, Jacques, *Margins of Philosophy* (Chicago: Chicago University Press, 1982)

Dery, Mark, 'Public Enemy: Confrontation', in Forman and Neal (eds), *That's the Joint!*, 407–20

During, Élie, 'Appropriations: Morts de l'auteur dans les musiques électroniques', in *Sonic Process*, 93–105

Ford, Simon, *Wreckers of Civilisation: The Story of COUM Transmissions and Throbbing Gristle* (London: Black Dog, 1999)

Forman, Murray, and Neal, Mark Anthony (eds), *That's the Joint! The Hip-Hop Studies Reader* (New York and London: Routledge, 2004)

Foucault, Michel, *Discipline and Punish* (London: Penguin, 1991)

——, *History of Sexuality*, vol. I (Harmondsworth: Penguin, 1978)

Freeman, Alan, 'Rock in Opposition, part 1', *Audion* 30 (spring 1995), 7–13

——, 'Rock in Opposition, part 2', *Audion* 31 (winter 1995), 19–25

Frith, Simon, ' "The Magic That Can Set You Free": The Ideology of Folk and the Myth of the Rock Community', Middleton and Horn (eds), *Popular Music 1*, 159–68

Gates, Henry Louis, *The Signifying Monkey: A Theory of Afro-American Literary Criticism* (New York: Oxford University Press, 1988)

Genosko, Gary, *Mcluhan and Baudrillard: The Masters of Implosion* (London and New York: Routledge, 1999)

Gill, Carolyn Bailey (ed), *Bataille: Writing the Sacred* (London: Routledge, 1995)

Gordon, Mel, 'Songs from the Museum of the Future: Russian Sound Creation (1910–1930)', in Kahn and Whitehead (eds), *Wireless Imagination*, 197–243

Gracyk, Theodore, *Rhythm and Noise: An Aesthetics of Rock* (London: Duke University Press, 1996)

Hainge, Greg, 'No(i)stalgia: on the Impossibility of Recognising Noise in the Present', in *Culture Theory Critique: Noise*, 1–10

——, 'Of Glitch and Men: The Place of the Human in the Successful Integration of Failure and Noise in the Digital Realm', in *Communication Theory* 17 (2007), 26–42

Hamm, Charles, *Putting Popular Music in Its Place* (Cambridge: Cambridge University Press, 1995)

Hegarty, Paul, 'Full with Noise: Theory and Japanese Noise Music', in Kroker and Kroker (eds), *Life in the Wires: The CTheory Reader*, 86–98

——, 'Noise Threshold: Merzbow and the End of Natural Sound', in *Organised Sound* 6 (3), December 2001, 193–200

Hegel, G. W. F., *Aesthetics*, vol. II (Oxford: Clarendon, 1975)

Heidegger, Martin, *Being and Time* (Oxford: Blackwell, 1962)

Henritzi, Michael, 'Extreme Contemporary: Japanese Music as Radical Exoticism', in *Japanese Independent Music*, 31–7

Heuzé, Bruno, 'Home Studio', in *Sonic Process*, 61–7

Hollier, Denis, 'The Use-Value of the Impossible', in Gill (ed), *Bataille: Writing the Sacred*, 133–53

Hollings, Ken, 'The Solar Myth Approach: The Live Space Ritual: Sun Ra, Stockhausen, P-Funk and Hawkwind', in Young (ed), *Undercurrents*, 99–113

Holm-Hudson, Kevin (ed), *Progressive Rock Reconsidered* (New York and London: Routledge, 2002)

——, 'Introduction' in Holm-Hudson (ed), *Progressive Rock Reconsidered*, 1–18

Home, Stewart, *Cranked Up Really High: An Inside Account of Punk Rock* (Hove: CodeX, 1995)

Ihde, Don, *Sense and Significance* (Pittsburgh, PA: Duquesne University Press, 1973)

Jameson, Fredric, *Postmodernism: Or, the Cultural Logic of Late Capitalism* (London: Verso, 1991)

Japanese Independent Music (Bordeaux: Sonore, 2001)

Jost, Ekkehard, *Free Jazz* (New York: Da Capo, 1994)

Kahn, Douglas, *Noise Water Meat: A History of Sound in the Arts* (Cambridge, MA: MIT Press, 1999)

Kahn, Douglas, and Whitehead, Gregory (eds), *Wireless Imagination: Sound, Radio and the Avant-garde* (Cambridge, MA: MIT Press, 1994)

Kant, Immanuel, *Critique of Judgement* (Indianapolis, IN: Hackett, 1987)

Karl, Gregory, 'King Crimson's *Larks' Tongues in Aspic*: A Case of Convergent Evolution', in Holm-Hudson (ed), *Progressive Rock Reconsidered*, 121–42

Keenan, David, *England's Hidden Reverse: A Secret History of the Esoteric Underground* (London: SAF, 2003)

——, 'picks best of Merzbow', *The Wire* 198 (August, 2000), 32–3

——, 'The Primer: Fire Music', *The Wire* 208 (June 2001), 42–9

Kerman, Joseph, *Musicology* (London: Fontana, 1985)

Kofsky, Frank, *Black Music: White Business: Illuminating the History and Political Economy of Jazz* (New York: Pathfinder Press, 1998)

Kopf, Biba, 'The Autobhan Goes on Forever: Kings of the Road: The Motorik Pulse of Kraftwerk and Neu!', in Young (ed), *Undercurrents*, 142–52

——, 'Introduction: Bacillus Culture', in Neal (ed), *Tape Delay*, 10–15

Krauss, Rosalind, 'The Cultural Logic of the Late Capitalist Museum', in Krauss et al. (eds), *October: The Second Decade, 1986–1996* (Cambridge, MA: MIT Press, 1997)

Kroker, Arthur, *Spasm: Virtual Reality, Android Music, Electric Flesh* (New York: St. Martin's Press, 1993)

Kroker, Arthur, and Kroker, Marilouise (eds), *Life in the Wires: The CTheory Reader* (Victoria: New World Perspectives, 2004)

LaBelle, Brandon, *Background Noise: Perspectives on Sound Art* (New York and London: Continuum, 2006)

La Mettrie, Julien Offroy, *Man a Machine and Man a Plant* (Indianapolis, IN: Hackett, 1994)

Lancashire, Terence, ' "World Music" or Japanese—The *Gagaku* of Tôgi Hideki', in *Popular Music* 22 (1) (2003), 21–9

Lange, Art, 'The Primer: The Art Ensemble of Chicago', *The Wire* 198 (August 2000), 38–43

Leach, Neil (ed), *Rethinking Architecture* (London and New York: Routledge, 1997)

Leppert, Richard, 'Commentary', in Adorno, *Essays on Music*, 327–72

——, 'Desire, Power and the Sonoric Landscape: Early Modernism and the Politics of Privacy', in Leyshon, Matless and Revil (eds), *The Place of Music*, 291–321

Lévi-Strauss, Claude, *Race et histoire* (Paris: UNESCO, 1952)

Leyshon, Andrew, Matless, David, and Revil, George (eds), *The Place of Music* (New York and London: Guilford Press, 1998)

Macan, Edward, *Rocking the Classics: English Progressive Rock and the Counterculture* (New York and Oxford: Oxford University Press, 1997)

Marclay, Christian, and Yasunao Tone, 'Record, CD, Analog, Digital', in Cox and Warner (eds), *Audio Culture*, 341–7

Marinetti, Filippo Tomaso, 'The Founding and Manifesto of Futurism', in Apollonio (ed), *Futurist Manifestos*, 19–24

Martin, Peter J., *Sounds and Society: Themes in the Sociology of Music* (Manchester and New York: Manchester University Press, 1995)

McClary, Susan, *Conventional Wisdom: The Content of Musical Form* (Berkeley and Los Angeles: University of California Press, 2000)

McLuhan, Marshall, and Fiore, Quentin, *The Medium Is the Massage: An Inventory of Effects* (Harmondsworth: Penguin, 1967)

Middleton, Richard, and Horn, David (eds), *Popular Music 1: Folk or Popular? Distinctions, Influences, Continuities* (Cambridge: Cambridge University Press, 1981)

Miller, Paul, 'Algorithms: Erasures and the Art of Memory', in Cox and Warner (eds), *Audio Culture*, 348–54

Moynihan, Michael, and Søderlind, Didrick, *Lords of Chaos: The Bloody Rise of the Satanic Metal Underground* (second edition) (Los Angeles: Feral House, 2003)

Nancy, Jean-Luc, *À l'écoute* (Paris: Galilée, 2002)

Neal, Charles (ed), *Tape Delay: Confessions from the Eighties Underground* (London: SAF, 1987)

Negus, Keith, *Popular Music in Theory: An Introduction* (Cambridge: Polity, 1996)

Nietszsche, Friedrich, *The Birth of Tragedy and The Case of Wagner* (New York: Vintage, 1967)

Nyman, Michael, *Experimental Music: Cage and Beyond* (second edition) (Cambridge: Cambridge University Press, 1999)

Ouellette, Fernand, *Edgard Varèse* (London: Calder and Boyars, 1973)

Paynter, John et al. (eds), *The Companion to Contemporary Musical Thought* (London: Routledge, 1992)

Pouncey, Edwin, 'Consumed by Noise', *The Wire* 198 (August 2000), 26–32

———, 'Rock Concrète: The Counterculture Plugs in to the Academy', in Young (ed), *Undercurrents*, 153–62

Pratella, Balilla, 'Manifesto of Futurist Musicians', in Apollonio (ed), *Futurist Manifestos*, 31–8

Prendergast, Mark, *The Ambient Century: From Mahler to Moby—The Evolution of Sound in the Electronic Age* (London: Bloomsbury, 2003)

Rahn, John, *Music Inside Out: Going Too Far in Musical Essays* (Amsterdam: OPA, 2001)

Re:Search: Industrial Culture Handbook (San Francisco: Re:Search, 1983)

Reynolds, Simon, *Blissed Out: The Raptures of Rock* (London: Serpent's Tail, 1990)

———, *Rip It Up and Start Again: Postpunk, 1977–1984* (London: Faber & Faber, 2005)

Rose, Tricia, *Black Noise: Rap Music and Black Culture in Contemporary America* (Middletown, CT: Wesleyan University Press, 1994)

Rosenthal, David H., *Hard Bop: Black Music 1955–1965* (Oxford and New York: Oxford University Press, 1992)

Rousseau, Jean-Jacques, *Discourse on the Origin of Languages* (Oxford: Oxford University Press, 1999)

Russolo, Luigi, *The Art of Noises* (New York: Pendragon, 1986)

Rycenga, Jennifer, 'Tales of Change within the Sound: Form, Lyrics and Philosophy in the Music of Yes', in Holm-Hudson (ed), *Progressive Rock Reconsidered*, 143–66

Satie, Erik, *Écrits* (Paris: Éditions Champ Libre, 1977)

Scheinbaum, John J., 'Progressive Rock and the Inversion of Musical Values', in Holm-Hudson (ed), *Progressive Rock Reconsidered*, 21–42

Schoenberg, Arnold, *Style and Idea: Selected Writings* (London: Faber & Faber, 1975)

Shabazz, David, L., *Public Enemy Number One: A View Inside the World of Hip Hop* (Clinto, SC: Awesome Records, 1999)

Shafer, R. Murray, 'Music, Non-music and the Soundscape' in Paynter et al. (eds), *The Companion to Contemporary Musical Thought*, 34–45

———, *The Soundscape: Our Sonic Environment and the Tuning of the World* (Rochester, VT: Destiny Books, 1993)

Shapiro, Peter, 'Deck Wreckers: The Turntable as Instrument', in Young (ed), *Undercurrents*, 163–76

Shepherd, John, 'Music as Cultural Text', in Paynter et al. (eds), *The Companion to Contemporary Musical Thought*, 128–55

Shipton, Alyn, *A New History of Jazz* (London and New York: Continuum, 2002)

Shuker, Roy, *Understanding Popular Music* (London and New York: Routledge, 1994)

Smith, Nick, 'The Splinter in Your Ear: Noise as the Semblance of Critique', in *Culture Theory Critique: Noise*, 43–59

Sonic Boom: The Art of Sound (London: Hayward Gallery, 2000)

Sonic Process: Une nouvelle géographie des sons (Paris: Centre Pompidou, 2002)

Sons et lumières (Paris: Centre Pompidou, 2004)

Stump, Paul, *The Music's All That Matters: A History of Progressive Rock* (London: Quartet, 1997)

Tamm, Eric, *Robert Fripp: From King Crimson to Guitar Craft* (Winchester, MA, and London: Faber & Faber, 1990)

Thacker, Eugene, 'Bataille/Body/Noise: Towards a Techno-Erotics', in Woodward (ed), *Merzbook*, 57–65

Thomson, Phil, 'Atoms and Errors: Towards a History and Aesthetics of Microsound', in *Organised Sound* 9 (2) (2004), 207–18

Toop, David, *Haunted Weather: Music, Silence and Memory* (London: Serpent's Tail, 2004)

———, *Ocean of Sound: Aether Talk, Ambient Sound and Imaginary Worlds* (London and New York: Serpent's Tail, 1995)

Washburne, C. J., and Derno, M. (eds), *Bad Music: The Music We Love to Hate* (London: Routledge, 2004)

Watson, Ben, *Derek Bailey and the Story of Free Improvisation* (London: Verso, 2004)

Webel, Sophie, and Duplaix, Sophie (eds), *Jean Dubuffet: Expériences musicales* (Paris: Fondation Dubuffet, 2006)

Whiteley, Sheila, *The Space between the Notes: Rock and the Counter-culture* (London and New York: Routledge, 1992)

Whiteley, Sheila (ed), *Sexing the Groove: Popular Music and Gender* (London: Routledge, 1997)

Witkin, Robert, W., *Adorno on Music* (London and New York: Routledge, 1998)

Woodward, Brett (ed), *Merzbook: The Pleasuredome of Noise* (Melbourne and Cologne: Extreme, 1999)

Young, Rob (ed), *Undercurrents: The Hidden Wiring of Modern Music* (London and New York: Continuum, 2002)

Web Sites

www.asahi-net.or.jp
www.ctheory.net
www.culturemachine.tees.ac.uk
www.deeplistening.org
www.japanimprov.com
www.johnlydon.com
www.overwhelmed.org
www.sapaan.org
www3.sympatico.ca/pratten/NSB/
www.tate.org.uk/liverpool
www.ubu.com/sound
http://web.fm/twiki/Fmext/WebHome

Index